Voices
of
Tomorrow

**The 24th Congress of the Communist Party
of the Soviet Union**

Editor: Jessica Smith

A New World Review Collection

Published by: NWR Publications, Inc.
156 Fifth Avenue, New York, N.Y. 10010
1971

Printed in the U.S.A.

Library of Congress Card Catalogue No. 71-177990

VOICES OF TOMORROW

The 24th Congress of the Communist Party of the Soviet Union

CONTENTS

NOTE TO READERS

WE ARE privileged to present this special enlarged issue of NEW WORLD REVIEW devoted to the 24th Congress of the Communist Party of the Soviet Union, which we are publishing at the same time in permanent form as a paperback book entitled *Voices of Tomorrow*. The project arose out of many questions from readers about the role of the Communist Party in the USSR, which are answered in this very full review of the Congress proceedings. Here we see in action how the Party performs its leading role in the life of the people, providing the basis for policies formalized into law by the Supreme Soviet of the USSR.

The main report of the Central Committee of the CPSU, delivered by General Secretary Leonid Brezhnev, covers Soviet internal developments and foreign relations for the past five years and charts the road ahead. The report of Premier Alexey Kosygin outlines the draft Directives for the 1971-75 Economic Development Plan.

In condensing these reports as necessitated by space limitations, we have sought to retain all essential points so that the reader will miss nothing except elaboration of certain details. These reports, taken together with excerpts from the discussions of delegates to the Congress, which adopted the reports, present in effect a whole course on the Soviet Union and its role in the world which no student of Soviet affairs and socialism can afford to miss.

This material has been prepared and edited by the NEW WORLD REVIEW staff: Jessica Smith, Editor, David Laibman, Assistant Editor. We have been fortunate in also having the help of our new Editorial Associate, David Buehrens. Mr. Buehrens is an English instructor and linguist, currently working on a Ph.D. in American literature. He has written articles and reviews for NWR and other publications.

We wish to express our special appreciation to Novosti Press Agency for securing the important article by Academician Pyotr Fedoseyev and providing translations of the Congress proceedings.

We are grateful to the English edition of *Soviet Literature* for permission to use the "Thoughts on the Party Congress by Writer-Delegates," published in their issue No. 7, 1971.

THE EDITORS

Thoughts on the Party Congress
By Writer Delegates

The survey printed in this book of the 24th Congress of the Communist Party of the Soviet Union, which took place March 30-April 9, 1971, gives a vivid picture of how the life of society is organized under socialism.

At this Congress, as at preceding ones, a great deal was said about the communist education of the people and about the significance of literature and art in this process. "With our society's advance along the road of communist construction a growing role is played by literature and art in molding the outlook, moral convictions and culture of the Soviet people," General Secretary Leonid Brezhnev noted in the Report of the CPSU Central Committee. "Quite naturally, therefore," he went on, "the Party continues, as it always has done, to devote much attention to the ideological content of our literature and art and to the role they play in society. In line with the Leninist principle of party spirit, we see our task in leading the development of all forms of creative art towards participation in the people's great cause of communist construction."

This idea was developed in the contributions made to the discussion by the writers Mikhail Sholokhov and Alexander Chakovsky, and a number of the delegates.

At the request of the magazine Soviet Literature *a number of other writers who were delegates wrote about what the Congress meant to them. We feel that this group of vignettes is the most appropriate introduction we can offer to our account of the proceedings of the Congress.*

MUSTAI KARIM

The First Day of Work

IT WAS a great day, that first day of the Congress's work. Not only was it a tiny bit longer than its predecessor—the sun rose two minutes earlier and set three minutes later; the main thing was that it pushed back the frontiers of time, drew within itself the thoughts, hopes and deeds of years and decades. It brought out the vistas of the five years lying ahead of us. And there was just as clear and broad a view of them as of the Agidel Valley from the Ufa hillside on a fine day.

Probably everyone, and especially every poet, has his favorite

---

Biographical sketches of the authors in this section will be found on page 16.

spot, a place where his gaze may take wing and his mind find quiet for reflection. For me one such place is the hillside where our Bashkirian hero, the bronze Salavat Yulayev, rides his rearing horse above the Agidel Valley. There I have a wider view of my land than almost anywhere else. I see its roads, I see its fields and meadows, I see the smoke rising from burning stubble and factory chimneys. I see my Bashkiria disappear into the blue distance beyond the horizon to join other lands, other peoples. Here, too, I hear the voice of history. For here by my side is Salavat. This wind that sweeps up from the lowland to beat in my face blows against his dark cheekbones. That wind once ruffled the mane of his steed, that wind, too, once swayed boughs that were to be cut for bows and arrows. In that wind, therefore, is the voice of my people's history, of their sufferings, of their glorious feats. It is also the voice of today, bearing on its wings from the valley the roar of a tractor, the swish of the waves, foaming swathes flung out by a motor boat towing rafted timber, and the distant, crystal-clear sound of a Young Pioneer's bugle.

I had this same sensation of breadth, a sensation of being present at a meeting with History itself on one fleeting day, when I listened to the report given by Leonid Brezhnev. As on that hillside, one could see everything, far and wide. . . . I could see my fellow-writers, could hear the echo of their thoughts and my own. I could feel their creative pangs, those pangs without which the happiness of achievement is unattainable. A deep interest, a demand for high standards and sincere concern have prompted the following words: "We are for an attentive attitude to creative quests, for the full unfolding of the individuality of gifts and talents, for the diversity and wealth of forms and styles evolved on the basis of socialist realism. The strength of the party leadership lies in the ability to spark the artist with enthusiasm for the lofty mission of serving the people and turn him into a convinced and ardent participant in the remaking of society on communist principles."

In front of our delegation was the delegation from Vietnam. Prolonged applause greeted the words: "The Democratic Republic of Vietnam may be sure that in its armed struggle and its peaceful endeavor it can continue to rely on the Soviet Union's fraternal support." At these words, resounding 8,000 kilometers from their native land, in a hall on which at that time the eyes of the world were riveted, I saw their faces quiver. Not only did their faces reflect the emotions evoked by the attention of the thousands of other delegates; the wind of war, blowing from the opposite end of the earth, swept over their features.

6

Many lands, many people passed before my eyes on that great day. I was also a delegate to the previous five party congresses. And I had the good fortune to rise to this height for a sixth time. Each time one can see further, and more clearly.

KONSTANTIN SIMONOV

A Little About Poetic Spirit

MANY thoughts, many recollections came crowding in on me as I sat in the hall where the Congress was being held and listened to people speaking from the rostrum, to good and diverse people—Mayakovsky once described poets thus, and I feel the words should be applied to everyone. Especially as the spirit of poetry is akin to the cause of socialism of which the delegates were speaking.

When a man thinks only of himself, of his own good, his own pocket, his own convenience, he can talk of all these things in the most eloquent and beautiful terms, but in all this selfish concern there is no place for poetic spirit. The real poetic spirit appears in a man's thoughts, words and deeds, when he takes into his heart and upon his shoulders the cares of others, when his concerns are concerns about their hopes, their happiness and their well-being.

And it was this really human poetic spirit, associated with the best and finest qualities of man's heart, with man's concern not for himself but for others, ultimately for society, that was felt in abundance in the Congress speeches.

I would add that the more straightforward, the more businesslike the speeches, the more openly people spoke about the practical mundane affairs necessary to our society, the more poetic spirit there was.

The clouds scudding overhead are also not devoid of poetic spirit. But somehow the silver birch, with its roots in our earth, says far more to our hearts. Its foliage rises into the sky, above it are the clouds, but its roots are in the earth. In this there is something deeply in harmony with man himself, of whom we often say when we want to speak of his strength, stability, constancy: here is a man with roots.

There are such people, with roots going deep into their native soil, and at the same time able to look high into the sky and far into the future, able, in their concern for their country, not to forget the needs and sufferings of mankind; these represent the real poetic spirit of life, which motivates the whole intellectual life of society, including the arts.

The arts must be truthful and fearless, they have no right to ignore earthy needs and cares or the imperfections of everyday life, but if at the very core of art there is no love for man and no faith in his power for good, art will be sterile.

As I listened to the speeches of the delegates, as I talked with many of those good and diverse people who had gathered at the Congress, I frequently thought how fruitful for art was that faith in man, in his strength, his ability to accomplish what he plans, that was ever present in the atmosphere at the Congress.

I listened to the speech made by Klavdia Smirnova, a milkmaid, who, after explaining briefly that she had been a machine-gunner during the war, went on to talk of the long-suffering Orel region from which she came and of how it had, because of war, "been turned to ashes, had dug into the ground."

This machine-gunner returned from the front and began with her fellow-villagers to resurrect this village which had "dug into the ground." That was done, and Klavdia Smirnova told the Congress how it had been accomplished. Behind her story was a whole lifetime of hard work, evoking the most sincere respect for this woman in her hearers, people who had themselves known hardship and trouble, and what it was like to be a machine-gunner at the front and what it was to follow that by reviving from the ashes a native village thrice seared by war.

When Klavdia Smirnova heard Leonid Brezhnev speak of those who fought at the front, saying that after the terrible strain of the war years they were not able to relax, they had found themselves at the front once more, this time the labor front, it is not surprising that she was moved to the heart. These words were in essence a reminder of the most difficult and lofty thing in the life of an individual—his readiness, after accomplishing a tremendous feat of heroism, not to sit back and ask to be allowed to take things easy, but to go straight on to further heroism, to a no less difficult feat, one that also demanded all of his physical and mental reserves—and not for one day, or even two, but for many long years.

Much was written about those who had fought at the front immediately after Victory, in 1945. Perhaps the boldest, the most forward-looking was the verse written at the time by Mikhail Lukonin, entitled *To Those Returned from the War.*

> *No passive, tranquil life of ease,*
> *No respite do we want.*
> *Those tired tributes spare us, please—*
> *"Old Soldier from the Front"!*

Our quest: exchange our arms for tools,
To prove our strength again.
To win, in toil for peacetime goals,
Awards from fellow men.

I recalled these lines as I listened to this modest Russian woman, a tower of strength, talking about herself, her comrades, her collective farm and her plans for the future. She drew strength from her entire experience of a life that had been difficult but lived honorably, decently, and also from her faith—based on that experience—in the future, in her comrades, in her Party and her country.

KAMIL YASHEN

The Image of an Epoch

THE PARTY and the people have entrusted the pen to us Soviet writers, confident that we shall use it with honor, with a high sense of responsibility, with burning hearts and an irresistible urge for creative activity in the name of communism. As Leonid Brezhnev said in the Report to the Congress: "Soviet writers and artists have been educated by the Communist Party. They draw their inspiration from the deeds and thoughts of their people, and their creative destiny is inseparable from the interests of the socialist motherland."

We writers have one desire—to link our creative plans more closely with the life of the country, with the problems of the Five-Year Plan. Each one of us has experienced a strong desire to follow in the fresh tracks of new construction work, to understand its rhythms, its spirit and its sweeping scale. In myself, a writer of the older generation, this is combined with an imperative wish to understand our own not-so-distant revolutionary past, in fact to take a flash-back of our romantic youth.

The basis of my earlier plays, as well as the later ones, was the chief conflict of our time—the conflict between implacably hostile classes, their fierce struggle. I was first aware of this conflict, I think, half a century ago. Then, an adolescent in Andizhan, I was accepted into a music and drama troupe to play the role of Eastern girls—at that time they themselves could not appear on the stage for fear of their lives. I traveled the fronts of the Civil War with this troupe, and I saw not only the Red Army's attacks but the triumph of the emergent new over what was old, defeated and crawling away into the past.

I grew to manhood, and even saw with increasing clarity the greatness of Lenin, his direct participation in the destinies of the peoples of the East, awakened from age-old slumber and now roused to struggle. I was seized with the idea of writing a play about Lenin, the great friend of our peoples, who had aroused the oppressed world to fight, and transformed Central Asia from a colonial backwoods to advanced Soviet republics. To me, a writer and a Communist, this was my principal responsibility to the party. And I put all my heart and soul into fulfilling it. My play *Guiding Star* is staged at many theaters in Central Asia.

Writing about Lenin means writing of the vitalizing force of Lenin's ideas, of the building of communism. All the valuable contributions made by our multinational literature to the revelation of this great character must be continued, given broader and more profound application in the socio-historic conditions of each nation. This is a happy but difficult task—to write about Lenin, to create the image of our time.

I feel deeply that the Congress decisions have given a new stimulus to my creative energies, have led me, a writer who is getting on in years, into new creative streams of thought and images, into a realm of fresh artistic quests.

SERGEY NAROVCHATOV

A Real Spring

MARCH this year turned out to be a month of blizzards and frosts. The winter was reluctant to give way, and only in the last week or so did the weather begin to get warmer. The snow began to disappear more quickly, moisture-laden clouds hung over the city, and unpleasant, raw weather seemed to have come to stay. But when I went out on the morning of March 30, I had to screw up my eyes because of the unexpected bright sun. It shone down from the blue, cloudless sky, was reflected in the windows of new blocks of flats and turned the blue puddles underfoot to gold.

It was spring! A real spring! Spring lit up the faces of passers-by, and when I was in the Metro and the train made its stop at the above-ground Lenin Hills station, I suddenly saw the Moscow River, with gleaming banks, shining brightly at us. The train slid into the tunnel again, but there was still a vernal glow on people's faces. Almost all of them carried the morning paper. "Greetings to the 24th

Party Congress!" ran big red banner headlines on the front pages. It was as though the speeding train itself was illuminated by these words.

The train hurried into my station, I emerged onto the surface, and the eternal miracle of the morning Kremlin was before me. The ancient battlements glowed and the red stars on the towers shone against the blue sky. The sanctum sanctorum of our people was awaiting the envoys of the Party!

I had the honor to be among them. With the other delegates I walked along the pavements of the Kremlin which had known the tread of fighters for the Revolution in October 1917, had known the tread of Lenin himself. The glass doors of the Palace of Congresses were open wide, and in the great halls of the Palace we again felt that festive spring atmosphere which that day seemed to infect both nature and people. And those who had gathered here were the cream of the people, the country, the Party. Men and women workers—the best of the best, pillars of the country and the Party, representatives of the leading class in Soviet society. Expert harvesters, cotton-growers, livestock tenders, thanks to whom we are fed, clothed and shod. Renowned scientists, by virtue of whose intellect and ability we stand on the heights of modern science. Our splendid soldiers on whom we can rely to defend our country of socialism from the encroachments of the imperialist predators. People of eminence in party and state affairs, to whom the country has entrusted the conduct of domestic and foreign policy.

In the eyes of the Party, workers and ministers are equal, as are collective farmers and academicians, writers and marshals—each is doing a useful job for the country in his own sphere. Now they had gathered together to review their achievements and to set new high aims in the building of communism.

The results of the Soviet people's achievements between the 23rd and 24th congresses were summed up exhaustively and with convincing force in the Report of the Central Committee, which was delivered by Leonid Brezhnev. The delegates all stood to applaud the General Secretary of the Central Committee of the CPSU, thus demonstrating their faith in the triumph of communism, in the victory of Lenin's ideas. The whole report was listened to with the utmost attention. In an extremely human way, appealing to both the hearts and minds of the working people, the report showed very powerfully that the supreme aim of the Party is the well-being of the Soviet people.

As a writer it was especially interesting for me to listen to the careful analysis given in the report of developments in literature and art

11

and to hear how the Party envisaged prospects for further development. I must emphasize that, like myself, every Soviet citizen can find in this Report not only a discussion of the broad, general problems affecting the entire country but much that is of particular personal interest to himself. In this lies the tremendous power of its impact.

I left the Kremlin that spring evening with a group of other delegates. All around people were speaking in a variety of tongues—Ukrainians, Georgians, Kazakhs, Latvians, Armenians and Uzbeks were talking over their impressions of the report they had just been listening to. Through their representatives the Soviet republics endorsed all its principles. The Congress was an example of the perfect unity in the views and opinions among Communists throughout the Soviet Union.

Spring stars lit up over Moscow. It was spring over the city, spring over the country, and spring in human hearts.

RASUL GAMZATOV

Confidence

IT IS a powerful word, confidence. Confidence in our strength. Confidence in victory. Confidence in our unshakable truth, in our thoughts, our deeds, our dreams.

It was a word heard many times from the rostrum of the Palace of Congresses. Those who used it were confident of the morrow of our vast Soviet land, for as Leonid Brezhnev said: "How we live today, and how we shall live tomorrow depends on us ourselves, on our successes in work."

Yesterday we were still reading the draft Directives. Then at the Congress they were approved by the delegates. Everything necessary is said in them, everything is taken into consideration. This is a tremendous program of action for the next five years. It gives birth to an immense amount of thought!

Thoughts and feelings come to us, like guests in the mountains, without invitation, without warning. And we in the mountains do not count our guests as being of lesser or greater significance, important or unimportant. The least significant guest is important—because he is a guest. We do not ask whence he has come, we lead him closer to the fire and show him the respect due to a guest.

These notes have come to me like a guest in the mountains. Do not ask why I write of this or of that. I shall not answer. I do not know.

I have lived on this earth more than 15,000 days. Along many, many roads of this earth have I walked or ridden. I have met no end of people. My impressions are countless, like the streams in the mountains in times of rain.

In these days of the Party Congress I have been overflowing with new impressions.

No matter where I have been cast by fate, everywhere I have felt myself a representative of that land, those mountains, that aul, where I took my first steps. I am a special correspondent of my Daghestan.

Two mothers have my people, my tiny land.

The first is our native Daghestan. Here I was born, here I first sang songs, here I first knew the taste of warm bread.

My second mother is great Russia, great Moscow. She gave me wings, opened up to me a broad highway, showed me boundless horizons.

Two mothers—they are like two wings, two hands, two songs, two strings stretched over the soundboard of the sensitive *chunguri*.

My Daghestan is growing, becoming richer, more beautiful. My heart overflows with joy—a son cannot help being proud of his own mother.

Forgive me, pyramids of Egypt, misty banks of the Seine, well-tended lawns of London, and screeching highways of America. You I have only admired. But my heart beats faster when I once again, for the countless time, see Red Square, the Kremlin. Someone long ago called Red Square the heart of Russia. During the time of the Congress it beat with thousands of hearts, the hearts of Congress delegates.

Friendship and brotherhood reigned in the Palace of Congresses.

Here I had thousands of brothers and sisters. From Russia, from the Ukraine, from Georgia, Turkmenia, Latvia and Moldavia. A host of new names and addresses have now appeared in my dog-eared address book—these are my friends.

I jotted down in my notebook: "The Party has a right to be proud of the young builders of communism." And another note: "This is our future, our replacements."

I remember the old verse:

> *"Where is your homeland, youth?" we ask.*
> *"All lands, all parts I'm from."*
> *"What do you bring the waiting world?"*
> *"The whole of time to come."*

One fifth of the deputies to the Supreme Soviet of the USSR are young people. They are entrusted with the running of the state. This is a sign of the times.

In our land people say: "If there were no words in the world, the world would not be what it is." They also say: "The poet was born a hundred years before the creation of the world."

The Daghestan poet Suleiman Stalsky once said: "As a poet I am neither Lezghin, Daghestanian or Caucasian. I am a Soviet poet. I am the master of all this vast country."

Leonid Brezhnev said: "It is a matter for great satisfaction that literature and art are developing fruitfully in all our republics, in dozens of languages of the peoples of the USSR, in a striking variety of national forms."

The languages of peoples are like stars in the sky. My star is the literature of Daghestan. Geologists say that even in a small mountain there may be a great deal of gold. I believe them.

Which comes first—the writer or his theme? Does the theme give birth to the writer or the writer to the theme? The theme is the writer's world. Without it he cannot exist. It is his sky, his air, the water he drinks, the bread he eats.

My theme is my homeland. I do not need to seek it out, to select it as a theme. We do not choose our homeland. Our homeland chooses us. There cannot be a writer without a homeland.

What have I jotted down in my notebook? Thoughts born during the Congress days, things heard, seen and remembered. Perhaps someone will tell me that I have not written an article but fragmentary notes. . . .

I do not object. Call these notes what you like. I have not written them according to journalistic rules, but in response to the dictates of my heart. And the heart makes its own rules.

MAXIM GETTUEV

Our Roads

WHAT were the thoughts and feelings of the delegates, of Communists, of all our people? Which of them were they to express at the Congress?

The roads leading to Moscow from all corners of our red-starred state ran across land and water, above the swan's down of spring clouds. Those roads converged in the Kremlin itself, at the threshold of the Palace of Congresses.

The thoughts come crowding in, like wave upon wave. In Kabardino-Balkaria special respect is shown to the traveler—the road is difficult, he must walk the edge of sheer precipices, pass through dark canyons slashing the mountain breast.

I remember—no, I don't remember, for in 1923 I was still a little boy. But people have told me how Nalchik was visited by the all-Union elder—that was what our folk called the Soviet President, Mikhail Kalinin, in those days. He saw that the mountains of the old life cut off people's view of the horizon. He called on my fellow-countrymen to climb to the summits of the new life so that endless vistas of a wonderful world would open up before them. The words of the all-Union elder have come true—the Communists of my republic were the first to begin the storming of the heights, and they drew the entire people after them.

Our people have a saying: a river between its banks does not lose it way, even at night. Hand in hand with all the nationalities of Russia, we have overcome poverty. We have driven out the invaders, we have raised our ruined villages from the ashes and built fine new ones, with clubs, schools and palaces of culture.

Throughout Leonid Brezhnev's Report ran the wise thought of Lenin—concern for every, literally every, person in our country. No one is forgotten—worker and collective farmer, the old soldier and the first-year recruit, the young woman expecting her baby, the scientist whose audacious ideas are being put into effect. The high demands made on the writer, the artist and the musician are accompanied by a warm, thoughtful solicitude on the part of the Party.

Roads are the beginning of our new life. With them my land grows younger, more beautiful, her sons come to manhood, throw back their shoulders and come to their fathers' assistance. Our children acquire wisdom—through love for their native land, their chosen task.

Nowadays our country roads are being asphalted. I recall how the workers at the Prokhladnensky Order of Lenin Repair Works, when they elected me deputy to the Supreme Soviet of the USSR, put forward the proposal that a new shop be constructed to build tractor trailers.

Today we have such a shop. And on mountain roads, still difficult to negotiate, our tractor drivers deliver goods right to cloud level. Today one may travel by bus through passes, across hills and mountains throughout the length and breadth of Kabardino-Balkaria.

Khabas Arkhestov, Hero of Socialist Labor, who is an electric fitter, and Nikolay Yevtushenko, a Candidate of Agricultural Science and Chairman of the Krasynaya Niva collective farm, were among the delegates sent by the Communists of my republic to Moscow for the Congress. An equal among equals, invested with the confidence of the republic's Communists, Kaziban Chechenova, another of my compatriots, took part in the work of the Congress. She is a milkmaid on the Krasnaya Balkaria collective farm, and has been awarded the Order of Lenin.

Just look at them. A worker hero, a peasant scientist, a milkmaid with a government decoration. These are the heights to which the Communist Party has raised my people.

In the conference hall I met fellow poets—Rasul Gamzatov, Semyon Danilov, Mustai Karim and Anatoli Sofronov. And I find joy and pride in knowing that poetry is also included in the Five-Year Plan of our country, that the best of our verse will help in construction work, will beautify our life, and strengthen the might of our multinational homeland.

RASUL GAMZATOV, an Avar by nationality, was born in Daghestan in 1923, and does his writing in Avar, often about his beautiful mountain homeland. Recipient of the Lenin Prize for his book of poetry *High Stars,* Gamzatov is also the People's Poet of Daghestan.

MAXIM GETTUEV, a Balkar writer, was born in 1916 in the Kabardino-Balkarsk ASSR, and graduated from the Lenin Pedagogical Institute in 1955. His works include a novel in verse, *Elbrus is Close By,* and much poetry in Balkar, also translated into Russian.

MUSTAI KARIM, born in 1919 in Bashkiria, is a noted writer of poetry, plays, essays, fairy tales and children's books, as well as an outstanding public and political figure. A People's Poet of the Bashkir ASSR, Karim writes in his native tongue, but his work has also often appeared in Russian.

SERGEY NAROVCHATOV, poet, critic and literary scholar, was born of Russian nationality in 1919. Active in socio-political work, Narovchatov, a graduate of the Gorky Literary Institute, has authored much poetry, including *Through War* and *Bitter Love.* His critical works include a study of *Lermontov's Lyrics.*

KONSTANTIN SIMONOV, one of the USSR's best known Russian authors, was born in Leningrad in 1915. A graduate of Moscow's Gorky Literary Institute in 1938, Simonov, now Secretary of the Board of the Soviet Writer's Union, this year completed his famous World War II trilogy begun with *The Living and the Dead* and *Soldiers Are Not Born.* Simonov's numerous poems, plays, novels and short stories have recently been reissued in a six-volume edition.

KAMIL YASHEN, an outstanding Uzbek playwright and academician, was born in 1909. His plays, repeatedly published in Russian and successfully produced, include *Nurkhon, Gulsara* and *General Rakhimov.* He is chairman of the Soviet Committee for Ties with Asian and African Writers.

ACADEMICIAN PYOTR FEDOSEYEV

Communist Construction: The
Party's Leading Role

THE 24th CPSU Congress was a major event in the life of Soviet society, in its advance to communism. In strict adherence to Marxist-Leninist principles and on the basis of the vast experience gained by our Leninist Party, the results of the devoted labor of over 14 million Communists and of all the working people of the Soviet Union were scrupulously analyzed in the documents and materials of the Congress. New great tasks were determined and majestic perspectives in all fields of communist construction were outlined. The Congress again revealed the great trust and support of the working people which the CPSU enjoys.

The 24th CPSU Congress was also an outstanding event in present-day world development and in the consolidation of the ranks of the anti-imperialist front. The historic significance of the Congress is first of all determined by the enormous and ever-growing role of the Soviet Union and our Leninist Party in the world liberation movement, in the struggle against imperialism, for peace, free national development and socialism.

The international significance of the Congress is further determined by the fact that it was the most representative forum of the communist, national-liberation and other revolutionary forces in history. All kinds of dissenters and renegades have been dispirited by this manifestation of mounting solidarity of the world anti-imperialist front and of the international communist movement. The main object of their slanderous attacks, the Communist Party of the Soviet Union, appeared before the world united, strong and with unprecedented creative initiative, enjoying growing respect and prestige in the ranks of the world liberation movement.

The successes achieved by the Soviet Union in economy, the

ACADEMICIAN PYOTR N. FEDOSEYEV, Vice President of the USSR Academy of Sciences, was formerly Director of the Academy's Institute of Philosophy and editor of the magazine *Bolshevik*. He has been director of the Institute of Marxism-Leninism since 1967. He is a deputy to the USSR Supreme Soviet.

various fields of science and culture, in the development of engineering, in increasing the welfare of the people and in perfecting forms of social life, aid the constant growth of forces in the international arena on the side of socialism and the liberation movement, and opposed to imperialism. But although the contraction of the economic base of imperialism and the strengthening of the material and technical base of socialism are substantially changing the correlation of forces in the interests of the world revolutionary process, a number of pseudo-communist "strategists" still deny the class nature and the revolutionizing importance of the economic and scientific-technological competition between the two systems, ignoring the real, substantial assistance which the Soviet Union and other socialist countries are rendering to the world liberation movement. Neither do they recognize the revolutionary content of the class struggle between labor and capital which has developed in the majority of capitalist countries. They would like to force upon the communist movement their theory of "prodding" the revolution by war, regarding revolution as a sort of military coup.

During the present period of the construction of the material and social basis for Soviet communism, the question of the *role* of the Communist Party in the socialist state is of tremendous importance, both from a theoretical and a practical point of view. As was emphasized in the Report of the CPSU Central Committee to the recent 24th Communist Party Congress, it is a fundamental and crucial question for the direction of social development as well as for the practical organization of the life and labor of the Soviet people.

The new society is built in every socialist country in forms conditioned by concrete historical circumstances. However, this diversity of forms is governed by laws which are common to all countries and among which the *leading* role of the Marxist-Leninist party ranks first. The reason for this is that the working class holds a leading position in the system of socialist production and social relations—and hence in political life. It is through its party that the working class exerts decisive influence on the rise and development of socialism and communism. The Communist Party's leading role in the building of socialism and communism, whether under a one-party system or a multi-party one, is thus a logical result of the fact that history itself makes the working class the vanguard of the revolution and the construction of a new society.

The assertion that the democratism of sociopolitical life depends on the number of political parties, or on their periodic replacement in office, is totally unfounded. There are a whole number of countries with many political parties where democracy is nonexistent. Moreover in those states where institutions of bourgeois democracy do function and where the population enjoys a certain minimum of civil rights, this has been achieved not as a result of a plurality of parties, but as a result of a stubborn struggle by the working class and other sections of the working people for their rights.

The record of the CPSU, as well as past and present experience in general, indicate clearly that only a Marxist-Leninist party can lead the working class and other working people to the victory of socialism and communism. Anyone who denies the necessity for the proletariat to have an independent party leading it and pursuing a class policy is placing himself, as Engels put it, "outside the proletarian movement and inside the camp of petty-bourgeois socialism" (*The Housing Question*). The actual role of the advocates of this kind of "socialism" has been amply illustrated by the experience of many countries. The Russian Mensheviks and Socialist Revolutionaries, for example, talked much about socialism, but when the opportunity presented itself of taking power and participating in the actual building of socialism, they capitulated by making common cause with the bourgeoisie, and were rightly swept away by the masses. It was the Bolshevik Party, not the reformists, which came out as a party of social revolution set on carrying this revolution through to the complete victory of communism. Similarly, in other countries spokesmen of petty-bourgeois parties and reformists regarding themselves as genuine democratic socialists have repeatedly been in power, as they are today, but when faced with the need to effect radical socioeconomic socialist changes, they have failed, as they fail now. Thus history has not recorded a single instance of socialism being built and its victory ensured without a revolutionary party of the working class playing the leading role.

In a number of socialist countries there are, alongside the working-class party, parties representing non-proletarian sections of the working people. They recognize the socialist road of development and cooperate with the Communists in a Popular Front. In this situation democratic parties are allies of the Communist Parties, not opposition forces. They recognize of their own free will the leading role of the Communist Parties, which exercise it not by pressure or injunction, but by virtue of the moral and political prestige which they enjoy among the masses. Relations between the parties in these socialist societies are based on regard for each other's interests and on mutual confidence. Cooperation between a Communist Party and other democratic parties is the political expression of the alliance of the workers, peasants, intellectuals and other working people who are building socialist society under the leadership of the working class. Modern revisionists, advocating the introduction of "new models" of socialism in the practice of the socialist countries, assert that only a "combination of competing political forces" in the manner of bourgeois countries can secure a "democratic mechanism of government." They favor "political pluralism" instead of the leading role of the working class and its vanguard—the Communist Party—totally disregarding the fact that the formation of a political system, one-party or multi-party, after the victory of the socialist revolution is not the result of subjective wishes, let alone of "Communist machinations," but of the specific historical features of the revolutionary process.

Thus in Russia, for example, the specific character of the revolutionary struggle led to the Communist Party becoming the only party that assumed full responsibility for the direction of society. For in the course of the revolution and during the Civil War, as we have seen, all the other political parties discredited themselves by their anti-popular policies and were rejected by the working masses. Even before the victory of October, Lenin, referring to the leaders of the petty-bourgeois parties, stressed that they "have killed themselves and their parties—the Mensheviks and the Socialist Revolutionaries—politically."

Although revisionists sometimes claim that increasing the leading role of the Party is necessary only at some particular stage—for example, before a revolution—the *growth* of the leading role of a Marxist-Leninist party in the whole course of building communism is an objective reality. Continually increasing the leading role of the party of the working class is a natural process covering all stages of the struggle of the working class and the working masses for a socialist revolution, for socialism and communism.

However, it is neither a spontaneous nor an automatic process but the result of conscious, vigorous and meaningful effort by all Communists. Marxism-Leninism considers social development dialectically, as a natural historical process which is determined by objective laws of development but influenced at the same time by the subjective factor: the revolutionary energy and creative initiative of the masses, as well as classes, parties and outstanding personalities who are capable of expressing the needs of social development and progressive class interests.

20

And the stronger and more harmoniously organized the Party is, the better it can accomplish its mission as the vanguard of the working class and the whole people. It is, as it should be, a living political organism developing in step with the building of the new society. It constantly reflects in itself the changes occurring in the socioeconomic field, the class structure and the spiritual life of the Soviet people. The economic, class, ideological and political changes brought about by the country's socialist progress over 50-odd years have extended and consolidated the social base of the Party and assured its further growth.

The period since the 23rd Party Congress has revealed more clearly than ever that in the conditions of further consolidation of the social, political and ideological unity of developed socialist society, the Communist Party is the vanguard of the *whole* people. It is still the party of the working class in its goals, tasks, ideals and class nature. But the point is simply that the Soviet people have assimilated the ideology and ultimate goals of the working class and have come to regard them as their own. And it would be wrong to ignore this in assessing the Party's role in the life of the people. The Party's revolutionizing power must be great indeed, its policy based on scientific foundations and its links with the masses extensive, if in decades of revolution, world war, grim class battles and tremendous economic and cultural building, millions, overcoming numerous obstacles, have carried forward the work of revolutionary transformation under the Party's leadership.

The opponents of communism, ignoring the fundamental class distinction between the leading cadres in the socialist countries and the ruling groups in the capitalist countries, spread theories alleging the rise of an "elite" in the Soviet Union. These attacks of bourgeois ideologists and the revisionists echoing them are plainly intended to antagonize leaders and masses, and to cause mutual estrangement among members of socialist society.

The elitist charge is plainly refuted by the entire history of the CPSU and the Soviet state, which shows that in training personnel great importance is attached to promoting active members of the working class and collective farm peasantry to key posts, thereby helping them to master the art of leadership, improve their knowledge and extend their experience. From their midst come many distinguished captains of industry and party and government leaders, closely linked with the people. A career ranging from the job of an ordinary worker to that of a high-ranking executive is typical of many Soviet men and women. More specifically, over 80 per cent of the secretaries of regional territorial and central committees of the Communist Parties of the Union Republics, as well as the Chairmen of Councils of Ministers and regional executive committees, are one-time workers or peasants. More than 70 per cent of the Ministers and Chairmen of State Committees of the USSR began their careers as workers or peasants. This is also true of most of the heads of research and design institutions.

Communism will be the result of the creative effort of millions. The more successful the development of socialist society and the more difficult and challenging the tasks it sets for itself, the larger are the sections of the masses brought into socialist construction. Strengthening socialist democracy—strengthening the Party's links with the masses—entails carrying on numerous complex and varied activities. But the emphasis is everywhere on drawing people into economic planning and control, on maintaining close contact with leaders and activists of mass organizations, and on propaganda and agitation to make the people aware of the opportunities for their participation in building the new society. This is true socialist democracy.

The main area of the Party's organizing effort is the working people's collectives—industrial enterprises, building sites, collective and state farms, and government offices and institutions. It is in such places that the Party has shown initiative and ability to inspire and lead people, to make the people's interests their own, and to detect and support whatever is new and progressive.

It is true that there are a number of theoreticians who would try to establish a kind of gradation of socialist democracy, depending on what were the democratic gains and traditions of the country concerned at the time of the proletarian revolution. Thus, according to them, the smaller these gains the country had in the past, the more noticeable the limited nature or "backwardness" of democracy in it. Those expressing this view see socialist democracy as a continuation of bourgeois democracy. Devoid of a class approach or class criteria, this view is far removed from reality. For with the victory of the proletarian revolution society makes a gigantic leap in its development, passing over to a qualitatively new state which differs fundamentally from the past in all spheres of life, particularly the political sphere. Precisely this law of development manifested itself most graphically in the experience of the USSR. It has *really* democratic traditions, created by the people, which have stood the test of time and embody the progressive character of socialism's political system. In the course of our revolutionary struggle the workers, soldiers and peasants of Russia passed through a great political schooling. Their class instinct and organizing talent found their most vital expression in the Soviets—the state form of dictatorship of the proletariat, which is a million times more democratic than any parliamentary republic of the bourgeoisie.

The Soviets embody the supreme constitutional principle of the Soviet system—genuine democracy. At present there are about 50,000 representative organs of power through which the Soviet people govern their state. At the 1969 elections to local Soviets alone 2,070,539 deputies were elected, of whom 44.6 are women, 45 per cent members and candidate-members of the CPSU, 55 per cent non-Party people, 35 per cent workers and 29.3 per cent collective farmers. The deputies include representatives of all the nationalities of the Soviet Union. The elections to the Supreme Soviet of the USSR in 1970 were also a vivid illustration of the political activity of the Soviet people and their devotion to communism. More than 99 per cent of the electorate went to the polls casting their vote for the candidates of the bloc of Communists and non-Party people.

In the light of these facts it is not difficult to see how far removed from reality is the view that with the end of the transitional period the state must wither away to avoid the "bureaucratic deformation of socialism." Such concepts have nothing in common with Lenin's teaching that "for the state to wither away completely, complete communism is necessary." They contradict also the experience of world socialism, as well as the lessons of history. These show that without the organizing role of the socialist state the tasks of economic and cultural development cannot be successfully accomplished either in the transitional period or in a developed socialist society. This is why problems connected with perfecting and strengthening the socialist state and its major link with the masses—the Soviets—are ever in the center of attention of the CPSU.

The CPSU can and must play an ever bigger leading role in the future. It represents a 14-million strong army of Communists and its membership comprises the foremost sections of the working class, collective-farm peasantry and the intelligentsia. Both the extended social base of the Party and the steady growth of its prestige among the people have prompted millions more of the Soviet people to link their destinies with the Party. But although numbers are not unimportant and are, indeed, an indication of the mass character of the Party and the deep roots it has among the people, the Party does not expect its organizations to lay unwarranted emphasis on quantitative growth. The important thing for the CPSU has always been to improve the qualitative composition and to increase the vanguard role of its members, raise their ideological standards and enhance their loyalty to principle and their sense of responsibility for the work of their organizations and the Party as a whole.

The report of the CPSU Central Committee and the statements of delegates and representatives of fraternal parties pointed out the vital importance of the struggle against right and "left" revisionism, and against nationalism. At the same time—and this is particularly important—the Marxist-Leninists strive not only to advance a well-argued criticism of erroneous and dangerous concepts, such as "the dissolution of the Party in society" or its "separation from power"; they also concentrate their efforts on the positive working out of problems of party guidance, on the improvement of all its aspects, organizing and inspiring the masses and directing public and state organizations. The Party does not substitute itself for these organizations, but rather coordinates their activity. In its directive activity it uses means and methods characteristic of the Party alone. Persuasion, explanation, political education, rallying together, organization and again persuasion—this is the basis of all the forms, means and methods of the work of the Communist Party as leader. This principle also exposes the departure from Marxism-Leninism of those to whom the army is higher than the Party, who regard the army as an example for the Party: as a result of the militarization of the Party and its subjugation to such an instrument of state power as the army, the Party unavoidably loses its characteristic forms, methods and means of work and is forced to carry out social functions not inherent in it.

At all stages of its history the CPSU has paid close attention to the need for improving its organizational structure and adjusting it to the tasks of the day. The assertion is groundless that Lenin considered the organizational structure he had elaborated immutable. Its authors would have us believe that the Leninist concept of the Party is out of date, that it should be replaced by another new concept. In effect, they are confusing Lenin's teaching about a new type of party and its organizational principles with ideas about some kind of fixed organization. Organizational forms can, do and must change. The main consideration is that as a result of the change the Party should become stronger, and that its unity, militancy and mobility should be safeguarded.

The Party has also worked steadfastly to improve the functioning of its leading committees on the principle of collectivism. As a result, Party meetings and committee plenums at all levels, from branch

24

organizations to the Central Committee of the CPSU, have come to play a bigger role. Party committees have been improving their work according to the principles of collective leadership. More and more Party members are drawn into studying and discussing various problems and carrying out decisions. The Party is concerned that Communists should be better informed of the work of their leading committees, and reporting of committee and bureau activities in the intervals between elections is becoming a regular practice.

The Party, however, categorically rejects all attempts at creating an atmosphere of "boundless collectivism" in which the personal responsibility of Party members is in fact reduced on the plea of collectivism. Understanding collectivism as Lenin did, the Party regards as imperative the personal responsibility of each Communist for the work entrusted to him. Moreover the Central Committee of the CPSU steadfastly promotes earnest criticism and self-criticism as important means of enhancing inner-Party democracy, of exchanging opinions and experience and of familiarizing Party cadres with rank-and-file suggestions and criticisms.

Vitally important is the position of the Congress that the ability of the Party to function is determined to a great extent by how correctly and consistently the principle of democratic centralism is implemented. Both anarchic looseness, presented as democracy, and bureaucratic centralization, hindering the initiative and activity of Communists, are equally injurious to the Marxist-Leninist party. The conclusion that principled criticism and self-criticism indicate the political health of a party organization is also important. The Congress pointed out that the development of democracy is inseparable from strengthening party discipline, meaning discipline based not on fear, nor on ruthless administrative methods which deprive people of confidence and initiative and give rise to overcautiousness and dishonesty, but on a high level of consciousness and responsibility.

The new period in the life of the USSR, the period of full-scale construction of communism, also makes new demands on the leading role of the Party, demands stemming from the growing scale and complexity of the tasks of communist construction. The one task alone of creating the material and technical base of communism is staggering, not only as regards the scale of what has to be achieved but also as regards the qualitative changes which characterize a higher level of development of the country's productive forces.

Among these qualitative changes is the fact that as society advances to communism the two forms of socialist property—state and cooperative-collective farm—will gradually merge into one form of

25

communist property. No less complex are the processes of perfecting socialist social relations, preparinig the conditions for transition to communist relations and educating the new man, the all-rounded builder of communism.

Other tasks are: erasing the basic difference between town and country, transforming the socialist state into communist public self-government, instilling a Marxist-Leninist world view in all Soviet people, and ending inequalities characterizing the lower phase of communism (socialism) in distribution of material wealth.

The vastly important work of educating the people, clearing their minds of the survivals of the past and fully satisfying the aspirations of the Soviet citizen for physical and spiritual well-being calls for maximum efforts by the Party on the ideological front. The molding of the new man proceeds from new social relations, but not spontaneously. According to Leninist teaching the Party continues in the new conditions to instill socialist consciousness into the spiritual development of the people. Moreover Lenin considered the molding of the communist man as a long process in which the participation of every member of society in productive labor and sociopolitical life is indissolubly combined with his education in the spirit of a high communist consciousness and morality.

The molding of the new man is the most important part of all our creative work. The CPSU takes account of the fact that the molding of the new man is taking place in conditions of an acute ideological battle between socialism and capitalism, in constant, uncompromising struggle against the survivals of the past. This explains the need for constant ideological and educational work of the Party, of all the conscious, advanced forces of society.

As pointed out in the Congress decisions, the most important thing in ideological work is propagating the ideas of Marxism-Leninism and uncompromising, resolute struggle against bourgeois and revisionist ideology. The fostering of the new, communist attitude to work in the Soviet people is one of the most important tasks.

The Party attaches special importance particularly to the education of the youth, for it is the rising generation which will have to continue the work of the older one. Soviet youth, true to Lenin's behests, are educating themselves in the spirit of communism. Industriousness, a thirst for knowledge, and a deep sense of patriotism and internationalism are characteristic of them, qualities which the Communist Party is developing still further.

The Party also displays constant concern for perfecting general and higher education so that it should more fully meet the demands of communist construction and of the contemporary scientific and technological revolution. Some 80 million people—about one-third of the country's population—are presently studying in its higher and secondary educational institutions, including a broad network of evening courses and schools.

Mastery of specialized knowledge combined with the molding of communist morality: this is the line of the CPSU in the sphere of culture and education. The Party does not hold with a narrow utiliarian approach, nor with the bourgeois view that the scientific and technological revolution leads to the "decline of ideology."

In accordance with its Leninist approach, the CPSU therefore pays the closest attention to the theoretical substantiation of practical activity, to party functionaries and rank-and-file Communists mastering the fundamentals of Marxist-Leninist theory, and to improving the whole system of mass political education, political information and the work of the press, radio and television.

The CPSU assigns literature and art an important place in creating the spiritual premises of communism and in the education of the new man. A society building communism is vitally interested in the flowering of literature and art and in all forms of artistic creative endeavor. Thanks to the efforts of the Party, literature and art have been placed at the service of the people.

In its work of guiding science, literature and art the Party follows Lenin's ideas. Lenin on repeated occasions warned against haste and methods of injunction in matters of culture. He particularly stressed the importance of methods of persuasion in this sphere, which calls for a particularly tactful and intelligent approach. For the cause of communist construction it is vitally essential that the Party support works of high artistic value, works imbued with communist morality, and that it criticize attempts to introduce in certain works views alien to the socialist ideology of Soviet society.

After the victory of the October Revolution and the establishment of the dictatorship of the proletariat, Party leadership in the period of building the new society was effected on an ever wider scale, becoming richer in content and more complex. Now the Party's task is to direct the socialist state, economic and cultural development—the entire process of creating new social relations. The Party bases its guidance on an overall, integrated approach to the development of society as a social entity. Alongside its efforts to increase the economic potential and defensive might of the country, it pays enormous attention to the problems of its sociopolitical development and of the education of the new communist man.

The Party's international responsibilities have also increased, responsibilities determined by the Leninist strategic policy of doing "the utmost possible *in one country* for the development, support and awakening of the revolution *in all countries.*" Of course Communists are working to achieve this not by "exporting revolution" but, first and foremost, by demonstrating a more rapid development of the productive forces, the flowering of democracy, culture and science and, in general, the advantages of socialism over capitalism.

In the case of the CPSU this was all the more difficult because it had to blaze the trail, and plow the virgin soil of history in conditions of capitalist encirclement, of bitter resistance by the class enemy within the country and the subversive activity of various anti-Party factions. The Party, however, overcame these difficulties and paved the highway to socialism.

True to its internationalist duty, the CPSU actively promotes consolidation of its ties with the great army of Communists of our planet, coordinates its activity with the other fraternal parties and struggles unflaggingly for unity of the Communist movement on the principles of Marxism-Leninism and proletarian internationalism. The Communist Party guides the foreign policy of the Soviet state, and, together with the fraternal parties, mobilizes the masses in defense of peace, against imperialist aggression, and supports the revolutionary struggle of the working people in the capitalist countries and the national liberation movement.

Our foes have for many years been claiming that Marxism has grown obsolete and does not reflect the requirements of life. But it is the critics of Marxism that grow old and disappear from the stage, whereas Marxism remains an eternally living, developing and all-conquering teaching.

Mankind discovers new sources and new kinds of energy in its struggle for mastering the wealth of nature and exploring space. But in the struggle for social emancipation, all thinking mankind lives and is moved on by the great energy of Marxism-Leninism. The CPSU regards itself as a contingent of the world army of Communists which has been entrusted by history with the honorable but difficult and responsible task of blazing the trail to communism. It is equipped with Marxism-Leninism and vast historical experience and, enjoying the confident support of the Soviet people, is resolved to fulfill its historic mission. And we are convinced that sooner or later all peoples, attracted by the powerful ideas of Marxism-Leninism, will rise to the summits of communism.

Leonid Brezhnev

GENERAL SECRETARY OF THE CPSU
CENTRAL COMMITTEE

*Report of the CPSU Central Committee
to the 24th Congress of the
Communist Party of the Soviet Union
Delivered March 30, 1971*

Extended Summary

THE INTERNATIONAL POSITION OF THE USSR

The Soviet Peace Program

THE Soviet peace program, consisting of the six immediate tasks undertaken by the 24th Congress of the Communist Party of the Soviet Union in the field of strengthening international relations, is of transcendent importance to all the world's people. No political party, no group or organization in the world, no government or state, has ever proposed any such sweeping program for world peace as this, which forms the basis of the foreign policy program of the USSR. We have taken the liberty of separating it from the main body of the Brezhnev report summarized in the following pages, and putting it at the beginning:

● **First:** To eliminate the hotbeds of war in Southeast Asia and in the Middle East and to promote a political settlement in these areas on the basis of respect for the legitimate rights of the states and peoples subjected to aggression.

To rebuff, firmly and immediately, all acts of aggression and international lawlessness. For this, full use must also be made of UN possibilities.

Repudiation of the threat or use of force in settling differences must become a law of international life. For its part, the Soviet Union suggests that the countries which accept this approach conclude appropriate bilateral or regional treaties.

29

● *Second:* To proceed from the final recognition of the territorial changes that took place in Europe as a result of the Second World War. To bring about a radical turn towards a detente and peace on the continent. To ensure the convocation of an all-European conference.

To do everything to ensure collective security in Europe. We reaffirm the readiness expressed jointly by the member countries of the defensive Warsaw Treaty to simultaneously annul this treaty and that of NATO or—as a first step—to dismantle their military organizations.

● *Third:* To conclude treaties banning nuclear, chemical and bacteriological weapons.

To work for an end to the testing of nuclear weapons, including underground tests, by everyone and everywhere. To promote the creation of nuclear-free zones in various parts of the world.

We stand for the nuclear disarmament of all states in the possession of nuclear weapons, and for the convocation for that purpose of a conference of the five nuclear powers—the USSR, the United States, the People's Republic of China, France and Britain.

● *Fourth:* To invigorate the struggle to halt the race in all types of weapons. We favor the convocation of a world conference to consider all aspects of disarmament.

We stand for the dismantling of foreign military bases. We stand for a reduction of armed forces and armaments in areas where military confrontation is especially dangerous, above all in Central Europe.

We consider it advisable to work out measures that would reduce the likelihood of accidental or deliberately fabricated armed incidents that could lead to international crises and war.

The Soviet Union is prepared to negotiate agreements to cut military expenditures, above all by the major powers.

● *Fifth:* The UN decisions to end the remnants of colonial rule must be carried out in full. Manifestations of racism and apartheid must be universally condemned and boycotted.

● *Sixth:* The Soviet Union is prepared for mutually advantageous cooperation in every sphere with other interested states. Our country is prepared to work with other states on such common problems as the preservation of the environment, the development of power and other natural resources, the development of transport and communications, the prevention and eradication of the most dangerous and widespread diseases, and the exploration and development of outer space and the world ocean.

Foreign Policy of the USSR

BREZHNEV'S report on the international position of the USSR dealt first with relations with the other socialist countries and their Communist Parties. Summing up the experience of 25 years of the socialist world system, the report found that:

1. The socialist social system "has proved its great viability in the historical contest with capitalism."

2. The formation and strengthening of a whole bloc of socialist

states has accelerated the historical progress toward socialism all over the world that began with the Russian Revolution and demonstrated that "the world socialist system is the decisive force in the anti-imperialist struggle."

3. The prevention of another world war has been one of the greatest contributions of the socialist bloc to the interests of the peoples of the world.

4. The lesson has been learned, both in theory and practice, that the building of socialism and the relations between socialist states depend on the correct combination of the general rules common to the development of all socialist countries and the different forms determined by the concrete historical conditions and the national specifics of each country.

While Brezhnev frankly acknowledged that both objective and subjective difficulties and complications had arisen in the socialist world, affecting relations between individual states and the Soviet Union, he stated that progress had been made in overcoming them and the dominant tendency remains that of strengthening friendship, unity and cooperation in every sphere among the socialist countries. The special attention given by the CPSU *to cooperation with the Communist Parties* of the fraternal countries had furthered joint efforts to work out the "fundamental problems of socialist and communist construction" and to coordinate activities in the realm of foreign policy.

The Warsaw Treaty organization is the main center for such coordination. It has proposed "a full-scale program for strengthening peace in Europe based on the immutability of existing state borders"; it has helped prevent realization of NATO plans "to give the FRG militarists access to nuclear weapons." Joint efforts by the socialist states contributed to defeat of the Hallstein doctrine [whereby the Bonn government sought to block recognition of the German Democratic Republic by other states] and to strengthening the international position of the GDR, now recognized by 27 states.

Active and consistent support from the USSR and other socialist countries has been a vital factor in the struggle of the people of Vietnam and other Indochinese countries; steps taken by the socialist states in the Middle East have helped frustrate imperialist plans of overthrowing progressive regimes in the Arab countries. In the UN the socialist countries have introduced numerous proposals of key international significance.

On advances made in economic cooperation through the CMEA (Council for Mutual Economic Assistance), Brezhnev said:

The Soviet Union and the fraternal states seek to help each other in every way to develop their national economies. In the last five years, over 300 industrial and agricultural projects have been built or reconstructed in the socialist countries with our technical assistance. We have been supplying our friends with many types of industrial equipment on mutually advantageous terms. The Soviet Union has met more than 70 per cent of the import requirements in some key types of raw materials and fuel of the CMEA countries and Cuba, and also to a considerable extent those of the Democratic Republic of Vietnam and the Korean People's Democratic Republic.

In return, the Soviet Union in the past five-year period has received from the CMEA countries equipment for 54 chemical plants; 38 per cent of the sea-going tonnage of the Soviet merchant navy; investments in the raw material, fuel and other branches of the Soviet economy; numerous consumer goods.

The USSR and other CMEA countries have coordinated their national economic plans for 1971-75 and will further develop the organizational and technical basis for multilateral economic cooperation. The Druzhba Oil Pipeline will be delivering almost 50 million tons of Soviet oil to the Eastern European socialist countries by 1975. The huge new pipeline being laid to carry natural gas from Siberia to the European part of the USSR will help increase gas deliveries to Czechoslovakia and Poland and to start supplying gas to the GDR, Bulgaria and Hungary. Integrated power grids have meant great economies for the CMEA countries. Among other multilateral ties are the International Bank for Economic Cooperation and the new common investment bank of the CMEA countries. All this has meant an increase of 49 per cent in the CMEA countries' industrial production in the past five years. Mutual trade relations have increased.

Brezhnev emphasized that the possibilities of the socialist division of labor were not, however, being fully used, and urged further advances toward economic integration of the socialist countries.

Brezhnev reviewed the strengthening of bilateral relations between the Soviet Union and other socialist countries in the period between the 23rd and 24th Congresses. New treaties of friendship, cooperation and mutual assistance concluded with Bulgaria, Hungary, Czechoslovakia and Romania, together with similar treaties with the GDR, Poland and the Mongolian People's Republic which entered into force earlier, "constitute a comprehensive system of mutual allied commitments of a new, socialist type."

He spoke of the deep satisfaction of the CPSU that recent difficulties in Poland had been overcome and that the Polish United Workers' Party is taking steps to have its ties with the working class and other working people strengthened.

On Vietnam:

Our Party and the Soviet people have relations of socialist solidarity and strong and militant friendship with the Working People's Party of Vietnam and the Democratic Republic of Vietnam. Following the precepts of Ho Chi Minh, great patriot and revolutionary, the Vietnamese people have raised high the banner of socialism and are fearlessly confronting the imperialist aggressors. The Democratic Republic of Vietnam may be sure that in its armed struggle and its peaceful endeavor it can continue to rely on the Soviet Union's fraternal support.

On Cuba:

Over these years, the Central Committee has devoted constant attention to strengthening cooperation with the Republic of Cuba and the Communist Party of Cuba. As a result of joint efforts considerable successes have been achieved in developing Soviet-Cuban relations. The peoples of the Soviet Union and of Cuba are comrades-in-arms in a common struggle, and their friendship is firm.

On Mongolia:

For half a century the CPSU and the Soviet State have had bonds of strong friendship with the Mongolian People's Revolutionary Party and the Mongolian People's Republic. The Soviet Union is a true friend and ally of socialist Mongolia and actively supports the efforts of our Mongolian friends to solve major economic problems and strengthen their own country's international position.

On Korea:

Our ties with the Korean People's Democratic Republic and the Korean Party of Labor have grown, and this, we are sure, meets the interests of the people of both countries. The Soviet Union has supported and continues to support the proposals of the KPDR Government on the country's peaceful, democratic unification and the Korean people's demand for a withdrawal of US troops from South Korea.

On Yugoslavia:

Soviet-Yugoslav relations have continued to develop. The Soviet people want to see socialism in Yugoslavia strengthened and her ties with the socialist community grow stronger. We stand for Soviet-Yugoslav cooperation and for developing contacts between our parties.

On the People's Republic of China:

It will be recalled that the Chinese leaders have put forward an ideological-political platform of their own which is incompatible with Leninism on the key questions of internal life and the world communist movement, and have demanded that we should abandon the line of the 20th Congress and the Program of the CPSU. They unfolded an intensive and hostile propaganda campaign against our Party and country, made territorial claims on the Soviet

33

Union, and in the spring and summer of 1969 brought things to the point of armed incidents along the border.

Our Party has resolutely opposed the attempts to distort Marxist-Leninist teaching and to split the international communist movement and the ranks of the fighters against imperialism. Displaying restraint and refusing to be provoked, the CC CPSU and the Soviet Government have done their utmost to bring about a normalization of relations with the People's Republic of China.

As a result of this Soviet initiative, a meeting took place of the heads of government of the two countries in September 1969, followed by negotiations in Peking between government delegations on border issues. They are proceeding slowly and "their favorable completion calls for a constructive attitude not only of one side." Ambassadors have been exchanged, trade agreements have been signed, trade has somewhat increased. Brezhnev said these were useful steps and the CPSU was prepared to continue to act in this direction:

> But on the other hand, comrades, we cannot of course fail to see that the anti-Soviet line in China's propaganda and policy is being continued and that the 9th Congress of the CPC has written this line, hostile to the Soviet Union, into its decisions . . .
>
> We resolutely reject the slanderous inventions concerning the policy of our Party and our state which are being spread from Peking and instilled into the minds of the Chinese people. It is more absurd and harmful to sow dissent between China and the USSR considering that this is taking place in a situation in which the imperialists have been stepping up their aggressive action against the freedom-loving peoples. More than ever before the situation demands cohesion and joint action by all the anti-imperialist revolutionary forces, instead of fanning hostility between such states as the USSR and China. . . .
>
> Our Party and the Soviet Government are deeply convinced that an improvement of relations between the Soviet Union and the People's Republic of China would be in line with the fundamental, long-term interests of both countries, the interests of socialism, the freedom of the peoples, and stronger peace. That is why we are prepared in every way to help not only to normalize relations but also to restore neighborliness and friendship between the Soviet Union and the People's Republic of China and express confidence that this will eventually be achieved.

On Albania, Brezhnev declared that the CPSU stood ready, as in the past, to normalize relations, which would be beneficial to both countries and the common interests of socialist states.

On Czechoslovakia: Brezhnev declared that the Czechoslovak events were a fresh reminder that whatever remained of anti-socialist forces within socialist countries "may, in certain conditions, become active and even mount direct counter-revolutionary action in the hope of support from outside, from imperialism, which, for its part, is always prepared to form blocs with such forces." These events also, he said, pointed up the dangers of right-wing revisionism which, on the pretext of "improving" socialism, paves the way for the penetration of bourgeois ideology.

The Czechoslovak events showed very well how important it is constantly to strengthen the Party's leading role in socialist society, steadily to improve the forms and methods of Party leadership and to display a creative Marxist-Leninist approach to the solutions of pressing problems of socialist development.

It was quite clear to us that this was not only an attempt on the part of imperialism and its accomplices to overthrow the socialist system in Czechoslovakia. It was an attempt to strike in this way at the positions of socialism in Europe as a whole, and to create favorable conditions for a subsequent onslaught against the socialist world by the most aggressive forces of imperialism.

In the light of this, the report continued, and in view of "appeals by Party and state leaders, Communists and working people of Czechoslovakia" and concern for the future of socialism and peace in Europe, "we and the fraternal socialist countries then jointly decided to render internationalist assistance to Czechoslovakia in defense of socialism." He expressed CPSU agreement with the assessment of this action as set forth in the document "Lessons of the Crisis Development" of a plenary meeting of the Central Committee of the Communist Party of Czechoslovakia, which he quoted as follows:

"The entry of the allied troops of the five socialist countries into Czechoslovakia was an act of international solidarity, meeting both the common interests of the Czechoslovakian working people and the interests of the international working class, the socialist community and the class interests of the international communist movement. This internationalist act saved the lives of thousands of men, ensured internal and external conditions for peaceful and tranquil labor, strengthened the Western borders of the socialist camp, and blasted the hopes of the imperialist circles for a revision of the results of the Second World War."

Thus, concluded Brezhnev: "The peoples of the socialist countries have clearly demonstrated to the whole world that they will not give up their revolutionary gains, and that the borders of the socialist community are immutable and inviolable."

He emphasized that the socialist world is still a young and growing socialist organism with still unsettled problems, developing "through struggle between the new and the old." Accumulated experience will help the parties of the socialist countries find the correct resolution of their internal contradictions, and to deepen their mutual help and cooperation. He drew this picture of the future of the socialist world:

We want to see every fraternal country a flourishing state harmoniously combining rapid economic, scientific and technical growth with a flowering of socialist culture and rising living standards for the working people. We want the world socialist system to be a well-knit family of nations, building and defending the new society together, and mutually enriching each other with experience and knowledge, a family strong and united, which the people of the world would regard as the prototype of the future world community of free nations.

The Struggle Against Imperialism

IN ITS assessment of modern imperialism and the peoples' struggle against it, the report said that under today's conditions of confrontation with socialism, the ruling class fears more than ever the development of the class struggle into a mass revolutionary movement. Hence the bourgeoisie tries to use more camouflaged forms of exploitation and oppression of the working people and to keep the masses under its political and ideological control by partial reforms. This adaptation to new conditions has not meant the stabilization of capitalism as a system. *"The general crisis of capitalism has continued to deepen."*

Simultaneous growth of inflation and unemployment has become a permanent feature of even the most developed capitalist countries, with the USA foundering in one of its economic crises for almost two years.

Neither processes of integration nor the pooling of imperialist activities against the socialist world has eliminated inter-imperialist contradictions. The three main centers of growing imperialist rivalry are the USA, Western Europe (above all the six Common Market countries), and Japan.

The continuing reactionary and aggressive nature of imperialism is embodied above all in US foreign policy,

which in the last few years has reasserted its urge to act as a kind of guarantor and protector of the international system of exploitation and oppression. It seeks to dominate everywhere, interferes in the affairs of other peoples, highhandedly tramples on their legitimate rights and sovereignty, and seeks by force, bribery and economic penetration to impose its will on states and whole areas of the world.

Forces of war and aggression also exist in West Germany, where the revanchists have been increasingly ganging up with the neo-Nazis; in Britain they are the executioners of Northern Ireland, arms suppliers to the South African racists and supporters of the aggressive US policy; in Japan, the militarists who seek once again to embark on expansion and aggression.

Militarism has grown at an unprecedented rate since World War II. In 1970 alone NATO countries invested 103 billion dollars in war

36

preparations. The USA has spent almost 400 billion dollars for military purposes in the last five years.

The imperialists are willing to commit any crimes to preserve or restore their domination of the former colonial countries of Asia, Africa and Latin America. Their annual plunder of Third World countries amounts to billions of dollars, while according to a 1970 UN report, 375 million people of those continents live at starvation level.

Condemning imperialist aggression against the Arab states, the colonialist attempts to invade Guinea and the subversive activity against progressive regimes in Latin America, Brezhnev charged:

> The continued US aggression against the peoples of Vietnam, Cambodia and Laos is the main atrocity committed by the modern colonialists; it is the stamp of ignominy on the United States.

Declaring that "it is hard to keep a calm tone when speaking about the atrocities committed by the interventionists," Brezhnev recounted the sadistic murders of old men, women and children at Songmy, the turning of huge areas into wasteland, the million and a half Vietnamese poisoned by US chemicals and other horrors committed by those who claim to represent the "free world."

However difficult the struggle, the anti-imperialist front steadily widens, with the *international working class movement* in the vanguard of the revolutionary forces and the trade unions playing an increasingly important role. Adducing examples of working class action against monopoly capital in many countries, including the United States, Brezhnev emphasized especially the US Black liberation struggle and the role of US youth in the movement against the war in Vietnam. At the same time anti-imperialist pressures are intensifying from the national liberation forces, especially in the young states of Asia and Africa:

> The main thing is that the struggle for national liberation in many countries has in practical terms begun to grow into a struggle against exploitative relations, both feudal and capitalist.

Quite a few countries in Asia and Africa have taken the non-capitalist road of development, leading toward socialism. Property of imperialist monopolies is being nationalized. In the UAR the state sector now accounts for 85 per cent of total industrial production; in Burma the state sector controls over 80 per cent of the extractive and almost 60 per cent of the manufacturing industry. Algeria has taken new steps in nationalizing imperialist property. In Guinea, the Sudan, Somali and Tanzania many foreign concerns have been taken over by the state. Serious land reforms have been carried out in the UAR and Syria, have started in the Sudan and Somalia and are announced for this year in Algeria. In the Congo (Brazzaville) all the land and its minerals are now state-owned.

Serious progressive social change is taking place in many other countries and the fight for liberation intensifies in countries still under the colonial yoke:

> As for our country, it fully supports this just struggle. The USSR's political and economic cooperation with the liberated countries has been further developed in the last few years. Our trade with them is growing. Dozens of industrial and agricultural enterprises have been built in many countries of Asia and Africa with our participation. We have also been making a contribution to the training of personnel for these countries. All this is being done in the mutual interest.

Among the changes taking place in a number of Latin American countries, the victory of the Popular Unity forces in Chile "was a most important event." The fact that "the people have secured, by constitutional means, the installation of a government they want and trust," has "incensed domestic reaction and Yankee imperialism," which seek to deprive the Chilean people of their gains. The governments of Peru and Bolivia are fighting against enslavement by the US monopolies. Lenin's prediction that peoples struggling for national liberation would go on to fight against the very foundations of capitalism is thus coming true.

Brezhnev stressed the efforts of the CPSU and the parties of other socialist countries to strengthen the cohesion of anti-imperialist forces, above all of the world communist movement, on which the success of the anti-imperialist struggle largely depends. This task has been complicated by splitting efforts of the Chinese leadership, the Trotskyites and others, tendencies toward nationalistic self-isolation and the revival of both "Left" and Right-wing opportunism.

A major step in strengthening international unity of the Communists and consolidating the anti-imperialist forces, according to Brezhnev, was the International Meeting of Communist and Workers Parties in 1969 and various other meetings which preceded it. Worldwide celebrations of the Lenin Centennial also contributed greatly to unity. Brezhnev reiterated the continuing urgency of fighting against revisionist and nationalistic tendencies, especially those taking the form of anti-Sovietism, which bourgeois ideologists and propaganda rely on in their fight against socialism and the communist movement.

The CPSU is increasingly finding allies in the struggle against imperialism in the revolutionary democratic parties, many of which have proclaimed socialism as their goal. The CPSU has been actively developing ties with them as well as with Left Socialist Parties in some countries. Further, said Brezhnev:

The CPSU is prepared to develop cooperation with the Social Democrats both in the struggle for peace and democracy and in the struggle for socialism, without, of course, making any concessions in ideology and revolutionary principles. However, this line of the Communists has been meeting with stubborn resistance from the Right-wing leaders of the Social Democrats.

Expressing the high regard of the CPSU for the work of its brother parties and its dedication to the pursuance of a strengthened, united anti-imperialist struggle, Brezhnev declared:

The full triumph of the socialist cause all over the world is inevitable. And we shall not spare ourselves in the fight for this triumph, for the happiness of the working people!

The Soviet Struggle for Peace

THE REPORT set forth Soviet efforts in the five-year period "to ensure peaceful conditions for communist construction in the USSR, to expose and frustrate action by the aggressive imperialist forces, and to defend socialism, the freedom of the peoples and peace." It has consistently followed the Leninist principle of the peaceful coexistence of states, regardless of their social systems, and maintaining normal relations wherever the situation allows.

Placing the Vietnam war in the forefront of pressing international problems, Brezhnev warned the United States that no steps it would attempt in its aggressive war in Southeast Asia "will break down the Vietnamese people's determination to become master of its own country":

The so-called Vietnamization of the war, the plan to have Vietnamese kill Vietnamese in Washington's interests, and the extension of the aggression to Cambodia and Laos, none of this will get the USA out of the bog of its dirty war in Indochina or wash away the shame heaped on the country by those who started and are continuing the aggression. There is only one way of solving the Vietnamese problem. It is clearly indicated in the proposals of the DRV Government and the Provisional Revolutionary Government of the Republic of South Vietnam, proposals which we firmly back.

The Soviet Union resolutely demands an end to the imperialist aggression against the peoples of Vietnam, Cambodia and Laos. Our country has been and will be an active champion of the just cause of the heroic people of Indochina.

Turning to the Middle East, he declared:

The crisis which has arisen as a result of Israel's attack on the UAR, Syria and Jordan has been one of the most intense in the development of international relations over the past period.

The USSR and other socialist countries took all possible measures to stop and condemn the aggression. They raised the question in the UN Security Council and at an extraordinary session of the UN General Assembly called at their demand. They broke off relations with Israel, which ignored the UN decision for a ceasefire. The USSR helped restore the defense potential of the Arab states subjected to invasion, the UAR and Syria in the first place.

Brezhnev expressed satisfaction with the UAR initiative in supporting the proposal of special UN representative Gunnar Jarring, stating its readiness to conclude a peace agreement with Israel once its troops are withdrawn from the occupied Arab territories, and in proposing steps to resume navigation along the Suez Canal. He continued:

> The Israeli Government's rejection of all proposals, and Tel Aviv's now openly brazen claims to Arab lands clearly show who is blocking the way to peace in the Middle East, and who is to blame for the dangerous hotbed of war being maintained in that area. At the same time, the unseemly role of those who are instigating the Israeli extremists, the role of US imperialism and international Zionism as an instrument of the aggressive imperialist circles, is becoming ever more obvious. . . .
>
> The Soviet Union will continue its firm support of its Arab friends. Our country is prepared to join other powers, who are permanent members of the Security Council, in providing international guarantees for a political settlement in the Middle East. Once this is reached, we feel that there could be a consideration of further steps designed for a military detente in the whole area, in particular, for converting the Mediterranean into a sea of peace and friendly cooperation.

On Soviet peace efforts in Europe, the CPSU General Secretary spoke of recent improvement in Soviet-French relations as a contribution to European security and noted possibilities of further growth of Soviet-French cooperation.

A substantial shift in Soviet relations with the Federal Republic of Germany has opened up new prospects in Europe. Treaties of the Soviet Union and Poland with the FRG have confirmed the inviolability of the postwar borders, including those between the GDR and FRG and the Western borders of the Polish state. Noting differences in West Germany over ratification of these treaties, Brezhnev warned:

> Delay over ratification would produce a fresh crisis of confidence over the whole of the FRG's policy, and would worsen the political climate of Europe and prospects for easing international tensions.

The CPSU report advocated serious measures for the convocation of an all-European Security Conference, now backed by a majority of the European states. It underlined that the problem of West Berlin could be solved if the USA, France and Britain would proceed "from respect for the allied agreements which determine the special status of West Berlin and respect for the sovereign rights of the GDR as an independent socialist state." There should also be equitable relations between the GDR and the FRG, and both should be admitted to the United Nations. Disarmament, to curb the arms race and reduce the danger of war, continues to be a cardinal point in Soviet foreign policy. The treaty on non-proliferation of nuclear weapons which entered into force in the period under review must be ratified by the FRG, Japan, Italy and other signatories. Treaties banning nuclear weapons in outer space and on the ocean floor are only a first step. Our aim is "to bring about a situation in which nuclear energy shall serve peaceful purposes only."

The CPSU, said Brezhnev, seeks a favorable outcome of the SALT talks, in order to avoid another round in the missile arms race and release large sums for constructive purposes. Success is only possible if no one seeks unilateral advantages:

> The struggle for an end to the arms race, both in nuclear and conventional weapons, and for disarmament—all the way to general and complete disarmament—will continue to be one of the most important lines in the foreign policy activity of the CPSU and the Soviet state.

Reviewing improved relations with various capitalist nations, Brezhnev took up relations with the United States:

> An improvement of Soviet-American relations would be in the interests of the Soviet and the American peoples, the interests of stronger peace. However, we cannot pass over US aggressive actions in various parts of the world. In the recent period, the US Administration has taken a more rigid stance on a number of international issues, including some which have a bearing on the interests of the Soviet Union. The frequent zigzags in US foreign policy, which are apparently connected with some kind of domestic political moves from short-term considerations, have also made dealings with the United States much more difficult.
>
> We proceed from the assumption that is possible to improve relations between the USSR and the USA. . . . But we have to consider whether we are dealing with a real desire to settle outstanding issues at the negotiating table or attempts to conduct a "positions of strength" policy.

Brezhnev spoke wryly of the well-known proclivity of the imperialists to try to revive the "Soviet menace" to cover up their own aggressive schemes, seeking evidence of this threat "in the depths of the Indian Ocean and on the peaks of the Cordilleros," while those who look through NATO binoculars "see nothing but Soviet divisions set to march against the West in their field of vision." The CPSU answers:

41

We have everything necessary—a genuine peace policy, military might and have no intention to attack anyone, we stand for the free and independent development of all nations. But let no one, for his part, try to talk to us in terms of ultimatums and strength.

We have everything necessary—a genuine peace policy, military might and the unity of the Soviet people—to ensure the inviolability of our borders against any encroachments and to defend the gains of socialism.

Brezhnev hailed as the greatest achievement of the Party's foreign policy the 25 years their people had lived in peace and mankind had been safeguarded from world war. Yet the forces of aggression had not yet been rendered harmless. They have started 30 wars and conflicts in the postwar years. Not yet has the threat of a new world war been completely eliminated. It is the vital task of all the peoples to prevent this threat from becoming reality.

The Soviet Union has countered the aggressive policy of imperialism with its policy of active defense of peace and strengthening of international security. [The six-point peace program placed at the beginning of this report follows here.]

II. MAIN QUESTIONS OF PARTY'S ECONOMIC
POLICY AT PRESENT STAGE

BREZHNEV opened his review of economic policy by recalling Lenin's urging fifty years ago, when presenting for broad discussion the GOELRO plan, the first state plan for economic development in history, that Party Congresses and conferences should be turned into "bodies that will verify our economic achievements . . . in which we can really learn the business of economic development" (*Collected Works*, Vol. 31, p. 514).

"Our Party Congresses," Brezhnev declared, "have in fact become such bodies in the full sense of the word!" He proceeded to report on the successful completion of the Eighth Five-Year Plan by the Soviet people, "thereby taking another major step in building the material and technical basis of communism, strengthening the country's might and raising the people's living standards."

Main Results of Eighth Five-Year Plan, 1966-1970

THE Directives of the 23rd Congress have been successfully fulfilled in all the main economic targets. The national income, to have increased by 38-41 per cent, has grown by 41 per cent; industrial production, targeted at 47-50 per cent, increased by 50 per cent. Key indicators relating to the working people's living standards have been overfulfilled. On the whole results were considerably greater than those of the preceding five-year plan, with the aggregate social product rising by 142 per cent instead of the previous 137 per cent. The national income used for consumption and accumulation increased at an average rate of 7.1 per cent a year as against 5.7 per cent in the preceding period. Productivity of social labor increased by 37 per cent as against 29 per cent.

The share of products turned out by those branches of heavy industry which determine technical progress—electric power, the chemical and petrochemical industries, engineering, especially radio-electronics and instrument-making—increased from 28 to 33 per cent of total industrial output. Output of consumers' goods rose 49 per cent as against 36 per cent in the previous five years. Industrial output in 1970 alone nearly doubled that of all the prewar five-year periods taken together.

In agriculture, which has been and remains the most difficult and complex sector of the economy, efforts of the Party and the working people have resulted in an increase of 21 per cent in average farm output as against 12 per cent in the preceding five-year period. Annual average gross output of grain has increased by 37 million tons, or 30 per cent. In 1970 a record 186 million tons of grain and 6.9 million tons of raw cotton were harvested, with grain averaging 15.6 centners and cotton 25 centners per hectare. (One hectare=2.47 acres.)

In large-scale capital construction, almost 1,900 large industrial enterprises and installations have been commissioned.

The economic potential of Siberia, the Far East, Central Asia and Kazakhstan has markedly increased and the national economy of all the republics has advanced, thus enlarging "the economic foundation of the union and brotherhood of all our peoples."

Brezhnev then reviewed those areas especially connected with people's living standards. In the five years, real income per capita increased by 33 per cent as compared with 30 per cent envisaged by the 23rd Party Congress and 19 per cent in the previous plan period. The minimum wage for workers and office employees was raised to 60 rubles a month; the average wage increased by 26 per cent; collective farmers' incomes from social production increased by 42 per cent. In the collective farms guaranteed payment has been introduced, the pension age lowered, and payment of sick benefits and disability allowances for members inaugurated.

In these five years social consumption goods have increased by 50 per cent, amounting to almost 64 million rubles in 1970. Retail trade increased by 48 per cent in 1966-70; meat consumption per capita increased in 1970 by 17 per cent over 1965, milk and milk products by 22 per cent, eggs by 23 per cent, fish and fish products by 14 per cent, with a simultaneous reduction in consumption of bread and potatoes. Sales of such articles as radios, TV sets, washing machines and refrigerators all increased.

On housing, the Soviet state has spent nearly 60 billion rubles in the past five years, representing 500 million square meters, the equivalent of over 50 cities with a million people each. In 1966-70, 151,000 doctors were trained, 22,000 more than in the previous period. Length of paid annual leaves has been extended for many working people; most are now on a five-day week.

Alongside these successes, the CPSU report noted shortcomings and unresolved problems. Production targets for some important items not fully met; delays in expanding production capacity in chemical, machine-tool, light and a few other industries; failure of many ministries to fulfill plans for new equipment and labor productivity targets; electricity and machinery for agriculture still behind plan. Within overall average wage increase, rates and basic wages of some categories fell below plan. Within overall rise in food and consumer goods, supplies of meat and other products and goods are still below demand.

Aside from objective causes, external and internal, the Congress, said Brezhnev, must focus attention on any deficiencies in the work of economic, government and Party organs responsible for these shortcomings.

In the past five years much has been done to rectify shortcomings in management of industry and agriculture. In particular great advances have been made under the economic reform (see the article by Alexander Birman, NEW WORLD REVIEW, No. 1, 1971) and in formulating new long-term development plans for agriculture.

The Tasks of the New Five-Year Plan

BREZHNEV emphasized that the immense economic strength built up in the Soviet Union meant entering upon an entirely new stage of development with hitherto undreamed of potentialities. *This economy daily produces a social product worth nearly two billion rubles, ten times more than at the end of the thirties.*

[Detailed figures for the ninth five-year plan are given in Kosygin's report and will not be repeated here.]

In the earlier stages it was necessary to concentrate on the top priorities on which the very existence of the Soviet state depended.

Now, said Brezhnev, we can and must deal simultaneously with broader problems:

> While securing resources for continued economic growth, while technically re-equipping production, and investing enormously in science and education, we must at the same time concentrate more and more energy and means on tasks relating to the improvement of the Soviet people's well-being. While breaking through in one sector or another, be it ever so important, we can no longer afford any drawn-out lag in any of the others.
>
> The high degree of economic development has yet another important effect: The demands on planning, guidance and economic management techniques are rising substantially. The interdependence of all the economic links is enhancing, adding to the importance of long-term planning, of forging a system of inter-industry connections and of improving material supplies.
>
> Important specific features of the present stage of the country's economic development are also traceable to the rapidly unfolding scientific and technical revolution. Socialism, the planned socialist economy, offers the broadest scope for all-sided progress of science and technology. However, the scientific and technical revolution requires the improvement of many sides of our economic activity. In other words, it is a huge force favorable for socialism, but one that has to be properly mastered.

External conditions which must be taken into account in facing new economic tasks are the developing economic integration of the socialist countries and the economic and technico-scientific competition between the two world systems. In sum:

> The main task of the Five-Year Plan is to secure a considerable rise in the living standard and cultural level of the people on the basis of high rates of growth of socialist production, increase in its effectiveness, scientific and technical progress and accelerated growth of the productivity of labor.

Raising the Standard of Living the Supreme Aim

THIS MAIN task of the Ninth Five-Year Plan, said Brezhnev, will determine the Party's activity not only for the coming five years, but over a long term:

> In setting this task the Party proceeds primarily from the postulate that under socialism the fullest possible satisfaction of the people's material and cultural requirements is the supreme aim of social production.

Higher living standards, Brezhnev explained, were not only based on the Party policy of further accentuating the role of material and moral labor incentives; it was not a question of sitting back and taking things easy. They are a precondition for the rapid growth of production, "for the all-round development of the ability and creative activity of Soviet people . . . that is, to develop the main productive force in our society." Modern production sets rapidly rising demands not only on machines, on technology, but primarily on the workers.

Specialized knowledge and a high degree of professional training, man's general cultural standard, are becoming an obligatory condition of successful work. And this enhancement of man's creative, productive capacity depends in turn to a considerable extent on how fully material and spiritual requirements can be satisfied.

After reviewing measures to increase substantially the income of the Soviet people, extend house building and improve the towns and villages, Brezhnev outlined the Central Committee's plan for *satisfying the growing solvent demand of the population for foodstuffs, manufactured goods and services.* Contrary to the situation in the past, consumer production must go up at a higher rate than the cash incomes of the Soviet people. The production potential now makes possible a higher rate of growth for light industry and consumers' goods in relation to heavy industry.

This means no slackening of concern for heavy industry. Priority development of heavy industry in the past alone has "enabled us to safeguard the gains of the socialist revolution, to end the centuries-old backwardness, to achieve gigantic economic, social and cultural progress."

High rates of growth in heavy industry retains its importance since all future economic growth including improvement in the standard of living and the building of the material and technical basis of communism are all largely dependent on this, and "because without developing heavy industry we cannot maintain our defense capacity at the level necessary to guarantee the country's security and the peaceful labor of our people." But, while "we must be prepared for any possible turns in the train of events," the Soviet Union is ready to support "realistic disarmament measures that consolidate peace and do not impair our security."

Program of Further Agricultural Development

MUCH ATTENTION has been given to agriculture in the period under review. On its successful development the rates of growth of the economy as a whole and of the people's living standards largely depend.

An important step taken by the March 1965 CC plenary meeting was to make decisions on stable procurement plans (i.e., amounts to be sold to the state) for collective and state farms for a number of years, incentive prices for products delivered in excess of plan to stimulate growth of production and other measures. Further, following a thoroughgoing analysis of the needs of agriculture and the means to meet them, the CC plenary meeting of July 1970 worked out a comprehensive, long-term plan for the development of agriculture, including supplying the countryside with the necessary machinery and fertilizers, expanding capital construction and electrification, land improvement, personnel training and improvement of organization of production, and further expansion of grain, animal husbandry and industrial crops. Brezhnev warned the delegates, however:

> The problems of agriculture are such, comrades, that they cannot be completely resolved in a year or two, or even in five years; it will take a much longer time and require huge investments and enormous effort not only by the farm workers, but by all our industry.

In the future, specialization of farming and industrial methods of producing meat, milk and other products will be further developed, but only as thoroughly prepared in each case and economically substantiated. All this is leading increasingly to the spread of inter-collective farm and state-collective farm production and the establishment of agro-industrial complexes, able to make more effective use of equipment, investments and manpower, and broader use of industrial methods.

In outlining the need for increasing the quantity and improving the quality of consumer goods, Brezhnev spoke of the need for a radically changed approach to consumer goods production on the part of planning and economic authorities and Party, trade union and government organizations:

> We have many years of heroic history behind us, comrades, when millions of Communists and non-Party people consciously accepted privations and hardships, were content with the bare essentials and denied themselves the right to demand any special amenities. This could not but reflect on their attitude to the production of consumer goods, to their quality and range. But that which was explicable and natural in the past, when other tasks, other undertakings stood in the forefront, is unacceptable in the present conditions. And if some comrades tend to overlook this, the Party is entitled to regard their attitude as stemming either from a failure to understand the substance of its policy, oriented on a steady rise of the living standard, or as an attempt to vindicate their inactivity. The Central Committee considers it necessary to raise this issue incisively and frankly.

Brezhnev excoriated those administrators, in the center as well as locally, who managed to "coexist peacefully" with shortcomings, reconciled themselves to the low quality of some goods, cut back or stopped production of essential items on the pretext of replacing outdated goods with new ones, etc.

In order to meet the needs of the people, nearly twice as much is being allocated for the development of the light and food industries as in the preceding five-year plan. The Party and economic bodies

FOR THE NEW MAN

IN THE DOMAIN of social policy the Party line is a line for the further strengthening of the unity of Soviet society, bringing still closer together the classes and social groups, all the peoples and nationalities making up Soviet society. It is a line for the consistent development of socialist democracy, for enlisting ever wider masses for the solution of public and state matters; it is, further, a line of raising the communist consciousness of all working people, the all-out development of science and culture, of the intellectual development of the Soviet man, of asserting the moral and political atmosphere in the country in which people find it easy to breathe, joyous to work and peaceful to live.

L. I. BREZHNEV, closing speech, April 9

have the responsible task of seeing that these sums are used correctly, that "cases where prices are inflated should be firmly combated," and that retail prices remain stable, with price reductions put into effect when economic preconditions are created.

On Trade and Community Services

MANY NEW stores and trading facilities have been opened. Yet there are still many flaws in the domain of trade and services, which unfortunately the people concerned accept as being perfectly normal. Trading establishments do not properly study market demand, stock up with too many non-essential and not-enough-needed goods. Consequently production is sometimes curtailed, creating shortages of items like sewing machines and irons. Managers of trading organizations must give attention to improving service in shops, the organization of trade and introduction of modern methods.

Much attention is being paid to public catering, but still more must be done, especially in enterprises, offices, factories, state and collective farms, and educational organizations, and capacities must be enlarged to meet the demand. Often the fare is not tasty, which is "not to be tolerated." Brezhnev called for stricter dealing with the ministries, local authorities and management and urged that the trade unions take a strong hand in correcting unsatisfactory cuisine.

Substantial improvement is necessary in all the services that deal directly with the people, "with the diversity of their tasks, feelings and moods." This applies to tailoring and dressmaking and repair services as well as recreation and entertainment facilities. Paid services to the population will be doubled in the next five-year plan. Much depends on local initiative, including the local Soviets. More must be done to make it possible for pensioners, housewives and invalids to work in this sphere. It is necessary to raise the social standing of people working in the services, so that young people will not think it beneath them to do service work and the public will not look down on those who do.

Resources for the ever-expanding tasks that lie ahead must be found mainly in increasing the productivity of labor and in acceleration of scientific and technical progress.

The Scientific and Technical Revolution. Fusion of Science and Production

BREZHNEV laid great stress on the need for a high scientific and technical level of production as a whole, rather than on separate scientific achievements, at this time when "the role of science as an immediate productive force keeps growing."

There must be further unfolding of scientific research, concentration on the most important long-term trends in scientific and technical progress, on new machinery and production processes. Greater tasks than ever face the State Committee for Science and Technology, the Academy of Sciences and the ministries.

Our weakest link is the speedy adoption of scientific achievements in mass production. Everything possible must be done to concentrate attention of scientific organizations on the most important production problems, and to make sure that our enterprises fight for modernizing plant and production processes and "not shy away from them, figuratively speaking, as the devil shies from holy water."

Economic plans must reckon more fully with achievements of science and technology. Failure to do this has resulted in the Ministries of the Timber and Woodworking Industry, Tractor and Farm Machinery, Engineering, and others falling short of their targets.

There must be an extension of research and studies within industry, design bureaus, experimental bases. A large number of researchers should go directly into industry. "In many cases good results may be obtained by merging research institutions with enterprises, creating powerful science-production complexes." Since "scientific and technical progress is the main lever for building the material and technical basis of communism," it is essential that all Party cadres pay special attention to accelerating scientific and technical progress and take long-term prospects into account in their practical work. Brezhnev told the Congress:

> The task we face, comrades, is one of historical importance: *organically to fuse the achievements of the scientific and technical revolution with the advantages of the socialist economic system;* to unfold more broadly our own intrinsically socialist forms of fusing science with production.

At the same time, Brezhnev emphasized the need to combine with this task *a rational treatment of natural resources that should not cause dangerous air and water pollution or exhaust the soil.* The Party, he said, demands that all economic and scientific organizations and cadres must keep the question of nature protection in mind in designing and building new enterprises or improving existing ones, so that "not we alone but coming generations should also be able to use and enjoy the gifts of our country's special natural environment."

Brezhnev spoke of the need for improving the structure of industrial development and the proportions in the economy of various branches, economy of raw materials, a high rate of expansion of the extractive industries, reducing per unit consumption of materials on a countryside scale, more rational use of manpower resources by cutting down on manual and physically arduous labor. Necessary is all-round development of industries manufacturing new highly productive equipment, whole systems of machines facilitating conversion to comprehensive mechanization of jobs and automated processes. (Measures for improving specific industries and whole complexes of related industries and improving the utilization of production assets and investment, discussed by Brezhnev, are here omitted since they are covered also in the Kosygin report.)

In his discussion of the Party's economic policies Brezhnev emphasized the necessity for a decisive change in the approach of Party cadres to economic questions. In the past, due to historical reasons and special conditions, quantitative assessments had always been given priority: to produce so many tons of steel, of oil, of grain, so many tractors, and so on. Quantity remains important. But the new situation today requires emphasis on quality and on the economic aspect of industrial operations. Whereas executives in the past won praise by quantitative achievement, today, where the cost has been excessive, where the executive has fulfilled the plan itself but failed in inter-enterprise delivery commitments, letting down other enterprises, where success in one sector has concealed a shortfall elsewhere, in such cases not praise but criticism is required. The standard of exactingness must be raised. "There must be criticism not only of those who make mistakes but also of those who fail to use all

50

the possibilities for developing production, refuse to display initiative, and sit on their hands."

To Improve the System of Economic Management

IMPROVEMENT of the system of economic management "is essentially a matter of how best to organize the activity of society in accelerating economic and social development, in ensuring the fullest use of the available possibilities, and in rallying even closer together hundreds of thousands of collectives and tens of millions of working people around the main aims of the Party's policy." It is a matter affecting not only a narrow circle of executives and specialists, but all Party, government and economic organizations and all collectives of working people. It is an important part of the Party's entire activity in directing the economy. The growing scale and qualitative shifts in our economy make it impossible to depend on existing forms and methods. Higher levels of knowledge and training of cadres and working people and the rapid development of the science of management and computer techniques have created new potentialities. We have succeeded in raising the level of centralized direction of the national economy along with much greater operational independence for the enterprises.

Brezhnev dwelt also on the political aspects of the question. Bungling and bureaucracy create apathy, waste labor and resources. An efficiently operating economy creates enthusiasm, spurs initiative, and benefits everybody.

Much has been accomplished in improving economic management. But it must be a continuing, dynamic process of solving problems brought up by life.

On planning. Under socialism planning is the core of national-economic guidance, and both its theory and practice must be continually improved; especially today its scientific level must be raised. "Planning must rest on a more precise study of social requirements, on scientific forecasts of our economic possibilities, on all-round analysis of different variants of decisions and of their immediate and long term consequences. . . . National economic development requires long-term planning and constant coordination of long-term with five-year and annual plans." We have already had much positive experience in this sphere. In the future we must take fuller account of local specifics and improve the territorial location of production. There must be wider use of methods of economic-mathematic modelling, systems analysis and so on. Sectoral automated management systems must be created more rapidly in preparation for a nationwide automatic system for collecting and processing information, for which necessary equipment must be produced and skilled personnel trained. *On improving the organizational structure of management.* This means enhancing the role and improving the work of the State Planning Committee and other all-Union state organs as well as of the ministries and departments, and extending the independent initiative of the latter. The line of forming amalgamations and combines should be followed more boldly in industry and agriculture, since only large associations can embrace sufficient numbers of qualified specialists, insure rapid technical progress, and make the best use of all resources.

Brezhnev spoke of the necessity of consistent practice of "the Leninist principle of individual responsibility for assignments." It must be made perfectly clear who is responsible for fulfillment, and for failures and delays. *It is important to define at every level of management the volume and balance of rights and responsibilities,* in order to avoid arbitrary administrative acts, subjectivism and ill-considered decisions. It is necessary to eliminate too many levels of management, to have decisions final on most questions, instead of being passed from one level to another.

On increasing economic incentives. In accordance with the decisions of the Central Committee's plenary meeting in September 1965 on improving industrial management, the Party has accumulated considerable experience in combining directive assignments by central organs and the use of economic levers such as cost accounting, prices, profit, credit, forms of material incentives and so on. Many problems remain to be solved. It is necessary to create the economic conditions which would enable enterprises "to adopt maximum plans and make more rational use of capital investments and labor resources, ensure the maximum acceleration of scientific and technical progress and the growth of labor productivity and facilitate a consistent drive for higher quality in production." Brezhnev declared:

> The consistent implementation of the principles of operation on a profit-and-loss basis remains an urgent task at industrial enterprises, at collective and state farms and at higher economic levels. The role of economic contracts and the responsibility for honoring them must be enhanced.

Brezhnev cited the experience of the Shchekino Chemical Works as an example of the importance of giving greater material incentives to those workers and collectives who make the greatest contribution to the development of production, while at the same time promoting moral incentives.

On broader participation of the people in economic management. Brezhnev emphasized the Party's concern for drawing the workers into the management of production on an ever larger scale. He cited Lenin's teaching that every working person, every politically conscious worker should feel "he is not only the master in his own factory but that he is also a representative of the country."

The people's participation in economic management is not confined to their role in individual enterprises. The economic policy of Party and state is dictated by the basic interests of the working people, and charted by representatives of the working people in elective organs, with masses participating broadly in the discussion of major plans and decisions, and in checking up on their fulfillment.

A large role is played in economic management by the primary Party organizations uniting millions of workers, collective farmers and office employees; also by trade unions in resolving economic problems, promoting socialist emulation and mass technical innovation and strengthening labor discipline, and in concluding and checking collective agreements. Procedures for the latter should be improved.

The period under review has seen a marked upswing of activity of production conferences [in which workers participate jointly with management in solving production problems], workers' meetings and general meetings of collective farmers. There must be encouragement of the practice of heads of amalgamations and enterprises and top-level ministry officials regularly accounting for their work directly to the workers. Questions of labor protection and living conditions must of course receive the closest attention of the collectives of working people. In the final analysis, everything depends on the people themselves

---

CHANGES IN CPSU RULES

1. Congresses of the CPSU and of the Communist Parties of the Union will convene every five years, to dovetail with the five-year plans. Territorial, zonal, town and district Party conferences will be held twice in the five-year period, with corresponding election meetings; primary (local) party organizations must hold election meetings every year.

2. The control or checking-up functions of the Party in relation to design, research, educational, cultural, medical and other establishments will be shifted to the primary party organizations from higher bodies, in all cases where such establishments function within the sphere of the local party collective. Primary organizations can now be formed within the framework of several enterprises belonging to a production association, and party committees can be formed at individual shops within one large primary organization.

Adapted from Pravda, *April 10*

and their conscious and persevering labor. Brezhnev concluded this section of the report as follows::

> Our purpose is to make the life of the Soviet people even better, even more attractive, even happier. We are marching forward to many years of selfless and inspired labor, giving fully of our creative energy. For this is the only way to welfare and happiness, to a radiant communist future.

SOCIO-POLITICAL AND CULTURAL DEVELOPMENT AND THE TASKS OF THE PARTY

Changes in Social Structure, Strengthening of Unity

IN PURSUANCE of the Party's policy of taking fully into account both the interests of the entire people and of various classes and social groups, it seeks to bring the working class, the collective-farm peasantry and the intelligentsia closer together, *gradually erasing the distinctions between town and countryside and between labor by hand and by brain.* This is being achieved on the basis of Marxist-Leninist ideology which expresses the socialist interests and communist ideals of the working class.

During the past five-year plan the number of workers grew by about 8,000,000. Including state-farm workers, workers now comprise 55 per cent of the employed population. The leading role of the working class as the main productive force in society is further enhanced by the growth of its general cultural and educational level. In 1959 there were 386 workers per 1,000 with a higher or secondary education; now the figure tops 550. Numerous workers with a secondary education, who have mastered their trade, are continuing their studies while on the job and studying the advanced achievements of science and culture. The stratum of workers has been steadily growing in the Communist Party, the Soviets and public organizations.

The alliance of the working class with the peasantry, the political foundation of Soviet society, has been further consolidated. With the gradual conversion of agricultural labor into a variety of industrial work through increased mechanization, the cultural upsurge in the countryside and the transformation of rural life, the peasant now has more and more features in common with the worker. On the eve of World War II only six per cent of the rural population had a higher or secondary education; today this true of more than half.

An increasing number of inter-collective and mixed state-collective farm production associations and enterprises has brought industry and agriculture closer together. New and more complex farm machinery, the growth of the peasants' standard of living and gradual improvement of cultural and everyday conditions have made agricultural labor more attractive, particularly for young people, who today return more willingly to the countryside after graduating from educational institutions.

The new Model Rules of the Collective Farm adopted by the Third all-Union Congress of Collective Farmers and the election of a Union Council of Collective Farms and collective-farm councils of district, regional, territorial and republican levels have contributed to the development of life in the countryside and collective-farm democracy. Much of course still remains to be done.

The intelligentsia continues to grow quickly, and in recent years the growth of the scientific and technical intelligentsia has exceeded that of all other social groups. The fact that this group is replenished increasingly from the ranks of the workers and peasants is itself a big factor in reducing the gap between workers by hand and by brain.

The Party, Brezhnev declared, will continue to pay special attention to the interests of young people, women and pensioners. More than half of the country's population are under 30—"they are our future and our replacement."

The Party has initiated a series of important measures to improve the working conditions of women and lighten their household chores; maternity leave procedures have been extended to collective-farm women; more crèches, kindergartens and everyday service establishments have been opened. Much more is planned for the new period, declared Brezhnev:

> The aim of the Party's policy is that Soviet women should have further possibilities for bringing up their children, for taking a larger part in social life for recreation and education and that they should have greater access to the blessings of culture.

Pensioners and war veterans have been given wider opportunities to take part in social and labor activity and steps must be taken to employ their experience and energy even more extensively.

Practical implementation by the Party of the *Leninist national policy,* a policy promoting equality and friendship among peoples, is demonstrated in recent celebrations of the 50th anniversaries of many of the fraternal republics. All the nations and nationalities of our country, declared Brezhnev, and above all the great Russian people, have played their role in the formation and development "of this mighty union of equal nations that have taken the road to socialism." The General Secretary continued:

> Further progress along the road of the all-round development of each of the fraternal Soviet republics, along the road of the further gradual drawing together of the nations and nationalities of our country, has been made during the past few years under the Party's leadership. This drawing together is taking place under conditions in which the closest attention is given to national features and the development of socialist national cultures. Constant consideration for the general interests of our entire Union and for the interests of each of its constituent republics forms the substance of the Party's policy on this question. . . .
> The Party will continue to educate all the working people in the spirit of socialist internationalism, intolerance of nationalism, chauvinism, national narrowness and conceit in any form, in a spirit of profound respect for all nations and nationalities.

Strengthening the Soviet State. Development of Socialist Democracy

THE BASIS of the work accomplished in the recent period in strengthening the Soviet state, the report noted, has been and remains the further development of socialist democracy, which has its main embodiment in the Soviets of Working People's Deputies. They comprise over two million deputies "who administer the affairs of our state of the entire people at all its levels," aided by 25 million voluntary activists.

Following decisions of the 23rd Congress, powers of local Soviets have been extended in many ways, including greater responsibilities in coordinating the work of factories and economic organizations in their territories, enlargement of their material and financial resources and trained personnel. Deputies meet more regularly with the electorate and account for their work to them. Increase in standing commissions and more efficient organization of their activities have developed more initiative on the part of the deputies. Greater control is exercised by the Supreme Soviets of the USSR and the Union Republics over the work of ministries and departments and in the key sectors of economic and cultural development.

Pursuing its concern for perfecting Soviet legislation the Party has initiated important new legislation, which has become law after broad discussions in which millions of citizens participated. This includes government decrees in the sphere of improving public health services, strengthening family relations, improving labor relations and ensuring nature conservation and the rational utilization of water resources and other natural wealth.

56

Important steps have been taken to improve the work of the state apparatus by use of modern means and methods of administration:

Most of the employees of the state apparatus are highly trained, conscientious and considerate people. Their work merits the highest appreciation and respect. But it must be admitted that there still are callous officials, bureaucrats and boors. Their conduct evokes the just indignation of Soviet citizens. The Party has been and will go on making a resolute effort to achieve more efficiency in its administrative apparatus. The way we see it, efficiency in administration organically combines an attentive, solicitous attitude to the needs and cares of the working people with a prompt consideration of their applications and requests.

The organs of people's control, through which millions of factory and office workers and collective farmers continually check up on fulfillment of tasks by both officials and rank and file, will find continued support and strengthening on the part of the Party.

An important feature of the socialist system is the working people's participation in the administration of society not only through state organs, but through a network of mass organizations, especially the trade unions and the Komsomol (Young Communist League).

The 93 million trade union members include practically the entire working class, all the working intelligentsia and numerous sections of rural workers.

The trade unions are one of the key links in the general system of socialist democracy, in drawing the working people into the administration of the affairs of the state and society. They participate in solving production problems, drawing up state plans, questions of management; they help to inculcate a socialist attitude to labor and social property, to satisfy the cultural and everyday and health requirements of the people; to safeguard the legitimate interests of the workers and prevent violations of their rights. The Party's line is to continue enhancing the role of the trade unions:

Without assuming petty tutelage over the trade unions, the Party organizations must do everything to promote their activity and initiative . . . seeing to it that they are able to fulfill their role of school of administration, school of economic management and school of communism more fully and successfully.

The Lenin Komsomol (to be considered more fully below), which unites over 28 million young men and women, plays an important part in the country's social and political life:

It would be hard to name a sector of economic and cultural development where the energy, creative efforts and ardor of Komsomol members have not been displayed. Komsomol shock building projects, team contests of skill by young workers, students' building detachments, youth production brigades and summer work and recreation camps are among the concrete and vital tasks being accomplished by the Komsomol, the leader of the Soviet young people.

In recent years Party organizations have been assigning increasingly responsible tasks to the Komsomol on questions of labor, education, recreation and everyday life of young people. Over half a million young people have been elected to organs of state power. Nearly 20 per cent of the deputies to the Supreme Soviet of the USSR are young people. Since the 23rd Congress 45 per cent, or 1,350,000 new members of the Party have come from the Komsomol. The Party is proud of the young builders of communism and relies on them "to be worthy continuers of the cause of the great Lenin."

Brezhnev reported that in this past period the Central Committee and the Soviet Government have continued measures *to strengthen legality and law and order.* This is not only the task of the state apparatus, but the Party organizations, the trade unions, the Komsomol, all persons in office, all Communists. Stressing the need to insure the strictest observance of law, Brezhnev also declared that no "violation of the rights of individuals" or "infringement of the dignity of citizens" could be tolerated. In the fight against crime, along with measures taken for stricter punishment, there is also great concern "to find ways and means of discouraging and preventing crime."

In face of "continuing subversive activity by imperialism," the organs of state security are educated by the Party to act "'in the spirit of Leninist principles, of absolute observance of socialist legality, in the spirit of unremitting vigilance in the struggle to safeguard Soviet society against the actions of hostile elements and against the intrigues of imperialist intelligence services."

In this troubled world, everything created by the people must be reliably protected. To strengthen the Soviet state means to strengthen its *armed forces,* and "raise our country's defense capability to the highest possible level." Said Brezhnev:

> The Soviet people may rest assured that our glorious Armed Forces are prepared to repel an enemy attack at any time of the day or night from any quarter. Any possible aggressor is fully aware that in the event of attempting a nuclear-missile attack on our country he will be dealt a devastating counterstrike.

Brezhnev said that the Party's constant concern was that socialist democracy should steadily develop and that every person should feel he is a citizen in the full sense of the word.

Molding the New Man

THE BUILDING of communism "cannot be advanced without the harmonious development of man himself." One of the paramount objectives of the Party's ideological work is to *foster in Soviet people the new, communist attitude to work.* Evaluating the essence of the new type of human being, Brezhnev said:

> Comrades, the new make-up of the Soviet man, his communist morals and outlook, are consolidated in constant and uncompromising struggle with survivals of the past. Communist morals cannot triumph without a determined struggle against bribe-taking, parasitism, slander, anonymous letters, drunkenness and the like. The struggle with what we call survivals of the past in the minds and actions of people is a matter that requires constant attention by the Party and all the conscious, advanced forces of our society.
>
> During the period under review, the Party CC has taken steps to create in our society a moral atmosphere that would help establish a respectful and solicitous attitude to people, honesty, exactingness to oneself and others, and trust, combined with strict responsibility and a spirit of true comradeship in all fields of social life, in work and everyday relations. In short, our aim has been that in our country everyone should live and work better.

The 23rd Congress set the task of completing the transition to universal secondary education by the end of 1970. While not achieving the set target, today about 80 per cent of the pupils completing eight-year school go on to complete secondary education. More than 60 new institutions of higher learning, including nine universities, were opened during the past five years. All Union Republics and many Autonomous Republics have their own universities today. Curricula of schools and higher educational institutions have been brought more into line with the general level of modern scientific knowledge. Over seven million specialists with a higher secondary special education have been trained in the last five years.

The total number of Soviet scientific workers has increased 40 per cent during the past five years, reaching nearly 930,000. New scientific centers are being opened in the Urals, the Soviet Far East and the North Caucasus. Much fruitful work has been accomplished by the Soviet Academy of Sciences and Soviet scientists in general, in scientific progress on the earth and in outer space and in the introduction of scientific achievements in production.

Brezhnev noted at the same time that there were still shortcomings in the work of scientific institutions, that many scientists were still occupied on work divorced from the practical needs of the country which was in fact wasted effort. On the growing role of literature and art in "molding the outlook, moral convictions and spiritual culture of the Soviet people," Brezhnev made these observations:

> The Party continues, as it has always done, to devote much attention to the ideological content of our literature and art and to the role they play in society. In line with the Leninist principle of partisanship we believe that our task is to direct the development of all forms of creative art towards participation in the people's great cause of communist construction.
>
> During the past five years our literature, theater, cinema, television, fine arts and music have given the Soviet people many new, interesting and talented works. New works and productions have appeared which deal with our people's past and present realistically, from Party positions, without embellishment and without playing up shortcomings, and concentrate attention on truly important problems of communist education and construction. These works are further confirmation that the closer the artist is to the many-faceted life of the Soviet people the surer is the road to creative achievement and success.

He mentioned particularly the fruitful development of literature and art in all the republics, in dozens of languages of the peoples of the USSR and in all the vivid diversity of national forms.

Declaring that it could not be said that all is well in the realm of creative artistic work, especially as regards quality, Brezhnev said that there were still many works "shallow in content and inexpressive in form," that sometimes even in work that had a good theme, the artist had approached the task superficially and not put all his effort and talent into it.

Criticizing both those who still laid too much stress on the Stalin period and those who tried to whitewash the past, he said:

> There were some people who sought to reduce the diversity of present-day Soviet reality to problems that have irreversibly receded into the past as a result of the work done by the Party to surmount the consequences of the personality cult. Another extreme current among individual men of letters was the attempt to whitewash past phenomena which the Party had subjected to emphatic and principled criticism, and to conserve ideas and views contravening the new creative elements which the Party had introduced into its practical and theoretical work in recent years. Essentially, both these cases were attempts to belittle the significance of what the Party and the people had already accomplished, and divert attention from current problems, from the Party's constructive guidelines and the creative work of the Soviet people.

Development of the Party. Questions of Inner Party Life

THE PERIOD under review witnessed the further growth of Party membership and qualitative improvement of its composition. The CPSU now has 14,455,321 members of whom 645,232 are candidates, or probationary members. Nine per cent of the adult population are Communists. The Party composition is: 40.1 per cent workers, 15.1 per cent collective farmers, 44.8 per cent office and professional workers, including engineers, agronomists, teachers, doctors, scientific workers and workers in literature and art.

Three million people have been admitted to the CPSU since the 23rd Congress, of whom 1,600,000, or more than half, are workers. The Party, said Brezhnev, cleanses its ranks of those who violate Party or state discipline, or abuse their office, whose behavior casts a slur on the name of Communist. *We have been undeviatingly further developing inner-Party democracy, observance of Leninist norms of Party life and increase in the activity of Communists.* The principle of electivity and accountability of leading organs is implemented consistently and the spirit of collective leadership and collective work has been consolidated. Questions concerning the Party's work are discussed and decided on a broad democratic scale.

During the five years under review there have been 16 plenary meetings of the CPSU Central Committee. Regular weekly meetings of the Politburo consider the most important and pressing problems of the Party's home and foreign policy. There is also a weekly meeting of the CC Secretariat, centering chiefly on selection of cadres and fulfilment of assignments. Local Party committees likewise hold regular plenary meetings and bureau sittings and operate as organs of collective leadership.

The democratic principles in the life and work of the Party were strikingly demonstrated during the election campaign for this Congress. Party meetings were attended by over 90 per cent of the Communists, more than three million people spoke. Party Congresses and conferences of the Union Republics thoroughly discussed the Party's policy, their own work, successes and shortcomings, unresolved problems and future plans.

Many new people have been elected to leading Party organs— workers, collective farmers, intelligentsia, workers of all social strata and groups and of all the nationalities of the country; 423,000 workers and collective farmers have been elected to the bureaus of Party organizations and Party committees. Members and alternate members of district and town Party committees are 40 per cent workers and collective farmers.

Inner-Party information on key problems of the Party's work and on the domestic and international situation has been improved, both from the Central Committee to local organizations and information going from bottom to top. Brezhnev declared that criticism and self-criticism, "a tested method of eradicating shortcomings and improving the work," has been further developed:

61

Most Party committees have become more attentive to the critical remarks and suggestions of Communists and have intensified control over their realization. At the same time it must be emphasized that not all Party organizations and their leading organs have drawn the proper conclusions from the instruction of the 23rd Congress on this question. Some leaders lack restraint and tact, the ability to hear out critical remarks attentively and correctly react to criticism. But those who underestimate or ignore criticism wittingly doom themselves to failure. Broad development of criticism and self-criticism is a sign of political health of the Party organizations, of their correct understanding of their duty towards the Party and the people.

Brezhnev spoke of the need for strengthening Party discipline and correct adherence to the principle of democratic centralism and avoidance of either anarchic lack of discipline, presented as democracy or of bureaucratic centralization. Changing of Party membership cards, not done for 17 years, should be approached as an important organizational and political measure. Brezhnev said the Party could not accept passivity and indifference on the part of Party members; the moral prestige of the Party requires lofty ideological and moral qualities in all members:

Regrettably, we still have Party members who do not show themselves to be real political fighters. When they come across shortcomings and other negative phenomena they pretend to notice nothing, adopting the position of the philistines, who say, "This does not concern me, let others worry about it." There are also some whose activity is for the purposes of show, of creating an outward impression. They talk more than others about the need for doing one thing or another, always lecture and exhort everybody. But as soon as the time for practical action comes they manage to remain on the sidelines. . . . If you are a Communist your duty is not to shirk difficulties, not to encourage backward attiitudes, but to be a politically conscious and active fighter for the Party.

Brezhnev stressed the importance of the primary organizations of the Party, of which there are 370,000—45,000 more than on the eve of the 23rd Congress. In improving their work special stress is laid on the right of the Party organizations to check on the activities of management in production enterprises and to extend this right to primary Party organizations at research, educational, cultural and medical institutions and in central and local government and economic institutions and departments.

In connection with improving the structure and activity of Party organizations Brezhnev noted that whereas in the past 14 years CPSU membership has doubled, increasing from 7 to 14 million, the Party apparatus was reduced by more than 20 per cent. There are now in the CPSU 14 Central Committees of the Communist Parties of the Union Republics, 6 territorial committees, 142 regional committees, 10 area committees, 760 town committees, 448 urban district committees and 2,810 rural district committees.

He spoke with approval of many important suggestions put forward by Communists for strengthening the Party work, which must be utilized. He said the Central Committee approved the proposals for convening Party Congresses every five years instead of every four, in order to bring it in line with the period of the five-year plans and be in a better position to assess their results and prospects. Organizations below the republic level could hold them twice in the same period.

On training of cadres and raising the level of leadership, the rise of the political consciousness, education and professional training of workers, collective farmers and intellectuals, there are now immense possibilities. From 70 to 80 per cent of the top central, republic and regional leadership of the Party and government began their careers as workers and peasants. More than half of the directors of the largest industrial enterprises were once workers. Local functionaries are constantly being promoted, with a special policy of bringing forward young cadres along with maximum use of the experience of veteran functionaries. Initiative, a feeling for the new, are valued qualities of leadership, which must also combine managerial and educational work. Brezhnev said:

> It sometimes happens that a leading cadre suddenly gets the idea that all the secrets of life are open to him, that he knows everything. That is when he begins issuing instructions on all questions, ordering people about, instead of skillfully using the experience and knowledge of others. We have long had skilled cadres capable of resolving problems within their competence directly.

We must put more trust in them and, correspondingly, more must be asked of them.

The combination of collective leadership with personal responsibility for assigned work is indispensable. Discipline and responsibility of cadres must be enhanced—not discipline founded on fear or ruthless administration, but on a high level of consciousness and responsibility of people. During the period under review nearly 200,000 Party and government functionaries were trained or retrained to improve their work. Refresher institutes, departments and courses have been set up for economic executives and specialists. An Institute for National Economic Management for leading cadres in industry, including ministers, has recently been opened.

The Marxist-Leninist Education of Communists

REGARDING the Party's ideological and theoretical work, Brezhnev stated:

> Comrades, our Party is a party of scientific communism. It is steadfastly guided by Marxist-Leninist science, which is the most advanced, revolutionary science of modern times, and does everything for its further development. Theoretical understanding of the phenomena of social life and its main trends enables the Party to foresee the course of social processes, work out a correct political line and avoid errors and subjectivistic decisions.

The Party's theoretical thinking, along with the Party's and the people's "multiform experience of revolutionary struggle, the building of socialism and communism, the problems of the world revolutionary process and the specifics of the present stage of international relations, have all found expression in the decisions of the CC and in the Party's documents commemorating the 50th anniversary of the Great October Revolution and the Centenary of the Birth of V. I. Lenin," as well as in connection with the International Meeting of Communist and Workers' Parties in 1969, and also in connection with the 150th birth anniversaries of Marx and Engels and the centenary of the Paris Commune.

Commenting on new fundamental works on Lenin's role as leader and theoretician published during this period, Brezhnev continued:

> As an eternally living and developing teaching, Leninism has been, remains and will be in the center of the Party's ideological life and the foundation of all its revolutionary, transformative activity. While drawing on Lenin's ideological legacy, the Party holds that its cardinal task is to find solutions to pressing problems of communist construction on the basis of Lenin's ideas and Lenin's methodology.

Much attention was given to the further development of teaching on the role of the Communist Party which today has become the pivot of the struggle between Marxist-Leninists and representatives of the various forms of revisionism. The Party attached immense importance "to the accurate, unbiased presentation of the history of our state." Individual attempts to assess the history of the Soviet people from non-Party, non-class positions, and to belittle the history of their socialist gains, were sharply criticized, as well as "dogmatic notions which ignored the great positive changes that have taken place in the life of our society in recent years." On the question of the Stalin and Khrushchev leadership [although not mentioning their names] Brezhnev said:

> The experience of the past years has convincingly shown that the surmounting of the consequences of the personality cult and also of subjectivistic errors has favorably affected the general political and, above all, the ideological situation in our country. We have been and remain true to the basic principles of Marxism-Leninism and shall never make any concessions in questions of ideology.

Together with other governing Communist Parties, the CPSU has continued to elaborate the fundamental questions of the development of the world socialist system and to specify the characteristics of the general laws of socialist construction and the main features of socialism that has already been built, on the basis of study and generalization of each other's experience. Particular attention has been given to the working out of principles of economic integration.

Attention has also been given to analyzing new phenomena in the development of modern capitalism and ways and means by which socialism influences the development of the non-socialist part of the world. Terming theoretical work a major element of "our internationalist, revolutionary duty," Brezhnev continued:

> The struggle between the forces of capitalism and socialism on the world scene and the attempts of revisionists of all hues to emasculate the revolutionary teaching and distort the practice of socialist and communist construction require that we continue to pay undivided attention to the problems and creative development of theory. Repetition of old formulas where they have become outworn and an inability or reluctance to adopt a new approach to new problems harm the cause and create additional possibilities for the spread of revisionist counterfeits of Marxism-Leninism.

While much has been accomplished, the Central Committee does not consider that everything in our theoretical work is satisfactory; "The ideological steeling of Communists is an indispensable condition for enhancing the militancy of the Party ranks."

Much has been done in the improvement of Marxist-Leninist education, with a comprehensive system of Party education of three stages —primary, middle and higher. Textbooks and manuals have been published in mass editions for all levels. More than 16 million people now study in the system of Party education. The attitude of some Party committees which do not give this work proper attention must be corrected. Summarizing the results of the last five years of ideological work, Brezhnev declared:

> The unity of interests between the Party and the entire Soviet people makes our society invincible and gives it the ability to withstand any test. It is the indissoluble unity between the Party and all the working people that allows us to forge confidently ahead and resolve the most complex tasks. Our Party values and treasures that trust of the working people above all else. To strengthen our great Party in every way, to deepen its bonds with the people, with the masses—that is the behest left to us by the great Lenin— and we shall be true to this behest of Lenin.

Concluding his report, Brezhnev reminded the delegates of the importance in Lenin's view of the work of Party Congresses in summing up the results of practical experience and all that has been found to be valuable and instructive, as well as criticizing shortcomings and finding ways of removing them. He called for a principled, responsible discussion of the report on this basis. The conclusion of his report follows:

> Comrades, we have inexhaustible possibilities. Our country's economic might is greater than ever before. New heights have been attained by Soviet science and culture. The moral and political unity of our people is unbreakable. We are moving forward shoulder to shoulder with our socialist friends and allies. Our militant alliance with the revolutionary forces of the whole world is growing stronger.
> We know that we shall achieve all that we are striving for, and successfully carry out the tasks we are setting ourselves. The guarantee of this has been, is and will be the creative genius of the Soviet people, their selflessness and their unity around the Communist Party which is steadfastly advancing along the course charted by Lenin.
> Long live the Communist Party of the Soviet Union—the Party of Lenin, militant vanguard of our entire people!
> May the Union of Soviet Socialist Republics, mainstay of peace and friendship among nations, live long and grow stronger!
> May the mighty alliance of revolutionary forces—the world socialist system, the international working-class movement and the fighters for the national and social liberation of people—grow stronger and advance from victory to victory!
> Hold higher the banner of the eternally living, invincible teaching of Marx-Engels-Lenin! Long live communism!
> Glory to the great Soviet people, the builder of communism!

Speeches of
Congress Delegates

In the pages which follow we present excerpts from some of the speeches made at the Congress. Presented as comments on the main report, delivered by Leonid Brezhnev, and on the report on the draft Directives of the Ninth Five-Year Plan, delivered by Alexey Kosygin, these comments all make special contributions in the speakers' areas of competence and experience. Our selection from them continues on page 111, following the summary of Kosygin's report.

ANDREY A. GROMYKO

USSR Foreign Minister

THE fraternal socialist countries continue to be a reliable barrier against any aggressor. Those who tried in one way or another to probe the strength of the borders of the Warsaw Treaty states have seen for themselves that the socialist countries take the defense of these borders seriously, as they do the defense of their socialist system.

Mention must be made of the contribution by the socialist states to the defense of other countries of the world from aggression. No one will ever be able to erase from the awareness of the peoples of Asia, the Middle East, Africa and Latin America the steps that our country has taken time and time again, jointly with its allies, to protect the victims of aggression.

Things are shaping up well with relations with most of our neighbors, as indeed with most of the countries of the world. The following figures indicate the scope of our activity abroad. Today we have 144 embassies and consulates representing the USSR's state interests abroad. The Soviet Union is taking part in the work of more than 400 international organizations. More than 7,000 operative international treaties and agreements have been signed by our country.

Today nothing of any degree of significance in world relations can be decided without, or in defiance of, the Soviet Union. Indeed, anyone today who might try to prove that the Soviet Union could be dispensed with in deciding such matters would be considered cockeyed. On the contrary, our proposals for strengthening peace and European security, for ending the arms race, for firm measures against colonialism, and for many other measures, are at the very pivot of political debates and discussions and they help in reaching the needed solutions. This is admitted by all, including our political and ideological opponents.

The strength of Soviet foreign policy is due not only to the might that stands behind it. We all know that certain other powers also possess economic and other potentials of no mean magnitude. The main thing is that our policy is the expression of the very nature of our social system as the most peace-loving in history.

In the USA millions of volumes are published which extol the foreign policy of imperialism. Add to that the almost daily official or semi-official utterances in the same vein, and the vast newspaper and magazine editions with the same content. The ordinary man's head simply buzzes with all this cacophony, designed to confuse him. However, it has a deadly fault: it is a tissue of lies because behind it all are the definite class aims of those who pursue an aggressive policy. When Washington says that the USA would like to pull its troops out of Vietnam, but at the same time commits aggression against Cambodia and Laos as well, what is one to call that? In whatever colors this policy is depicted, lies can never be passed off as truth or the aggressor as a peace-maker.

The revolutionary nature of our country's foreign policy, its consistent championship of peace, its firm defense of the Soviet Union's state interests, and its genuine internationalism are all fused together in a single entity. Soviet foreign policy is honest and forthright in action as well as aims.

The call for peace was inscribed on the banner of the Soviet Republic the day it was born. Today our country continues along this road. With every year and indeed, with every day, it is acquiring more and more new friends throughout the world.

Small wonder, therefore, that in the most far-away places, in Africa, say, a person who is still unable to show where different countries are located on the map, because the colonialists did not want to teach him such things, knows that there is a country in the world which spurns racial inequality and aggressive wars and which stands for freedom for all peoples.

We have no territorial claims against any country in the world and no intention of infringing on anyone's legitimate rights and interests. But we also demand that our own country be treated in the same fashion.

Anyone really prepared to come to terms with us on questions requiring a solution will always find the Soviet Union a serious and responsible partner. But anyone who tries to encroach upon our interests and security, and the interests and security of our friends and allies, will soon see the futility of such an attempt.

"Marxism," V. I. Lenin teaches us, "requires of us a strictly exact and objectively verifiable analysis of the relations of classes and of the concrete features peculiar to each historical situation. We Bolsheviks have always tried to meet this requirement, which is absolutely essential for giving a scientific foundation to policy." (V. I. Lenin. *Collected Works*, Vol. 24, p. 43, Engl. ed. Progress Publishers, Moscow, 1964).

Motivated by this thesis of Lenin's, the Party has placed before Soviet foreign policy the task of securing the most auspicious conditions for building socialism and communism, the task of averting the danger of another world war. Two things are equally alien to us, either to succumb to imperialist threats or to engage in ultra-revolutionary phrase-mongering.

The USA and some of its allies in its aggressive military blocs use every possible device to camouflage their line in world affairs. At the same time they try to discredit Soviet foreign policy and distort its content and aims.

Here are a few examples.

The key decision taken jointly by the great powers, the former wartime allies, to bring lasting peace to Europe and pull out the roots of aggression for all time to come was the Potsdam decision, taken immediately after Hitler Germany was defeated. But instead of collective security and cooperation with the Soviet Union on the basis of the Potsdam decision, the Western powers divided Europe into military blocs and undertook a policy of intensifying tensions in Europe.

The 1954 and 1962 Geneva Accords were reached to promote peace in Indochina and to ensure independence to the peoples of Vietnam, Cambodia and Laos. The USA took part in the drafting and adoption of these agreements. However, Washington policy-makers were in no way embarrassed by that when they decided to unleash the most dangerous and bloody armed conflict since the second world war.

Without the USA's direct support, Israeli aggression against its Arab neighbors would have fizzled out at once, indeed, would probably not have been undertaken at all. Without such support the Israeli extremists would never have dared to flaunt their refusal to implement the UN decision to withdraw from the occupied Arab territories.

Our Party draws a distinct line of demarcation between the ideological struggle, in which there can be neither peace nor truce, and our international relations with the capitalist states, relations that are built on the Leninist principles of peaceful coexistence. The Soviet

Union and its allies propose settling all international disputes by peaceful means through negotiations. On our part we are doing everything in our power to search for such solutions.

If we take the work done by the Politbureau in foreign policy alone, it must be said outright in the Party's highest forum that this steering body has the enormous energy and skill necessary for the complexity of the tasks facing it.

In the entire range of the Soviet state's moves in the international arena, the actions and steps taken within the framework of the USSR Supreme Soviet occupy a great and responsible place. The diversified activities of its Presidium, the work of its Commissions for Foreign Affairs and its Parliamentary Group, the latter's visits, talks and exchange of delegations: all these greatly enrich our state's activity on the international scene and serve the cause of peace.

Day after day the Soviet Government, the USSR Council of Ministers, occupies itself with foreign affairs in conformity with the line adopted by the Central Committee and the Politbureau. This work, which deals not only with politics but many highly important matters in the sphere of economic contacts, trade, scientific and technical cooperation and cultural relations with other countries, calls for the personal participation of a large number of responsible representatives from our country and experts in various fields. One can say that the government's representatives have continuous dealings with more than 100 states, reflecting in their daily practices our policy and what we usually call the Center's directives. Meanwhile, the core of this Center is the will of the Party, as expressed above all in the decisions adopted in its congresses.

Altogether thousands of people, including Members of the Central Committee and the Soviet Government and the Deputies of the USSR Supreme Soviet are directly involved in one way or another in all the complex and responsible undertakings in our country's foreign policy.

Our Soviet diplomatic corps is also discharging its duty as helper of the Party and Government. I almost said our legion of diplomats, but then I remembered that the offices in charge of personnel matters might pick that up, which could mean a rough time for those of us who work in this field!

In the pursuit of its peaceful foreign policy our country attaches great significance to searching for agreement even with those who follow a different political course. The question is sometimes asked: "How reliable is this, what is the real value of agreements with certain states, if they do not always observe these agreements?" This point is sometimes raised in another, to put it bluntly, provocative manner, when any agreement with capitalist states is declared to be almost "collusion." Of course no one can guarantee that our partners will always duly carry out the treaties signed. Here we also have a struggle, in which the Soviet Union invariably proceeds from strict observance of international treaties and agreements. But as for the afore-mentioned claims about "collusion," even those who make them don't believe what they say.

Our country's moves in foreign policy since the 23rd CPSU Congress have greatly reenforced the hopes of the peoples for peace. In Europe our dealings with France are faring well. Affairs with Italy have made great progress. Millions of people outside the socialist countries as well, have characterized the signing of treaties with the FRG by the Soviet Union and Poland as a gain for themselves too, as an essential contribution to normalization in Europe. The entry into force of these treaties, the settlement of problems in relations between the FRG and the socialist states of Europe, the holding of an all-European conference on security, and the successful outcome of talks on West Berlin, are all important steps that must be taken to change a Europe of conflict to a Europe of lasting peace. These moves must be undertaken simultaneously without waiting for one to be concluded before taking up another.

The blows of the peoples have shattered those colonialist empires whose subjects once seemed doomed by their oppressors to live in everlasting misery. However, not all colonialist prisons have yet been destroyed. The Soviet Union has made a special contribution to the realization of this major international task not only because our practical moves in policy are so very important here, but also because our very world outlook, the example afforded by our multinational state exposes, in perhaps the most effective way, the policy of national and racial oppression.

Another great gain for the foreign policy of socialism and for the forces of peace is that today the overwhelming majority of states prefer peaceful coexistence as the sole sane alternative to war. Our Party and our country are doing everything they can to entrench this Leninist principle still more widely and firmly in international relations.

And in this connection there again arises the question of our relations with the United States. Time and again we have stated our policy in this matter. It has also been clearly and definitively expounded in the CPSU Central Committee report to this Congress. Washington must weigh with all seriousness everything that the General Secretary of the CPSU Central Committee has said in his report, in speaking for our Party and country.

The Soviet Union is for normal relations with the USA. It believes an improvement in Soviet-American relations possible. But Washington's statements in favor of talks must be supported by practical measures. Yet the Americans, to put it mildly, are far from always prepared to do that. We have little liking for talks that are more like fencing matches. We stand for serious talks. We want the parties to such talks to really seek agreement and not try to trip one another up.

As you well know, the Party and country have always attached and continue to attach great importance to our relations with China. Our policy, which was formulated in Leonid Brezhnev's report, clearly demonstrates the positive consequences improved relations would have for the peoples of both the Soviet Union and China, as well as the tremendous significance this would hold for the common struggle against imperialism and aggression. It depends on China's leaders, on the Chinese side, in what direction relations between the Soviet Union and the People's Republic of China will develop.

That we are a peace-loving country has been proved by word and action. Our foreign policy as well as our economy and mass well-being are advanced by each machine tool made in the country, each ton of metal smelted, each new computer manufactured, each kilogram of grain harvested.

On the international scene major complex tasks face the country. There will be much work to do and it will be hard work. To accomplish the tasks before us we shall have to continue the struggle against the forces of aggression. But we rest confident that in the years to come as well, our country will cope with its historic mission, as the bulwark of socialism, the freedom of the peoples, and peace.

MSTISLAV V. KELDYSH

President, USSR Academy of Sciences

ALLOW me, on behalf of our scientists, to express complete support for the Party's domestic and foreign policies.

One of the main levers for accelerated development of our national economy is technological progress. The foundation of technological progress is the discoveries in the natural sciences. In our time it is difficult to find new opportunities accessible to direct observation, and a profound penetration into the phenomena of nature is therefore necessary.

Such great discoveries of the past as electricity, electromagnetic

72

waves and the laws of aerodynamics have had an immense influence on people's entire way of life. Modern science is opening up increasing opportunities. The study of the atomic and molecular structure of matter lays the foundations for the development of new materials and substances for technology, agriculture and medicine. Today chemistry has provided opportunities for processing oil and gas into plastic materials and fibers, and has become a mighty stimulus for development of agriculture. The study of electrical phenomena in solids and gases has led to the development of electronics. The investigation of the structure of the atomic nucleus has helped to discover the use of nuclear energy. New discoveries in mathematics are playing an immense part in the development of very sophisticated structures and machines, means of automation and control.

Revolutionary changes in the science of living matter are taking place today. The physics of elementary particles helps to deepen our understanding of the microstructure of matter. Astounding discoveries are being made in astronomy. There is every reason to consider that the recently discovered pulsars are the neutron stars prognosticated by our theoreticians, stars with a density of matter so great that a single cubic centimeter weighs a hundred million tons. Some other amazing astrophysical objects and processes have also been discovered. Perhaps we are on the verge of discovering new laws of the transformation of matter. Much is being done in our country to extend research in all the areas of science. The further strengthening of the experimental facilities of medium-energy nuclear physics is also important in the current five-year period.

Our country has blazed the trail into outer space, and has achieved in the past half decade some outstanding successes in the establishment of orbital stations, in the exploration of the moon and planets. In developing the utilization of cosmic means for the exploration of the universe we should increasingly employ them for the solution of practical problems in communications, meteorology, navigation, for investigating natural resources and for geographic and oceanographic research.

Marxist-Leninist teaching is the foundation for the entire development of our society. The past few years have seen expansion of research in the social sciences. Our task is to keep raising the level of research in philosophy, economics, sociology and the study of historical processes, especially those in the modern world. The social sciences, developing on the basis of Marxist-Leninist theory, should help to intensify the struggle for the victory of communist ideology the world over.

The tasks formulated in the draft Directives, for the development of the natural and social sciences and the tasks of accelerated progress in industry and agriculture, place immense responsibility on the scientists. The decision of the Party Central Committee and draft Directives stress the need of paying special attention to raising the level of management in all areas of the national economy. This is a major guarantee of progress in our highly developed socialist economy. It is the job of economists and sociologists to investigate further the advantages provided by the socialist system for the boosting of development rates and the speediest possible utilization of the results of science.

National economic plans and the regulation of interbranch ties are the foundation of economic management. At the present level of development of the country it is necessary to have long-range forecasts, as well as five-year plans. In recent years, forecasts have been worked out for the development of long-term trends in certain areas of science and technology in the closest possible connection with the development of branches of the national economy. Yet it is necessary to intensify research in working out long-term general socio-economic forecasts.

Vladimir Ilyich Lenin said that "socialism means accounting first of all." Modern information and computing equipment opens boundless possibilities in this area. Scientific research and concrete economic management should make full use of these opportunities. One can confidently say that the utilization of computers in all areas is one of the determining factors in the present scientific and technological revolution. Recently some substantial advances have taken place, with the active participation of scientific institutions, in the utilization by ministries and enterprises of information and computing equipment for planning and control. Successes have also been scored in the development of computing machinery. I would like to mention the need for extending the use of computers in design work not only in technical-economic calculation, but also in the process of developing the design of structural parts themselves.

In the new five-year period it is necessary to intensify our efforts in developing more sophisticated machinery, and in expanding production and utilization of electronic computers. At the same time we must try to reach the point where these machines will be produced in complete sets, including electronic processes, advanced external devices, instrumentation for control of production processes with mathematical precision, and so on.

The use of computing devices in the management of technological processes is a mighty lever for increasing labor productivity. Thus, for instance, their utilization at a single pipe-rolling mill of the Pervouralsky Novotrubny Plant has helped to increase substantially the precision of production of piping, to save 2,000 tons of high quality steel, and to save half a million rubles a year. The automation of the numerous processes helps to economize labor effort and at the same time to ensure higher quality of the product.

An indispensable condition for raising the level of management, especially automated management, and for intensifying economic and social processes in our country, is the extensive development of means of communication. Immense opportunities in this respect are provided by new achievements of physics and the use of space craft. We believe that in carrying out the five-year plan it is necessary to seek opportunities for a sharp rise in the development rates of means of communication.

A *sine qua non* for automating production processes and generally raising standards of modern production is the extensive use of instruments devised on the basis of the latest achievements in physics, including optics, radioelectronics and nuclear physics. In recent years major advances have been made both in the Academy of Sciences itself and in a number of specialized institutes in the designing of new up-to-the-minute instruments. However, in a number of areas, specifically in optical spectroscopy, the results are still inadequate. Absolutely inadequate—and this is the main thing—is industry's output of instruments already designed—which are not only needed for promoting science and production, but which also could be exported. The draft Directives provide for swift advances in instrument manufacture. Obviously special mention ought to be made of the development of optical instrument production.

Electronics is the basis for evolving sophisticated systems of control and instrumentation. It is gaining increasing application in the power industry and machine building. Much has been done in the country to strengthen the electronics industry. Soviet scientists have contributed signally to the development of semi-conductor theory. A key trend in radio-electronics is the miniaturization of electronic instruments. And though our scientists report progress in this field, we are taking steps to expand research considerably in this area. Our scientists have fathered electronics, which in recent years has paved the way for solving crucial problems of new machinery, technology and even medicine.

I would also like to mention an interesting recent discovery called holography, which enables us to get a three dimensional picture of various objects through a special image on photographic film. This is very promising for instrument production and the development of the 3-D cinema. Color holography is a discovery of Soviet scientists.

Science must play a decisive role in further developing the electric power industry. This more specifically refers to the tasks of raising the unit capacity of steam-turbine units for conventional power stations and of reactor-turbine units for atomic stations. Special heed should be paid to setting up atomic power stations based on fast-neutron reactors that reproduce nuclear fuel. Looking far ahead, we should pay great attention to employing the phenomenon of super-conductivity in order to devise highly economical electrical machines and devices. In the new five-year period we are planning to generate electric power on experimental installations that use the more economical methods of direct heat transformation. It is to be noted with satisfaction that Soviet scientists are in the front ranks in the search for peaceful ways to employ thermonuclear energy.

The integrated processing of raw materials, improvement in the quality of materials and in new production processes all play an enormous role in the intensification of our national economy. By synthesizing new compounds and the use in production of elements in the Mendeleyev Table never before used, scientists are discovering more and more sophisticated materials. For example, the use of a recently created alloy in the manufacture of permanent magnets with doubled magnetic force paves the way for designing new and still better instruments. The elimination of undesirable admixtures or the addition of small amounts of specially selected substances can sharply improve the qualities of a material. By employing the effects of low and high temperatures, vacuums, high pressures, electro-magnetic fields, plasma, and various radiations and emissions, we can obtain directed changes in physical properties and undertake new chemical processes. There should be dissemination of such novel metallurgical and technological processes as electric-slag re-smelting and casting, the rolling of metal directly from liquid aluminum and steel, electronic-beam and laser technology, etc. Scientists are confronted with important tasks in evolving highly efficient chemical production processes. A problem of paramount importance is to devise and produce far more effective catalysts that would enable us to greatly intensify chemical engineering processes.

It is necessary to draw special attention to the development of branches of industry capable of producing great economic gains from a small investment, in particular, small-scale chemical industry, which turns out small-tonnage products—admixtures for polymer materials and oil products, dyes for natural and synthetic fibers and physiologically active substances for medicine and agriculture. Products of the small-scale chemical industry are manufactured by a number of ministries and obviously the coordination of this work should be improved.

As is known, industrial production of synthetic diamonds has been extensively developed in our country. In recent years, the production process has been developed for obtaining large lamina of sapphire, ruby, garnet, emeralds and many other crystals. These are very important in modern engineering. What is needed now is to improve the industrial production of artificial crystals.

In our time, biology is acquiring ever greater importance not only in farming and medicine, but also in the light and food industries; this has been reflected particularly in the creation of a special branch —the microbiological industry. In recent years, biological research has expanded considerably and its level has been raised; what is needed is to step up its practical application.

The intensive development of Soviet economy confronts science with ever more urgent questions of tapping new natural resources of the land and the ocean and their rational utilization.

Research facilities have been strengthened in recent years. Special mention should be made of the development of science in the outlying areas and of the great importance of the creation of scientific centers in the Urals and the Far East.

The role played by science in technological progress and the great outlays needed for its development sharply pose the question of enhancing its effectiveness and speeding up the utilization of scientific results in practice.

Scientific instruments and the automation of research, which permit increasing the productivity of scientific endeavor dozens of times over, are a determining factor in enhancing the efficiency of the work done by scientists and raising the level of research. If scientific instrument-making is not developed in a proper manner, science will be doomed to lag behind. It is common knowledge that the Council of Ministers of the USSR has adopted a special resolution on the development of scientific instrument-making, and its translation into life is a major task.

In recent years, the Party and the Government have taken a number of measures to increase the effectiveness of scientific research. Of major importance here is the decision of the CPSU Central Committee and the Council of Ministers of the USSR on enhancing the efficiency of research, passed in September 1968. We still have to do much, however, to fully implement this decision. We are still making inadequate use of competitive examinations and the re-certifying of staff workers of institutes to improve the selection of scientific cadres, although these means may prove very effective. Nor are we making full use of the possibilities of economic and moral incentives and measures to enhance responsibility for work on scientific and technological problems. Specifically, the financing of related research through the parent organization, which is provided for in the decree, is not practiced everywhere. This measure will substantially improve the organization of work on large projects, which normally call for extensive cooperation between institutes and enterprises.

Experience has shown that the elaboration of scientific and technological problems proceeds more effectively when institutes are directly linked with production.

I would like to voice my support for the system being introduced by way of an experiment for the organization of scientific research, in the Ministry of Electrical Engineering, under which the subject matter, financing and economic incentives for scientific research are organically linked with the branch's technological progress and the economic gain obtained therefrom. We believe that the initial results already available here provide grounds for this system to become more widespread.

The main lines of technological progress must be planned, and it is necessary that our economic development plans reflect more fully the introduction of new techniques not only in new enterprises, but also in the reconstruction of existing ones. The organization of ministries has most certainly led to an acceleration of technological progress. However, it is necessary to have long-term plans for the technological modernization of the branches. There should be greater responsibility for the fulfilment of plans for technological progress, and for raising the level of production and quality of output.

At the same time, as stressed in Comrade Brezhnev's report, the material interest of the enterprises themselves in mastering new technology plays an immense role. I believe that in this area we are still not making use of all that was stipulated in the decisions of the September 1965 Plenary Meeting of the CPSU Central Committee. Notably, prices should stimulate new technology to a greater degree, as should the fuller implementation of measures provided for the crediting system.

Obviously we should pursue more boldly the policy of organizing production associations. This will bring science and production closer together, and create better opportunities for the reconstruction of individual enterprises. In order to speed up technological progress, it is very important to promote in every possible way the balanced nature of plans for production, modernization of enterprises and capital construction.

Comrades, our country is on the upgrade; its economy is being strengthened, its science, technology and culture are developing, and its international prestige is growing. The complicated questions which at times rise before us are difficulties of growth, which are connected with the rapid pace of development of our national economy.

The fulfilment of the tasks set for the five-year period will signify a major advance in the upbuilding of a communist society. Soviet science has been entrusted with highly important tasks. The Communist Party gives every possible assistance to the scientists and displays constant concern for the development of science.

Permit me to assure the 24th Congress of the Communist Party of the Soviet Union that the scientists will exert every effort for the further development of science, for the acceleration of technological progress for the good of our people, for the sake of the great cause of communism.

A. V. SMIRNOVA

*Weaver of Yakovlevsky Linen Combine
In the Ivanovo Region*

L IKE ALL the rest of you, I listened attentively and with great emotion to the report of the Central Committee of our Party delivered by Leonid Brezhnev. As I listened to it I kept finding thoughts just like my own and those of my fellow shopworkers.

For me, taking part for the first time in the work of the supreme council of the Communists of the country, it was a special joy to realize that the Party talks to the people in the Leninist language of truth, that it sees the vastness of the life of the people, of each one of us, meaning my life, too.

All the speakers who preceded me fervently endorsed the tireless, transforming activity of the Central Committee of the Party. I too am happy to have the chance to express my heartfelt opinion. The noble profession of a weaver prompts me to make a professional comparison: like an experienced weaver, our Party, day after day, weaves the strong cloth of a new society, the name of which is communism. We are summing up today the results of what has been achieved since the 23rd Congress. How much has been accomplished in this period by the Party and the people can be seen everywhere, including my native town of Privolzhsk.

It is a small community. Only 20,000 people live there. Such places are not always found on maps. Officially they are called small towns, but I will not exaggerate if I say that they are famed for deeds just as big as those of major industrial centers.

The whole life of Privolzhsk, like other towns of its kind, centers around an industrial enterprise. In the case of Privolzhsk it is the Yakovlevsky textile mill. It marked its centenary last December, but actually all that remains of the old enterprise is its walls. The mill has been completely modernized, and is, as it were, going through its second youth. New bright, spacious buildings have sprung up. Many production processes are mechanized and automated.

Production standards have risen noticeably. Daylight lighting fixtures, pure cool air, flowers, colorful stands and recreation and reading rooms all help to build up a buoyant and happy mood. To this I should add that preventive clinics have been opened at the mill, maternity consultation centers are functioning, and public services are improving, which for us women workers is particularly important. We no longer have a shortage of children's pre-school facilities. Our young production hands have ample, well-appointed dormitories. Workers' apartments are well provided with heat, gas and many other conveniences.

We listened yesterday with special excitement to the proposals of the Central Committee, outlined in Leonid Brezhnev's speech, aimed at improving the living conditions of large families and of women engaged in production. All this fills our hearts with boundless joy, and makes us want to work still better. Allow me, on behalf of all Soviet women, to express heartfelt gratitude to our beloved Party for its special concern for working women, for mothers.

The pride of the mill is its people. Practically every family in Privolzhsk has someone, its plenipotentiary, so to speak, in our establishment. The townspeople are great patriots of our factory, which they built with their own hands. Thanks to them, Russian linen cloth has won world prestige; goods bearing our mill's trademark are eagerly bought in 20 countries.

The traditions of the older generation are being followed and enhanced by the younger people who make up 40 per cent of our personnel. These young men and women are wonderful! They are thirsty for knowledge. Among our weavers and spinners we have more and more girls with technicians' diplomas. Our evening textile school graduates 60 to 70 specialists every year. The latest defense of diploma work took place on the eve of the Congress, and I myself was one of the graduates! I now have a specialized technical education, which will make my life and work even more engrossing. And I shall do everything to help my husband, a bricklayer, to finish successfully his education in a civil engineering correspondence school.

The eighth five-year plan is vividly marked in my life by a number of milestones. Not so long ago we worked on four looms turning out towelling. Our weavers have now begun operating three times as many looms. Back in 1966 I was one of the first to go over from six to eight looms, and two years later I began operating a dozen. All 510 weavers in our mill are operating more looms now than ever before. This alone has raised labor productivity by 21.3 per cent.

At the beginning of the five-year plan period, my looms turned out 49 meters of textiles per hour. This average shot up to 110 meters by the end of last year, when preparations for the 24th CPSU Congress were in full swing. I finished my own five-year plan assignment on the eve of the Lenin centenary. My extra contribution to the labor gifts fund consisted of 126,000 meters of cloth.

I am always full of excitement when I leave home for the morning shift. Beside me are friends—those I know and those I don't know. They start the workday with dignity, with a feeling of pride for belonging to the working class. In such moments another picture springs up in one's mind from Maxim Gorky's novel *Mother*. You think of the opening lines of that work, and they immediately sear your heart [See box following page.—Ed.]. How wonderful it is that all this belongs to the distant past, and that there will never be any return to it!

The Soviet worker of today is the real master of the country, a creator actively taking part in running production. He is well brought up and educated. For the Soviet worker labor is not only a source of earning power, but also a powerful means of becoming a part of that sacred comradeship that is setting up the most just social system on earth. It is a great honor to be a part of the Soviet working class! And I wish to express the deepest gratitude of a worker to the Leninist Central Committee of our Party for the high assessment of the role of the working class which Leonid Brezhnev gave in his report.

I understand that all I have said here is a usual thing for you and me. But I still want to say it because from this rostrum I will be

> Every day the factory whistle shrieked tremulously in the grimy, greasy air above the workers' settlement. And in obedience to its summons sullen people, roused before sleep had refreshed their muscles, came scuttling out of their grey houses like frightened cockroaches. They walked through the cold darkness, down the unpaved street to the high stone cells of the factory, which awaited them with cold complacency, its dozens of square, oily eyes lighting up the road. The mud smacked beneath their feet. They shouted in hoarse, sleepy voices and rent the air with ugly oaths. . . .
>
> In the evening . . . the factory expelled the people from its stone bowels as though they were so much slag, and they climbed the street again—grimy, black-faced, their hungry teeth glittering, their bodies giving off the sticky odor of machine oil. . . . The day had been devoured by the factory, whose machines sucked up as much of the workers' strength as they needed. The day was struck out, leaving not a trace, and man had advanced one more step towards his grave.
>
> *Mother,* by Maxim Gorky, Chapter 1, page 1.

heard far and wide. The enemies of our country will hear it abroad too. Let them know that their efforts to slander Soviet reality, the Soviet way of life, are in vain. They can never shake our love for our socialist motherland and the Leninist Party.

The feeling of being master of your country and of the enterprise where you work was again brought home in the days of the pre-Congress emulation drive. The very fact that the Congress was near, and the preparations for it, left an indelible impression on all our hopes and deeds. We reckoned what each of us was able to do and what reserves should be brought into play to make a bigger con-tribution to the common cause. To fulfil the target set for this whole year by the Great October Revolution holiday—this is my resolve. That means I must produce 22,500 meters of cloth beyond the plan. I am determined to fulfill the five-year plan in four years!

Dear delegates, discussing the draft Directives, the Communists and all the workers of our mill understood that this document is addressed to the people and everything in it is for the people. To us textile workers, the task of achieving a faster growth and increas-ing the share of the consumer goods industry is very close.

We are also very much concerned about adequate provision of raw materials. The linen workers expect that their raw materials base will enable them to produce a wide variety of high-quality linen: fine fabric, bath towels, sheets, bedspreads and tablecloths. Thus the people's demands for these articles will be more fully satisfied.

We also ask the leaders of the Ministry of Machine Building for

Light and Food Industries and Household Appliances of the USSR to provide us as soon as possible with more efficient equipment. Our next request is addressed to writers and workers in the arts. Surely textile workers deserve more attention from writers, painters and film-makers than they are now getting! A long time ago a movie called *The Bright Way* was shown, a very good picture about the origin of the Vinogradova movement in the textile industry.* Since then this film has been left in proud solitude. You know how many good songs have been composed about girls spinners in the old days who toiled in small dark rooms. But now my contemporaries, intelligent and beautiful people with clever fingers and ardent hearts, are not given worthy attention by poets and composers.

Comrade delegates, everything I learn from the Congress, all the energy I draw from it, I will take back to my work-mates. There is no higher duty for a Communist than to work in a creative way, always setting an example for others. The strength of Communists, of the whole Party, is that they have deep roots among the masses.

ALEXANDER CHAKOVSKY

Editor-in-Chief, Literaturnaya Gazeta

A S A WRITER I naturally listened with special interest to those passages in Comrade Brezhnev's report that spoke of literature and art.

Today one recalls with particular clarity the feelings that filled the minds of Soviet writers and, first of all, party members, in the years before the 23rd Congress. We writers, party members or not, who have committed ourselves and our work to the Party and the great cause of communist construction, greatly desired clarity in certain important ideological matters, consistency and the elimination of those erratic excesses of which we had seen more than enough and of which, frankly speaking, we were sick and tired in those years.

The 23rd Party Congress and later party documents on ideology introduced this needed lucidity. As regards artistic creativity the Party then stated firmly and calmly that though our literature on the whole is faring well, a few alarming phenomena could be observed, and that in its evaluation of people and writings bearing the influence of bour-

---

*Vinogradova was a famous textile worker whose work methods and help to others started a nationwide movement in her name, similar to that named after the coal miner, Stakhanov.

geois ideology, misrepresenting Soviet reality and indiscriminately flirting with our class enemies, the Party would be consistently irreconcilable.

Today, at this 24th Congress of our Party we Communist writers, all who work in the field of art and, I am sure, the entire people, can say with feelings of profound satisfaction that the clear-cut Leninist line of the party in ideology has yielded beneficial results. The well-conceived and consistent activity of the Central Committee has shown that it is both necessary and possible to carry out the complex work of state guidance without any return either to the methods of crude administrative decree condemned by the Party or to the practice of arbitrary, capricious decisions, but rather by the use of persuasion and appeal to reason, combined with a principled and exacting approach as the basic method of leadership.

The Party and its Central Committee have demonstrated what enormous successes can be achieved by employing this only correct method, bequeathed to us by Lenin. The present development of our multinational Soviet literature is a glowing testimonial to this.

To my mind, Comrades, we should especially single out the fact that the writers of all the Soviet sister republics are making a daily contribution to the efforts to build up a literature worthy of our times.

So-called "intellectual" anti-communism has a carefully worked out strategy and tactic for seeking to influence our writers and artists, to drive a wedge between them and the Party, and demoralize Soviet intellectuals from within.

A current concept which our enemies actively propagate is that of the supposedly inevitable need for every artist to be in opposition to the state. We, of course, can understand the inevitable opposition of an honest and progressive writer or artist to the bourgeois society and state, which rests on violence, falsehood, the power of money and the exploitation of man by man.

Anti-communism wants to impose on us its own concept of "freedom," although it is interested in only one freedom, the freedom to propagate anti-Sovietism and undermine the socialist system. Who today, comrades, is not championing the freedom of creativity, the freedom of the writer and artist in the socialist world? Among these champions of freedom are the leaders of the CIA, the "Voice of America," the "Voice of Israel," "Radio Free Europe," the BBC, the *London Times, The New York Times,* the South African racists and the Portuguese colonialists. Poor things, they can't rest until they win freedom for us! But what sort of freedom can be offered by the capitalist world, which is going through such a profound spiritual crisis? Freedom for

84

violence and cruelty, for racism and pornography, for Zionism and neo-fascism? However, comrades, it was not for this that our fathers and grandfathers made the Great October Revolution, and that we fought against fascism for the freedom and independence of our country. Nor are we building the bright edifice of communism in order to let its foundations be washed away by the polluted torrents of bourgeois propaganda.

Soviet writers are well aware that in the same way that Antaeus drew his strength from his constant bond with his Mother Earth, so they draw their strength, their inner invincibility, from their cohesion and unity around the Party of Lenin, from their unbreakable bond with its great cause.

MIKHAIL SHOLOKHOV

Leading Soviet Writer, Nobel Prize Winner,
Author of **And Quiet Flows the Don** *Trilogy*

APPRAISING our literature in depth, we can say with pride that from the days of the establishment of Soviet power, it has served the people honestly and devotedly, and its voice, in the words of our great Russian poet Lermontov—has truly:

> *Sounded, like the bell on an ancient tower,*
> *In the days of both triumph and sorrow of our peoples.*

The voice, both in the past and today, has been heard far beyond the borders of our country. Without any false modesty we can say that we have done a great deal in the sense of reeducating people, influencing their spiritual awakening and growth through the medium of art. The militant role of Soviet literature and art in the world process of the development of artistic culture is determined above all by the charge of communist ideology and party spirit that permeates our best works. To put it bluntly, this is what most infuriates our ideological enemies and their accomplices, the revisionists. They would like to persuade us to abandon our clear-cut positions as convinced fighters for socialism and communism, and to renounce party spirit and kinship with the people as the basic principles of artistic creativity.

But it is time for us, too, under the present conditions of unprecedented and increasingly sharp ideological struggle, to go over more decisively to the offensive and oppose the efforts of the renegades and revisionists of all shadings with our unfailing weapon—the never-fading truth of Lenin. This is our paramount task.

Only our Party and the lofty ideals by which it is guided could achieve the fusing together of thousands of creative lives, from Maxim Gorky down to the healthy young writers of our time, and inspire them to serve the people and their interests. It's worthwhile, comrades, to give some real thought to this!

[Sholokhov deals caustically with some of the untalented, inept and too prolific current writing that also appears.]

How do we get rid of this trouble? I think we must insist on more exacting standards on the part of the editorial staffs of publishing houses and magazines—both in the provinces and in the capitals as well. Who, if not the publisher or magazine editor, should be the first barrier to the appearance of a poor book? Literary criticism should abandon the practice of remaining silent in dealing with an inferior work. Its direct obligation is to examine and appraise a work according to its true worth. No small share of the blame here rests with the writers' organizations, which fail to hold back useless books by their gray skirts.

There are still a number of imperfections and shortcomings in the work of our Soviet Writers' Union, but in order to save time I shall refrain from going into this. The All-Union Writers' Congress will be held in June of this year and we shall gladly invite all lovers of literature to attend our Congress. We'll certainly give our literary rugs a good beating then. The dust will fly!

The circulation of books in our country is truly gigantic, but the demand of our readers far exceeds what is printed. Even the libraries are kept on short rations. The desire of the worker, the collective farmer or the intellectual to have his favorite book in his own home must also be taken into account. One can sympathize with the comrades in the city or district party committees who sometimes have to ration out books as though they were the scarcest mechanisms or materials! There is not enough paper!

I remember how ardently Konstantin Ivanovich Galanshin advocated the cause of *belles lettres* at the last Congress. At that time he was First Secretary of the Perm Province Party Committee and he made a declaration of love to us. Now he is Minister of the Pulp and Paper Industry and he is as quiet as though his mouth were full of water.

Dear Konstantin Ivanovich! We took your love seriously at that time, and now we accuse you of inconstancy. Look, Konstantin Ivanovich, at how that one word—inconstancy—perturbs our women delegates! Like all other women in the world, they are constitutionally allergic to that word! And here I find true allies, in accusing you of inconstancy. Love demands not only declarations, but, at the very least, some expenditures. We are not expecting either bouquets or condescending manly smiles from you, Konstantin Ivanovich. Just give us more paper! Paper! In excess of the plan, which you fortunately are fulfilling, and of a better quality! And then we shall finally come to have faith in your protestations. Then we prose writers will get together and present you with some luxurious flowers, in no less luxurious wrapping paper, while some young poetess—you never can tell, you know—will write a love song in your honor. To be the recipient of a love song! That's quite a temptation! I wouldn't refuse one myself, in spite of my venerable age, and you, dear Konstantin Ivanovich, really ought to think seriously about this.

But, all joking aside, we do not make proper use even of the paper we have. And for this sin, neither Comrade Galanshin nor we writers are to blame. Paper is expended by just about anyone, in any amount and for any purpose. Paper, to be sure, can endure anything. It is no joking matter that almost half the book titles published in the country last year were so-called "departmental literature." What is hidden behind this screen? Here you can find fat official reports, scholarly notes in equally ponderous volumes, all sorts of "memorial" and gift chronicles—albums of one institution or another, which are placed in the archives to feed the mice immediately after publication. Everybody seeks to have his folio elegantly bound, with multi-colored lacquered dust jackets and, naturally, it must be printed on the finest paper. There is disorder in this matter, comrade delegates, great disorder! In order to eliminate it a strict, statesmanlike approach is needed. The tendency to publish departmental literature is growing.

A talented young generation is now growing up to replace us. The older generation of writers places great hopes in them. We are glad that the relay baton is being passed on to the kind of artists who are needed by our society. These are interesting, patriotically-minded people, probing into the depths of life. Young people are sometimes cocky and harsh in their appraisals of certain phenomena, but one valuable thing about them is that they are not indifferent. They are inquisitive, forever searching. Sometimes they lack experience. But the future of our literature lies with them, with the young writers. They will create that future, they will be responsible for it. You understand, of course that I am not here dividing our creative youth into the "clean" and the "unclean." I am speaking of young people as a whole. I am speaking about the new writers' reinforcements, the fresh forces of Soviet literature. But let me remind you, we writers of the older generation are also still worth something!

Alexey Kosygin

CHAIRMAN OF THE USSR
COUNCIL OF MINISTERS

Directives of the 24th Congress of the
CPSU for the Five-Year Economic
Development Plan of the USSR, 1971-75
Delivered April 6, 1971

Extended Summary

THE main report on the "Directives of the 24th Congress of the Communist Party of the Soviet Union for the Five-Year Economic Development Plan of the USSR for 1971-1975" was delivered on April 6 by Alexey Kosygin, Chairman of the Council of Ministers of the USSR.

The report began by noting the growth of the leading role of the Party in the life of Soviet society. In foreign policy and in internal construction, the Party's leadership has been decisive. Sound foundations have been laid for new steps along the road to communism, and the high ideological level of the Party and of Soviet people is reflected in the speeches made at this Congress. "Many useful and profound considerations have been expressed on questions relating to economic, social and cultural development. They will all be carefully studied." The discussion of the draft Directives shows a high level of understanding and support, and this is the main guarantee that the plan will be fulfilled.

The Eighth Five-Year Plan: Results

THE political and key socioeconomic tasks set in the plan have been successfully fulfilled. National income during the period rose by 41 per cent, and industrial output by 50 per cent (means of production, 51 per cent; articles of consumption, 49 per cent); these figures exceed the planned targets or just meet them. Other

88

indicators (1970 as a per cent of 1965, with the planned figure in parentheses) are: Capital investment, 142 (147); freight turnover for all types of transport, 138 (137); average wages of workers and employees, 126 (not less than 120); average monthly incomes of collective farmers, 142 (135-40); payments and benefits to the population from the social consumption funds, 153 (not less than 140); real income per capita, 133 (about 130). Average annual output in agriculture increased by 21 per cent, with underfulfillment appearing only in potatoes and vegetables.

Politically, the plan period witnessed a further consolidation of socialism, strengthening of the alliance between the working class and the peasantry, and deepening of socialist democracy. In the sphere of economic development, the Eighth Five-Year Plan raised the country to a higher level, with significant increases in labor productivity, scientific and technical progress, and the efficiency of the sectoral structure of the economy. In the social sphere, material and cultural standards have been greatly enhanced. Full employment of the work force has been ensured. The level of skill and training has increased. Progress has been made toward the gradual elimination of the distinctions between town and country, and between mental and manual labor. Greater priority was given to the growth of consumption, as an integral part of the accelerated economic development: ". . . in a developed socialist society accelerated national-economic development goes hand in hand with a rapidly rising living standard for the people. This flows from the nature of the socialist mode of production, which has done away with the appropriation by the exploiting classes of the results of the working people's production activity."

Almost three-quarters of the national income produced during the eighth five-year period went into consumption, with a large part going to meet requirements for education, health, cultural activities, the maintenance of incapacitated persons, grants to students, and scientific research. The rest, also a substantial amount, went into production accumulation (investment), housing and other construction, and into enlarging the defense capability of the country, a necessity in the current international situation.

The growth of retail trade is another indicator of the success of the plan. Output of some products, however, still lags behind the rising cash incomes of the population. Meat and meat products, in particular, are still in short supply, although their per capita consumption has increased by an average of several kilograms. The fulfillment of the housing construction plan is also noteworthy, and the USSR leads the world in the pace of housing construction. "But it is still too early to say that the whole population of our country has the normal amount of housing at its disposal. This problem remains a serious one for the years ahead."

By 1970, 75 per cent of the working people in the towns, and over 50 per cent in the countryside, had a secondary or higher education. The network of hospitals and polyclinics, sanatoriums, health resorts and holiday homes has been enlarged, testifying to the rise in health services to the population that has occurred during the period.

During the 1965-70 period, workers and office employees were switched to a five-day week, with two days off. The number of paid holidays has increased.

The vast increase in living standards is based on the successful development of socialist production, which was greatly enhanced by the introduction of the economic reform, approved at the 23rd Congress of the CPSU. Along with the great increase in total output, quality of industrial output has improved, with especially sharp increases in the engineering, metal-working, chemical and petrochemical, and electric power industries. The raw-materials base of industry has widened, due to discovery and exploitation of new gas, oil, ferrous and non-ferrous ore, diamond and other mineral deposits. Synthetic materials are playing a larger and larger role in Soviet industry. Industrial installations are rising in capacity, and this switch to larger units greatly increases potentials for raising labor productivity and reducing per-unit investments. It is no longer a question of manufacturing individual machines, but of entire automated machine systems, including machine tools with computer controls. This "complex mechanization" is reaching into agriculture as well as industry; the electrification of the countryside is now practically completed and this will greatly boost agricultural production.

The capital construction program of the Eighth Five-Year Plan was of course extensive, in order to support the huge increases in output which were cited. Capital investments during the five years came to almost as much as was invested in the preceding eight years. These investments include 35,400 kilometers of oil and gas pipelines, and the commissioning of the world's largest hydroelectric station at Krasnoyarsk, with a capacity of five million kilowatts. Along with capacity enlargement in almost every industry of the USSR, special attention has been given to increasing capacity in the automotive industry. The Togliatti works, started in 1967, was already turning out cars by 1970.

"At the same time, there have been substantial shortcomings in

90

capital construction. Construction periods for some enterprises and installations have run beyond the normal standards, and this has caused unproductive inputs and losses. There is a large volume of incomplete construction."

The growth rate of the productivity of social labor has accelerated during the past five years, increasing by 37 per cent, as against 27 per cent in the previous period. By 1970, the rise in productivity was accounting for 84 per cent of the growth of industrial output. Production costs have been reduced, and in the five-year period, profits of enterprises have more than doubled.

Against this background of the fundamental success of the Eighth Five-Year Plan, Mr. Kosygin turned to a discussion of shortcomings. In industry, agriculture, and in construction, labor productivity increases fell short of targets. The building ministries, in particular, did not fulfill their plans; this adversely affected plan fulfillment in many other industries, since planned installations and capacities were not commissioned. While the aggravated international situation, calling for additional diversion of resources and manpower to defense, was partly to blame, "we have quite a few shortcomings for which the reasons cannot be regarded as being objective." At the December

---

A WORKER'S BOAST

Novopolotsk, like our whole country, is one huge construction area. Just a little more than ten years ago there was nothing here but an impassable swamp. Now we have a shining city built of white stone, with 50,000 people, the largest oil refinery and chemical combine in our country, in all Europe. . . .

I could give you thousands of examples of the courageous, self-sacrificing labor of our construction and assembly workers. There was real mass heroism in getting the job done and putting the plants into operation. So you'll accuse me of boasting. Sure I'm boasting. But not about myself. I'm boasting about our native land! It brought us up, gave us the strength of Hercules! I'm boasting about our Party! It gave us wings, a high aim in life, steeled us in struggle, helped us find our place in society, made us part of a great endeavor!

We want to live and work still better.

To be a Soviet worker—that is the highest and noblest calling in our country!

FEODOR S. KURALENOK, petroleum construction
brigade leader, Vitebsky Province, Byelorussia

(1969) Plenary Meeting of the CC CPSU, criticisms were made of "breaches of state discipline" by some economic executives, including nonfulfillment of plans and targets, and "a weakened sense of responsibility to the people." Engineering industries, the light industry, and others were censured for failures. In some of these, the first batches of a new product were of high quality, but the quality subsequently declined below the level achieved. There have been losses of raw materials, failure to extend the range of products produced, unnecessary interruptions in production and marketing.

These, however, are blemishes on a generally favorable report card. "Drawing up the overall result, it is safe to say: our country has been successfully advancing in the political, economic and social respects along the way of communist construction."

The Ninth Five-Year Plan: Socioeconomic Tasks

TURNING to the prospects for the years 1971-75, covered in the draft Directives of the Ninth Five-Plan, Mr. Kosygin identified the solution of key socioeconomic problems as central to plan goals:

> The main task of the five-year plan is to ensure a considerable rise in the people's material and cultural level on the basis of a high rate of development of socialist production, enhancement of its efficiency, scientific and technical progress and acceleration of the growth of labor productivity.

The whole preceding period of socialist development has created the possibilities for not merely raising the standard of living in the material and cultural spheres, but for changing the whole *level* of life, a qualitative transformation in all areas of provision for human needs.

The foundation for this is the national income generated by the socialist economy, which will reach 325 billion rubles yearly at the end of the plan period. This figure represents the national income of a *socialist* country: "Our people is full master of its national income. In socialist society there is no antagonism between accumulation and consumption, as is inherent in the capitalist system: in this country both are used entirely in the interests of the whole people."

The new five-year period has two fundamental features, which in total distinguish it from previous five-year periods, and "*which are organically interconnected.*"

First, a massive new concentration on "improving the people's welfare and their working and living conditions." The increase in resources devoted to this purpose will amount to 75-81 billion rubles. (The qualitative aspects of this shift of resources are described in detail later in the report, in the section on the planned rise in living standards and cultural levels.)

Second, "greater intensification of the whole of social production and its greater efficiency on the basis of a substantial acceleration of scientific and technical progress." Growth rates of labor productivity in industry, agriculture and construction are planned at 36-40 per cent, up significantly from the previous period.

The sections of the report which follow are largely devoted to elaborating the forms of the interrelation between these two fundamental aspects of socialist construction. The dependence of the first —the rise in living standards—on the second—intensification and mechanization of production—has often been noted, and was a feature of the previous five-year plan periods. In this regard, what is new is the extent of the possibilities which now exist:

> It should be emphasized that never before have such vast monetary and material resources been allocated for the development of agriculture and branches connected with the manufacture of goods for the population as in the current five-year period. We are sure that this will soon yield results, and have a tangible effect on the further raising of the people's living standard in town and country.

What is qualitatively new, brought about by the new stage and the new potentials for the development of the productive forces, is the emergence of an intimate reverse dependence: The realization of the possibilities inherent in the scientific and technological revolution *require* a qualitative transformation of the *level of life* of the Soviet people; raising the material and cultural standard of the people, introducing creativity and knowledge into all aspects of life—these things are now not merely results of the progress of the productive forces, they are *preconditions* for that very progress. This is why capitalism cannot realize the potentials of the technological revolution:

> In the capitalist countries, the bourgeoisie has been using the achievements of this revolution in its own class interests. However, the scientific and technical revolution has been aggravating the social contradictions inherent in capitalism. Thus, for instance, some acceleration in labor productivity growth in the USA in the past few years has gone hand in hand with rising unemployment; millions of working people have been laid off from factories and plants.

By contrast, the socialist system is able to eliminate the contradiction between accumulation and consumption, between growth of the productive forces and meeting the needs of the people:

> The socialist system alone creates boundless possibilities for scientific and technical progress. In contrast to the capitalist economy, the high stable

growth rates in socialist production assure the Soviet people of full employment, with an accelerated growth of labor productivity.

Only thanks to socialism, and only within the framework of our social system, does the scientific and technical revolution attain its full and comprehensive development, whose results go to all the working people.

Specifically, during the ninth five-year period, "a major step is to be made in realizing the achievements of the scientific and technical revolution." What is envisioned is not merely more technology within the old framework, but a *radical transformation of production methods,* including new and highly productive instruments of labor, new materials, new industries. The branches which play a key role in technical progress will be given priority growth rates: electric power, chemicals, engineering, instrument-making, computers, etc., are scheduled for an overall 67 per cent increase in output.

The limitation of resources in the short run requires a "uniform state technical policy," including preferential development of priority sectors on the basis of planned projections of current and future needs in the economy as a whole, and using uniform and scientific criteria for evaluating and placing investments where they will yield the maximum benefit.

The draft Directives enumerate the tasks of the "uniform state technical policy." First, it aims at developing new instruments of labor "at a level that is above the best world standards." Second, the rate of renewal and replacement of obsolescent plant is to be speeded up. By 1975, new production assets commissioned will be 46 per cent of total assets in industry, and 60 per cent in agriculture. Extensive mechanization of operations that are still labor-intensive is to take place, and this includes widespread introduction of automated management systems. The introduction of chemical products and chemical technology is an important ingredient in the technical policy. The growing complexity of production requires a new kind of attention to development of back-up lines of production, storage and packing facilities. Hand in hand with all this goes perfection of the system of profit-and-loss accounting, economically warranted prices, new forms of crediting and financing, etc.

The role of science—scientists and scientific organizations—is obviously crucial. While appreciating the role of scientists in the past, shortcomings are noted. Research is sometimes divorced from practical needs, and insufficient for solution of key tasks. The system of remuneration of scientific workers should be improved, "so as to take greater account of the actual contribution made by each to scientific and technical progress." Where the bonds between science and pro-

94

duction are weak, they may be strengthened by the rise of *production amalgamations*, consolidated bodies intermediate between enterprises and the ministries, which can centralize research, design and experimental work.

The planned rise in labor productivity—36-40 per cent on the average, as against much lower increases in previous plans—is novel, crucial to plan fulfillment, and realistic. Some 80-85 per cent of the total planned increase in output must be achieved by means of increases in productivity, rather than by new capital investments. The plan aims at systematically improving the organization of production and labor, reducing lost time and idle time, improving the efficiency of materials handling and other ancillary operations which use up workers who otherwise could be devoted to basic production. This is especially important, since there is little prospect for greatly increasing the number of workers, and a larger proportion of the work force is slated for the service sectors.

It is important, in this regard, to reduce the material-intensiveness of products, and there are great untapped reserves in this area. Efficient and economical use of raw and other materials make possible large reductions in costs of production. There is need for "novel scientific, technical and design schemes, new technologies in the processing of raw materials, and a reduction in the weight of articles." Improvement in the use of production capacities and basic assets, and reduction in the time and cost of construction of new facilities, will result in a rise of the product-to-assets ratio.

This, in broad outline, is the foundation for the *social program* of the ninth five-year period, which embraces improvement of living conditions, accelerated rise in incomes, improvement of working conditions, an increase in appropriations for the upbringing of the rising generation, universal secondary education, evening up of the living standards of the urban and rural population.

Kosygin noted that doubling of the Soviet national income in the past took ten years, as compared with much longer periods for the western capitalist countries, an indication of the superiority of socialist, balanced development:

> Our enemies slander socialism in an effort to make uninformed people believe that the socialist system is, allegedly, incompatible with highly efficient labor organization and with incentives for the working people to display and develop ability. Actually socialism and communism signify the triumph of free, creative labor. The socialist state plans and creates the conditions for the growth of the labor productivity of every worker, for improving his qualifications, and on that basis insures the growth of incomes and an improvement of the living standard of the entire population. Much has already been done.

During the ninth five-year plan period much more will be done to promote the fruitful labor of all the members of our society. . . .

Ahead of us in the economic competition between the two opposite social systems still lies a long and hard struggle. We Communists are confident that the ultimate outcome of this struggle will be in favor of socialism.

Development of Material Production

THE GROWTH of the material base of the Soviet economy is the foundation for socialist and communist development, and the report by Kosygin went into the tasks mapped out by the draft Directives, branch by branch. First, it was noted that 1975 industrial output is planned at 528-544 billion rubles, compared with 248 billion in 1965; i.e., it is planned that industrial output will more than double in the decade 1965-75.

Heavy industry remains the foundation of the economic might of the country, and the basis for technical progress and the development of all other branches of the economy. Foremost among the heavy industry sectors are the *fuel and power industries*, and great priority is given in the plan to their development. The planned *increments* in the main outputs of these industries are as follows: Electric power, 290-330 billion kwh; oil, 131-151 million tons; natural gas, 102-122 billion cubic meters; coal, 61-71 million tons. New power stations with an aggregate capacity of 65-67 million kw will go into operation. Some 12 per cent of the total increase in power generation capacity will come from atomic power stations, and there is a broad program of atomic power station construction, especially in the power-scarce European part of the USSR. In the next decade, almost half of the new power capacity commissioned will be atomic, with enormous savings in capital investments in the coal industry. This program was not possible during the last five-year plan because the engineering industry was not then prepared to take it on.

The Integrated Power Grid of the European part of the USSR was completed during the Eighth Five-Year Plan. This grid is now to be continued. "We shall soon be able to transmit electric power from Siberia and Kazakhstan to the European regions. Almost all the collective and state farms are to be connected to the state power grids."

Oil production is to be greatly stepped up, particularly by using new methods of exerting pressure on oil-bearing strata; huge new oil-fields at Tyumen and Mangyshlak will account for 75 per cent of the total increase in oil output. Natural gas output will be increased by exploiting the remarkable deposits discovered in a number of areas, particularly in Uzbekistan and Turkmenistan. Construction of large-diameter pipelines will revolutionize pumping of oil and gas to the consumer areas of the country.

The draft Directives call for large-scale re-equipment of the coal industry, "in order to secure a considerable cut in the cost of coal extraction and improvement of the working conditions of the miners." Open-face mining in large quarries will come to account for nearly one-third of the coal output. This will raise labor productivity by 40 per cent, which means that the 11 per cent increase in coal output will be obtained with 20 per cent fewer miners.

The *raw materials industries* also have their work cut out for them. Steel output is targeted for 1975 at a maximum of 150 million tons, and 30 per cent of this will come from oxygen converters. In addition to continuous pouring techniques, the range of shapes and sizes of steel output is to increase greatly, along with the precision of the specifications. Completely new aluminum plants are to be built in Bratsk, Krasnoyarsk and Irkutsk. The chemical industry will turn out 80 per cent of the fertilizers in use by 1975, and there will be a doubling or near doubling of chemical fiber, plastics and synthetic resins, and household chemicals production. Ammonia production units are under construction in several places, each of which equals in capacity the entire Soviet ammonia production in 1948. The rubber and timber-and-woodworking industries have high targets for productivity improvement, and will especially benefit from the new capacities in the chemical industries as they come on line.

The *engineering industry*, as previously stated, is the key to the technical re-equipping of the entire economy, and its targets reflect the attention given to it in the ninth five-year plan. Output of the entire engineering and metalworking industries will rise from 88 to 148 billion rubles; motor vehicles, from .916 to 2-2.1 million units; instruments, means of automation and spare parts for them, from 3,102 to 6,155 million rubles; machines and equipment for the light and food industries, 771 to 1,564 million rubles; farm machinery, 2,115 to 3,500 million rubles; tractors, 458.5 to 575 thousand units; and grain harvester combines, 99.2 to 138 thousand units.

> The task confronting machine-builders is to supply all branches of the national economy more fully with machinery for the mechanization of arduous manual processes, and chiefly with systems of machines for the comprehensive mechanization of key production processes in all branches, particularly in agriculture.

Particularly noteworthy here are the planned doubling of the output of instruments and "means of automation," and the planned increase in computer output of 160 per cent. Among the instruments special emphasis is given to program lathes, which will increase by some 250 per cent, and which enable a three- or four-fold increase in labor productivity. Replacement of obsolete plant will affect one-fourth to one-third of the output of metal-cutting lathes and forging and pressing machines. There will be further specialization of production, unification of machine parts, standardization of technological processes, and expansion of the manufacture of materials handling equipment, power tools, special-purpose equipment and jigs and fixtures. The plan aims at a higher shift coefficient in the engineering industry; this means a larger proportion of calendar time during which the plant is in operation. This is made possible by mechanization of labor, which frees both production workers and people working in arduous auxiliary jobs, making it possible to open up a second shift, with a general upgrading of the skill qualifications of the work force. In this way, the increased productivity of the engineering industry is the foundation for further increases, in an upward spiral.

Here are the major annual output targets for the *consumer goods* industries (1970 to 1975): Light industry output, cultural and household articles, 76.5 to 112.4 billion rubles; furniture, 2.8 to 4.55 billion rubles; refrigerators, 4.14 to 6.686 million units; fabrics, 8.9 to 10.5-11 billion square meters; leather footwear, 676 to 800-830 million pairs; and food, meat-and-dairy, and fishing industry output, 78.8 to 106.6 billion rubles. Equipment for these industries will be doubled, making possible the increases in output envisaged. The textile industry will receive new highly efficient spinning frames, looms, etc., which will raise labor productivity 50-100 per cent. The output of foodstuffs will be considerably enlarged, with meat increasing by 40-43 per cent and fish by 47 per cent, and with a better internal assortment of meat and fish products. Goods which meet cultural and household needs will be increased by some 80 per cent.

The huge scale of production and modern scientific and technical progress require increasingly better organization of the work of industry. Particular importance attaches to precision and efficiency in the work of ministries, amalgamations and enterprises, to the absolute fulfillment of inter-enterprise delivery commitments, to the thorough study of the requirements of the national economy and the population, to the swift and flexible reorientation of production in accordance with changes in these requirements and to a sense of high responsibility to the state and the people for the introduction of the latest achievements of science and technology in production.

Agricultural output can be summed up in the following way. The first figure is the annual average output for 1971-75; the second is the average annual *increment* of output over the average annual output for 1966-70. Gross agricultural output (billion rubles), 96-98 and 15.7-17.7; grain (million tons), 195 and 27.5; raw cotton (million tons), 6.75 and 0.65; meat (slaughter weight; million tons), 14.3 and 2.7; milk (million tons), 92.3 and 11.8; eggs (billion), 46.7 and 19.9; wool (thousand tons), 464 and 67. "Increasing grain production remains the key problem. During the five-year period grain yields must be increased by at least four centners per hectare. Though not an easy task, this is quite feasible."

Crucial to increasing agricultural output is provision to the collective and state farms of tractors, harvester-combines, trucks, farm machinery and the necessary power capacity for the technical revolution in agriculture. Consumption of electricity in agricultural production will be doubled during the five-year period. Provision of fertilizers will rise from 46 to 75 million tons (1970-75). Broad programs of land improvement are being undertaken, together with construction of irrigation systems. One and a half million hectares of irrigated land are to go into use in the Volga area, the North Caucasus and South Ukraine, and 650,000 hectares in Central Asia. Five million hectares will be drained in the high-humidity zone, and pasture land of over 41 million hectares will be watered.

Along with a total capital investment in agriculture of nearly 129 billion rubles during the five-year period, new stress will be placed on crop and livestock selection, crop rotation, and sowing of only high-quality seed. To accelerate the growth of livestock farming, mechanized stock units will be built at collective and state farms and, near the towns, large state-and-collective farm and intercollective-farm livestock complexes, producing by industrial methods.

The plans for livestock output call for an increase in fodder resources, and "a radical change in the attitude to the growing of fodder crops." In addition, an increase in production and use of mixed feeds is planned.

"An increase of the number of livestock and poultry personally owned by the rural population must be encouraged (naturally, within definite limits) and help rendered in supplying their livestock with fodder and pastures."

In promoting labor productivity in agriculture, "better use must be made of economic levers, and the transfer of all the state farms to operation on a full profit-and-loss basis must be completed." The relative and absolute growth of the commonly owned sector of the collective farms (as distinct from the privately owned and worked plots) depends on improvement of labor organization and distribution of income, on the economic reform and on strengthening collective-farm democracy. The principle of establishing a stable procurement plan, in which the collective and state farms are given state procurement quantities and prices for the years ahead and thus stand to gain directly from any increases in productivity which they can bring about, has justified itself in the past and will be carried over into the new plan period. As the large-scale mechanized farm draws closer to the conditions of industrial production, the application of modern methods of industrial management and the provision of skilled personnel become critical needs.

The *transport and communications* branches have their tasks laid out for them: ". . . at present the railway and motor transport do not yet fully satisfy the requirements of the national economy, particularly in the autumn and winter." In the new plan period, freight transport will increase 32-35 per cent, with new lines laid, new tracks added to lines already in existence. The bus fleet will be enlarged, with a corresponding increase in hard-surface roads (110,000 kilometers) and "the establishment of a large network of service stations." The Soviet merchant marine fleet will be expanded to meet the needs of the USSR's growing international trade. The river fleet will be enlarged, and it has the particular task of relieving the railroads in the European part of the country of some of their burden by making better use of the Volga Basin and the Volga-Baltic waterway. A number of new ports will be commissioned in all parts of the country.

Oil pipelines will double. Air-borne passenger traffic will increase by about 70 per cent. Mechanization of loading and unloading operations for all forms of transport is to be undertaken, along with containerization.

Capital construction will be undertaken on a scale 40 per cent greater during the new plan period than during the preceding one. The proportions of capital investment going into the various branches of the economy are changing. State investments in agriculture are increasing by more than 70 per cent, in the tractor and farm machinery industries by approximately 100 per cent, in light industry 90 per cent, in the food and meat-and-dairy industry 60 per cent. Some 30 per cent of all capital investments will go into agriculture, food and consumer goods.

Special emphasis is placed on increasing capacities in the most up-to-date and modern technologies, and on enlarging the funds for technical re-equipment of already established facilities.

To get the greatest benefit from the planned capital investments, there must be a "drastic tightening of building schedules." The potential savings are enormous. The draft Directives also envisage the concentration of capital investments, and reduction of the number of projects under construction at one and the same time. The economic reform has just begun to be extended to the construction industry, and qualitative results are expected from this. The number of shifts should rise, idle time fall. The plan also calls for (and sets targets on the basis of) introduction of advanced methods of organizing work, such as the conveyer method of assembling and building large workshops, use of prefabricated structures, and lightened metal construction. Production of building materials must be greatly improved, and this problem cuts across a number of industries: cement, glass, slate, iron and steel, chemicals, timber. There are currently seven million workers in construction in all parts of the country; their training, wages, working and living conditions have improved substantially, and are slated for further improvement as an inducement for building workers to stay in the trade and meet the tasks of the five-year plan.

Special attention is being paid to the problem of the location of the productive forces, as an aspect not merely of the development of production, but also of "the unswerving implementation of the Leninist national policy." Great work is planned in the development of the huge natural resources of the European North, Siberia, the Far East, Kazakhstan and Central Asia. "The rational location of the productive forces will make it possible to speed up economic development and more correctly and fully to combine countrywide interests with the interests of the development of the Union republics and the economic areas."

Improvement of Management and Planning

THE economic reform was begun in broad outline by a decision of the 23rd Congress of the CPSU, and was set out in concrete form in the September 1965 Plenary Meeting of the Central Committee of the CPSU. The favorable impact of the reform on the development of the Soviet socialist economy can be seen in the results of the Eighth Five-Year Plan. The staffs of enterprises have become much more interested in the economic results of their work, and the participation of working people "in resolving questions of production economics" has grown.

At the same time, some ministries are still making poor use of the new methods of managing production—impinging on the rights of enterprises which have been switched to profit-and-loss accounting, and administratively usurping decisions which should be left to the enterprises' discretion according to economic criteria. Further improvement of the reform now involves strengthening of planning, tightening up the criteria for evaluating the activity of enterprises, and increasing material stimulation, not only at the enterprise level but also at the level of amalgamations and the ministries themselves. In sum, "the economic reform is not a single act. It is a process of improving economic management designed to secure the maximum use of all the advantages of the socialist mode of production."

In the new five-year period, all enterprises "in all fields of material production and in the service sphere" will be transferred to the new system. Qualitatively new needs have arisen in the area of inter-branch planning; the interconnectedness of the economy has reached a level at which plans must be drawn up not only "vertically" but also "horizontally":

> I shall cite the motor-vehicle industry as an example. The planned growth of motor-vehicle production determines the development not only of related branches, but also of road-building, of a broad network of various service stations, and of town-planning.

The importance of long-term forecasts is increasing, and the role of a long-term—10-15 year—development plan will grow in the near future. Long-term forecasts of the country's fuel balance are being drawn up, and a general plan for the location of productive forces is being studied.

In terms of the immediate future, further work remains to be done in improving the system of indicators of the national economic plan, in such a way that 1) the technico-economic norms are scientifically grounded—i.e., they reflect actual production conditions and are reviewed often enough so that they continue to stay in line with technical progress; 2) the needs of consumers are met more fully and promptly, and changes in this area are promptly transmitted to the planners—this necessitating "exhaustive study of social requirements and consumer demand"; 3) plans and norms are stable enough to secure the interest of enterprises and amalgamations in optimal plan assignments. Work must be done in tightening of state discipline, so that the work of enterprises, amalgamations and ministries can be correctly and consistently evaluated.

A central aspect of the economic reform is the improvement of commodity-money relations. Here confusion must be avoided; in a socialist economy these relations are not autonomous, but take their content from socialist planning. Prices, for example, reflect the needs of long-term planning in the interests of the entire working people as producer-consumers, not the power struggle of a capitalist society. Kosygin explained:

The Central Committee of the party and the Soviet Government hold that directive planning is the main and determining factor and commodity-money relations can and must be applied to strengthen planned guidance of the national economy and stimulate the initiative of enterprises and amalgamations operating on a profit-and-loss basis. In our country, commodity-money relations have a new, socialist content. It stands to reason that we reject all the erroneous conceptions that substitute market regulation for the guiding role of state centralized planning.

Far from counterposing the interest of the individual to that of society as a whole, "it is necessary to align more fully the individual and collective interests," to cultivate an attitude of working for society as the prime duty. As part of this bringing together of moral and material incentives, the material interest of people not only in current but also in *long-term* results will be stressed, and to this end the system of material incentives will be tied in directly with the fulfillment of five-year plan assignments. Individual interest is thus broadened to encompass the tasks of introducing the achievements of science and technology and improving the quality indicators of the work of enterprises.

Profit is the main indicator of the effectiveness of production, the source of funds of enterprises and amalgamations and the basic source of state revenue; its role will be increased. At the same time, the content of profit in a socialist economy is not the antagonistic appropriation of the fruits of the workers' labor for aggrandizement, but the wherewithal for social consumption and for the growth of the productive capacity of the economy. "Socialist society is not indifferent as to how, by what means and under what conditions profit is increased." Raising labor productivity, yes; illegally raising state-set prices or violating the quality or assortment norms, no. Properly used, the profit criterion is an effective way of enhancing the interest of production collectives in making good use of material, financial and labor resources. In 1970, nine billion rubles went into the funds of enterprises out of profits earned, including 3.6 billion into development funds; 1.4 billion into sociocultural and housing; and four billion into direct material incentives funds. Today one-quarter of the increase in wages and salaries comes from the material incentives funds. At the enterprises on the new system, these funds are distributed at the end of the year according to the overall yearly results, enhancing the interest of the individual worker in the results of the work of the entire collective, and providing incentives for the reduction of labor turnover, improvement of discipline, and growth of productivity. Moreover, the system places new demands upon socialist democracy: The stimulation funds of enterprises "come out of their receipts, and a broad *aktiv* of workers and employees must participate in the all-round discussion of how to use them rationally."

Continued work will be done in improving the system of price formation, bringing the prices of manufactured goods into line with socially necessary expenditures of labor. "As labor productivity rises and production costs decline we shall reduce the wholesale prices of manufactured goods." Prices must be used so as to stimulate the interest of enterprises in modernizing their products, improving quality and speeding up technical progress. The use of credit and circulating funds has grown greatly and will continue to grow. Nearly half of the circulating assets and a good part of the basic assets in the economy are now formed with the aid of credit, and more than 75 per cent of the payments for goods and services involve credits. The State Bank and the Building Bank are called upon to exercise greater influence over the choice of investment projects which they help finance.

The system of material and technical supply has been overhauled recently on a territorial principle.. The problem is to obtain the benefits of branch management of industry and at the same time avoid local departmental restrictions. Wholesale trading in means of production will be further developed in the new plan period, and stable ties between enterprises will continue to develop through the State Committee for Material and Technical Supplies.

A vital task in the economic reform, to be accomplished in the coming period, is the further rationalization of the administrative structure of the national economy. "We must review critically the present standard administrative structures, some of which are already obsolete." Special structures which suit the needs of particular branches are being studied. In places, i.e., the coal industry, unnecessary links were uncovered. In general, a two-or three-echelon system appears to be the most acceptable. Large-scale production amalgamations, mentioned previously, help avoid duplication and bring scientific research closer to the actual production problems. They also achieve economies by centralizing supply and sales functions, research, and the like. However, "the approach to forming amalgamations should be thoughtful and scientifically grounded. Amalgamations of enterprises should not give rise to additional intermediate echelons between ministry and enterprise, to expansion of administrative staffs and higher outlays for their maintenance." Creative search is needed to find the forms of amalgamation suitable for specific branches; in some cases, the central functions may

104

be performed at a head enterprise, or by a scientific organization, and amalgamations may open their own retail shops, to get close readings of demand.

Ministries are called upon to launch deep studies of their respective branches: to forecast social demand for their products, to introduce and carry forward a uniform technical policy, to solve specific problems (such as that of supplying spare parts for machines, an old headache), and to see to it that, at all levels of decision-making, the adopted decisions are, wherever possible, not merely *adequate* (consistent with physical possibilities, within the financial means of the planning unit, and within the overall targets to be met), but *optimal.*

The branch principle of administration must be combined with a system of rational ties within republics, economic areas and regions, and the ministries, organized on the branch principle, should be made responsible for developing inter-branch and territorial forms of organization and contact. "The socialist way of running the economy is in principle incompatible with departmentalism, which disrupts rational production ties, and with parochialism, which impairs unity in economic activity."

Broader application of electronic computers is required, and the socialist system makes possible their use on a countrywide scale. In the coming five years, it is planned to put into operation at least 1,600 automated control systems in industry, agriculture, communications, trade and transport. The further substantiation of nationwide planning demands the development of a nationwide system for information gathering and processing, a "state system of computer centers and a single countrywide automated communications network."

Qualitative new demands are now placed on the USSR's managerial cadres. "We are faced with the task of consistently extending and improving the system of training and retraining managerial personnel at all levels, including top executive cadres." The new management techniques involve thorough knowledge of Marxist-Leninist theory, management, labor organization, the new methods of planning and stimulation, economic-mathematical methods and computers.

Of overall vital importance is the drawing of millions of working people into the decision-making process:

> A further development of socialist democracy, broader participation of working people in running production, is an important condition for raising the effectiveness of the organization and management of the economy. This ensures

the implementation of that most important principle of our economic activity —the combining of the interests of society, of the collective, with the interests of each working individual.

Upon approval of the draft Directives by this Congress, the drawing up of the five-year plan must be completed quickly, including breaking it down into annual assignments; the amalgamations and enterprises must get it quite soon, so that it is ready for final ratification not later than August 1, 1971. Of course, the completion of the plan will not rule out the need for corrections during the course of the five-year period. Kosygin declared:

> Permit me to express the trust that Party and trade-union organizations, and government and economic executives, will display creative initiative and perseverance in fulfilling the tasks set by the Party Congress relative to improving management and planning.

Living Standard and Cultural Level

THE rising standard of living of the Soviet people is, as previously noted, both the central aim and the *sine qua non* of the Ninth Five-Year Plan. The rise during the five years will include growth of social consumption and falling prices of manufactured goods, but the bulk of it will take the form of rising wages, salaries and collective farm incomes.

Alexey Kosygin's enumeration of the specific steps envisaged is its own lesson on the nature of socialist society. The minimum monthly wage is to be increased to 70 rubles in 1971; and rates for middle brackets of railway workers and farm machine operators will go up the same year. As of July 1, 1971 minimum pensions for collective farmers will be raised, and regulations changed to bring them into parity with Soviet workers and office employees, whose minimums will also be raised on the same day. In 1972, a new minimum wage will be introduced, and middle-level wages and salaries in outlying areas of the country will be increased. On September 1, 1972, teachers' and doctors' salaries will rise by 20 per cent; scholarship grants to colleges and technical schools will increase by 25 and 50 per cent, respectively. In 1973, again new minimum wages and higher middle incomes in the production branches of Kazakhstan, the Central Asian republics and a number of other areas. All areas not covered by 1973 will be brought up to their original parity in 1974, with the overall increase to be completed by 1975. Zonal differentials will be increased, and payment for night work will be boosted. A whole variety of new pensions and benefits, including full-pay sick leave to attend sick children, will be introduced. Especially noteworthy is the gradual lessening of wage and salary differentials, with no provision for raising the incomes of the highest-paid workers, who will mark time, as it were, while the incomes of the lower-paid are increased. In addition, the income tax, already at very modest levels by Western standards, will begin to be phased out, with taxes reduced or abolished altogether on incomes below 90 rubles. Financing all of the new wages and benefits will require a 120 per cent increase in expenditure over the previous five-year plan.

The monthly cash wage of workers and office employees will rise by 20-22 per cent and collective-farm remuneration for work in the commonly-owned sector, 30-35 per cent. Social consumption expenditures—education, cultural facilities, roads, etc.—will go up by 40 per cent.

Between 1947 and 1956, in the years of postwar reconstruction, the Soviet state floated eleven loans, or bond issues, totalling 25.8 billion rubles. These are now to be redeemed six years ahead of schedule, returning their savings to Soviet citizens on terms more favorable than originally contracted. This plus the rise in remuneration for current labor will greatly increase the cash incomes of the Soviet population, and these cash incomes must be met by a corresponding increase in consumer goods output and trade turnover. In fact, the 40 per cent increase in cash incomes is to be matched by a rise in commodity sales of 42 per cent and a rise in the volume of services of 47 per cent. The planned percentage increases of *high quality* consumer goods are uniformly higher than the planned increase of consumer expenditure as a whole. Thus, supply of meat, fish, vegetable oil, eggs and vegetables will rise by 40-60 per cent; knitted goods, 56 per cent; cultural and domestic goods 80 per cent; refrigerators, TV sets, washing machines, and automobiles are all slated for large increases. Public catering, an as yet underdeveloped aspect of the Soviet consumer economy, will increase by 50 per cent. Attention will be given to the production of ready-to-cook and ready-to-serve foods, pre-packaged goods, everyday services, internal tourism, and other aspects of consumer needs.

Special emphasis will be given to housebuilding, with a planned total new construction of 565-575 million square meters, a new kind of attention to questions of design, layout and general esthetics, and the development of cooperative and individual forms of home-building and ownership.

The plan projects a milestone in the field of education: during the next five years, the introduction of universal ten-year secondary education throughout the USSR will be completed. Considerable attention will be devoted to the development of vocational and technical education, and to specialized secondary education, in addition to the expansion of the higher educational facilities of the country. Nine million new specialists will be trained during this period.

Those who will enter school during these years will be developing the country's economy and culture in the nineties and in the beginning of the 21st century. The curricula and teaching methods in general and technical schools and higher educational establishments must even now increasingly take into account future scientific and technological development.

Advances in the area of health protection have as a key task the drawing together of medical services in the rural areas and in the towns. Physical culture and sports will also be emphasized as a vital aspect of life. Avoiding pollution is a major component of the planned rise in the standard of living: "In the interest of public health, consideration must be shown for the natural environment, and the sanitary condition of all towns and villages must be improved."

The section of the report on living standards ends with a recapitulation of the interrelation between living standards and the growth of the productive forces:

It is necessary to ensure a harmonious combination of material and moral labor incentives. Better results at work and creative initiative should be encouraged by various material and moral incentives expressive of society's recognition of the individual's merits and rousing his professional pride.

Raising the people's standard of living and cultural level is indivisibly associated with the further consolidation and development of the socialist way of life. The Soviet people see the great advantages of socialism materializing with increasing effect in the course of communist construction.

Foreign Economic Ties

A N integral part of the economic development plan is the international division of labor, which "will help consolidate the international positions of the Soviet Union, to cement the unity and augment the economic power of the world socialist system." Trade with the member-countries of the Council for Mutual Economic Assistance will expand considerably in the five-year period, with the USSR exporting increased quantities of oil, natural gas, electric power and iron ore, and importing chemical-industry equipment, railway and water-borne transport facilities, and manufactured consumer goods. A program of socialist economic integration is currently being worked out, with a projected increase in joint projects, and increasing specialization and cooperation. Financing of these relations is facilitated by the founding, in 1970, of the International Investment Bank.

Non-CMEA socialist countries—the Democratic Republic of Vietnam, the Korean People's Democratic Republic, the Republic of Cuba and the Socialist Federal Republic of Yugoslavia—have also greatly increased trade and scientific-technical cooperation with the USSR. Trade with China, although far short of possibilities, will be promoted by the USSR "on the basis of equality and respect for mutual interests." Economic ties with most of the countries of Asia, Africa and Latin America will continue to develop; "our cooperation with them, based on principles of equality and respect for mutual interests, is acquiring the nature of a stable division of labor, counterposed in the sphere of international economic relations to the system of imperialist exploitation." The USSR also stands for broader commercial relations with the developed capitalist countries, and there is a tendency toward long-term agreements which create additional preconditions for the expansion of trade, especially between the USSR and Finland, France, Italy, Japan, the FRG and Austria. Much depends on resolving the problems in the present international situation, and in particular the convening of a European Security Conference. (The Soviet proposals in this regard are spelled out in Leonid Brezhnev's report to the Congress.) Relations with the United States of America are not ruled out by the USSR. The underlying principle is peaceful coexistence and mutual advantage in trade and other economic relations. The Soviet Union is opposed to closed groupings of the "common market" type, and to any form of discrimination in trade, and warns that any politically motivated discriminatory schemes aimed at the USSR are bound to fail; "the Soviet Union possesses resources that fully enable it to develop independently."

In Summary

THE five-year plans have been milestones in the construction of socialism and communism. The current plan is in that tradition, and epitomizes the will and wisdom of the Soviet people. The plans and achievements of the Soviet Union "add greatly to socialism's power of attraction. The example of the Soviet Union and other socialist countries exercises a tremendous influence, speeding up social progress throughout the world."

The five-year plan is a great step in the development of socialist democracy:

> The new five-year plan is to be a plan for the further development of socialist relations of production. It will assure the active participation of the

109

broad mass of working people in running production and administering society.

While the plan is a plan of peaceful construction, it is cognizant of world realities:

In the complicated international situation, with imperialist reaction resorting to military gambles and direct aggression, with the US imperialists, who trample the norms of international law, conducting an ignominous, dirty and piratical war in Vietnam, Cambodia and Laos, with tensions and the threat of war remaining in the world, we have no right ever to forget the need to strengthen our Armed Forces and enhance their combat readiness.

Fulfillment of the Ninth Five-Year Plan will have an immense effect on all the peoples of the Soviet Union. "It will increase still more (the USSR's) economic might, and make the life of all people better and still more attractive, materially more prosperous and spiritually more meaningful and interesting." In the nationwide emulation movement, the targets for the first three months of the plan for 1971 have been exceeded, getting the new five-year plan off to a good start. The key to success, and indeed the historical experience of the Soviet Union, are vividly expressed in these words of Lenin: "The greater the scope and extent of historical events, the greater is the number of people participating in them, and, contrariwise, the more profound the change we wish to bring about, the more must we rouse an interest and an intelligent attitude towards it, and convince more millions and tens of millions of people that it is necessary." We are grateful to our friends abroad, and their representatives our guests at this Congress, for their high appraisal of our policy; the international working class regards our five-year plans as great triumphs in the historic contest between socialism and capitalism. "By our plans, by our policy, we Communists say to the working people of the entire world that the welfare of the working man, the creation of conditions for the full and all-round flowering of the personality, is our main concern, our main goal." In conclusion, Alexey Kosygin declared:

Compared with all the previous five-year plans, which the Soviet people have successfully implemented, the present five-year plan stands out in scope, in the grandeur of its tasks and in the fact that it covers all the key aspects of the life of Soviet society . . .

Allow me to express the confidence that the Ninth Five-Year Plan will be successfully fulfilled through the will of the Party, and the will and selfless labor effort of the whole Soviet people.

The great Party of Lenin is leading us towards glorious new achievements, to new victories of communism!

Long live the great Soviet people, the builders of communism!

110

Speeches of
Congress Delegates

(Continued)

V. I. PROKHOROV

**Secretary of All-Union
Central Council of Trade Unions**

THE HIGHLY important Leninist tradition of taking counsel with the people has been fully carried out in the practical activities of the CPSU in recent years. The Central Committee initiates important general political, economic and inner-Party issues for nationwide discussion. The working people, considering the cause of the Party as their own cause, too, then express their wishes and advice. This course was followed by the Central Committee when it publicized the draft Directives for the 1971-1975 development plan well in advance of the Party Congress.

This program was studied and discussed by tens of millions of working people who contributed many proposals and much valuable advice. It is a matter of deep satisfaction that many proposals submitted by the trade unions were carefully examined by the Central Committee and the USSR Council of Ministers and taken into account in the draft Directives.

The constant attention paid by the Party to the activities of the trade unions raises the level of their organizational and educational work and expands trade union activity in all spheres of our society. Their membership has increased in the last five years by nearly 14 million. The work of the collective bodies—the trade union committees, almost 50 per cent of whose members are workers—has improved.

Guided by the decisions of the 23rd CPSU Congress, the trade unions concentrated their efforts on improving the forms and methods of socialist emulation. Presently involved in this drive are over 71 million, more than half of whom have joined in the movement for a communist attitude towards work.

There was a fresh upsurge in socialist emulation during the preparations for the 24th CPSU Congress. The trade unions organized competitions and instituted special prizes for the improvement of the scientific organization of labor and mechanization of arduous and manual operations. National reviews on the use of reserves of production and on the regime of economy are now being conducted.

During the last five years the trade unions were especially active in promoting technical innovations by factory and office workers. This has greatly influenced the successful development of social production, and the steady rise of labor productivity. Suffice it to say that the overall saving from the use of inventions and rationalization proposals in the national economy during this period added up to 12.5 billion rubles.

However, not everyone shows the right attitude towards technical innovations on the part of factory and office workers; this has led to the failure to introduce and use many of their proposals.

The speeding up of scientific and technological progress, improving efficiency of social production and labor productivity, ensuring a considerable increase in the output of consumer goods, improving quality and technical standards of output while reducing its cost: these are the most important trends on which the trade unions will concentrate their efforts.

As one of the major links in the general system of socialist democracy, the trade unions will exercise their right to participate even more actively in production management, in all affairs of society. Under the Party's leadership they will draw even more factory and office workers into the planning of production. They will improve the collective agreement system, work for the enhancement of the role of workers' meetings and permanent production conferences in the life of the collectives, and strengthen in every way their ties with the Soviets, Komsomol and public-control bodies.

The report of the CPSU Central Committee stresses that defense of the working people's legal rights remains one of the basic tasks of the trade unions. Important measures in this direction have been carried out in the past five-year period. State allocations for labor protection measures amounted to 5.4 billion rubles, more than 1.6 times the amount of the preceding five-year period. The number of workers receiving free work clothes and footwear increased by ten million. Outlays for these purposes increased by 50 per cent, reaching 5.4 billion rubles. Compared with 1965, occupational injuries were reduced by nearly 50 per cent and in some industries, 66.7 per cent and more.

But there are still many outstanding problems in this area. We are short of sanitary engineering and ventilation equipment. Certain problems remain in supplying workers more adequately with work clothes, footwear and so on. Leonid Brezhnev noted quite justly that there are enterprises that have made a practice of resorting to overtime work, depriving people unnecessarily of their free days and, in some places, failing to provide adequate safety measures. The trade unions are of course also to blame for this.

At the same time, it is necessary in our opinion that ministries and departments, in cooperation with trade union central committees, undertake comprehensive measures insuring the safety of industrial and office workers and collective farmers, the extensive mechanization of arduous and manual labor, and the introduction of progressive technological processes.

It is also necessary in the current five-year period to carry out additional measures for improving women's working conditions, professional training and skills. Executives and trade union organizations must see to it that during this period auxiliary service facilities and enterprise restaurants are brought up to established standards, and the level raised of everyday services to all personnel.

The Communist Party and the Soviet Government are constantly expanding public consumption funds. These funds constitute one of the great gains of socialism. Their expansion also means growth in the trade unions' activity in administering the state social insurance funds, supplying the working people with accommodations in sanatoria and health resorts, and developing tourism, physical culture and sports.

During the 1966 to 1970 period, 67 million workers of town and countryside were supplied with accommodations in sanatoria and vacation homes free of charge or at a reduced price, and 41 million children of industrial and office workers spent their vacations in Young Pioneer camps. In the new five-year period about 150 million people—one and a half times more than in the previous five-year period—will enjoy the same facilities.

We have also worked out a plan for the further expansion of health resorts. During the past five years the trade unions have made available new sanatoria, vacation homes, tourist centers and other institutions accommodating 165,000 persons. In this new five-year period our plans call for an additional 300,000 accommodations, and more than 1.5 billion rubles well be spent for these purposes.

The trade unions are paying considerable attention to educational work among personnel. For this purpose they provide a large number of cultural and educational institutions and sports facilities. But unfortunately these are distributed unevenly, and are lacking in places where they are most needed—at new enterprises and in newly developing remote areas. This situation must be corrected in the current five-year period.

It must be admitted, comrades, that the educational work of the trade unions sometimes lacks purposefulness and fails to yield the necessary results. Among our personnel, as was quite justly noted in speeches of some Congress delegates, we still find shirkers and job-switchers, people who, so to speak, know perfectly well all the rights of Soviet citizens, but at the same time forget that rights imply duties as well. This requires increased and improved educational work on the part of the trade unions.

While enthusiastically approving and completely supporting the new program of social and economic development outlined in the reports of Comrade Brezhnev and Comrade Kosygin, the Soviet trade unions clearly realize that the planned benefits will not come by themselves; they can be attained only by the determined labor of all the Soviet people. That is why the entire force of the trade unions, their entire experience, organizational and educational work, will be directed towards a new rise in the economy in view of the decisions of this Congress. The trade unions will fulfill even more actively their role as schools of administration and management, schools of communism.

VLADIMIR A. MATSKEVICH

USSR Minister of Agriculture

AGRICULTURE has been and continues to be the object of daily concern and attention of the Central Committee and of the entire Party because its state and rates of development have a direct bearing on the living standards of the Soviet people.

[Praising the Brezhnev report, the speaker enumerated the important measures taken by the CPSU in recent years opening up a new stage of intensification of agriculture in all its branches on the basis of mechanization, electrification and chemicalization.]

Consistent implementation of the measures to increase the material and technical facilities and strengthen the economy of the collective farms and state farms has ensured a continuous growth of gross and marketable produce of field-crop cultivation and livestock breeding.

There has been a substantial improvement of the situation in livestock breeding. Along with the quantitative growth of livestock, there has been a growth of its productivity. Whereas in 1965 the yield of

114

milk per cow on collective farms and state farms increased by 49 kg, as compared to 1960, in the past half-decade the increase amounted to 315 kg. The output of beef per cow and of pork per sow increased by one third. The live weight of cattle and pigs for slaughter was also increased.

The development of production was favorably influenced by strengthening of cost-accounting and the growing interest of the agriculturists in the development of the publicly owned economy. Whereas between 1961-1965 the state farm deficit amounted to 5.3 billion rubles, in the past half-decade we have received a profit of 7.5 billion rubles. Incomes of collective farmers have increased as well as their pay. Pensions and social insurance have been introduced for collective farmers.

We realize very well that by far not everything has been done of the things we can do, and we understand what we must do to meet more fully the requirements of the population in foodstuffs and the needs of industry in raw materials.

The machines which are being sent in increasing numbers to the countryside have not always been used with due efficiency. On some farms there are serious shortcomings in the expenditure of materials and money, in the organization of labor, in the utilization of land. Comrade Brezhnev was quite correct in criticizing us for this in his report.

There have been failures in ascertaining plans of purchases, and in implementing specialization—as when people on some farms too thoughtlessly and hastily curtailed certain branches of production. It would be quite just to mention also the drawbacks in the operation of planning agencies which allowed a substantial reduction of means for the development of agriculture in the annual plans.

With all due tribute to the efforts of industrial workers to reequip the countryside technically, I should say that some enterprises and branches have not been up to standard as regards the quality of the machines and chemical agents supplied to collective and state farms, which could not but affect technical progress and the size of output.

Much has to be done to increase the quantity and improve the quality of raw materials for the manufacture of consumer goods. Yet, the most acute problem is to increase output of highly nutritive products of which man has a daily need.

By fulfilling the targets of the five-year plan we shall be able to increase substantially consumption of meat and fruit, to actually achieve optimum standards in consumption of milk, sugar, vegetables and vegetable oils, and to reduce somewhat the consumption of flour and potatoes.

The growth of the output of grain and other field crops is based primarily on sound utilization of land. And from this high rostrum I would like to make a particularly urgent call for the most thrifty attitude toward conservation and sensible utilization of land, this precious treasure of the people. In recent years the CPSU Central Committee, the USSR Supreme Soviet and the Government have adopted some very important decisions in this matter.

The issue deserves the closest and most responsible attention. Unfortunately, not everyone has a proper understanding of the problem. It is common knowledge, for example, that two-thirds of this planet are under water and only a third of the solid ground is arable. Yet structures are being designed that flood thousands of hectares of bottom land and turn them into swamps and shallow lagoons.

All this, of course, is done with the laudable purpose of increasing our power resources. Yet, let us take a deeper approach to this problem. Increasingly taking the place of firewood and peat, in addition to hard coal and water, are such sources of power as oil and gas, as well as atomic energy. Whereas in addition to raw materials used to make clothing for man, chemistry and synthetic materials can also serve this purpose to some degree, we have nothing comparable in the foreseeable future to take the place of vegetable and animal food. Therefore, we must seek new ways and use other sources of energy that would not reduce the basic foundation for the production of foodstuffs.

Besides, with some expenditure, modern technology helps to reduce the flooding of lands. Moreover, there are cases when hard ground is wrested from the sea. It is the sacred duty of every Soviet citizen to preserve the land.

An equally important problem is the *sound* utilization of land. In the previous half-decade a lot has been done to increase soil fertility, to protect it from erosion, to increase standards of cultivation. There has been a sharp reduction in the various and sometimes ill-considered associations, mergers and reorganizations of farms. As a result there is better order in land tenure, and 87 per cent of our cultivated land now has correct crop rotation.

The growing supply of mineral fertilizers and machinery, increase of irrigated areas, and new high-yield varieties produced by our world famous selectionists have resulted in yields of from 50 to 60 and more centners of grain per hectare. All this means that specialists and scientists must develop new technology, ensuring rapid growth and high quality of production, reduction of costs, and at the same time the preservation and increase of soil fertility. This and this alone—the

116

steady raising of the yields of grain, technical and fodder crops—is the basic and practically the only way for increasing the productivity of agriculture.

In livestock breeding, the growth of output in the current five-year plan will be achieved through substantially raising productivity and increasing the head of livestock. The process of specialization, extensively developed in the previous half-decade, has resulted in the appearance of large factory-farms, complexes, organized on an industrial foundation. Several years ago we had no industrial poultry breeding. Now the country has 500 poultry factories where yields are 50 per cent higher than in small farms, labor expenditure only one-fourth and fodder expenditure one-half.

Industrial fattening of cattle and pigs is being developed. The five-year period will see the construction of about 1,500 large complexes and factories for meat, milk, eggs and vegetables. These will make use of sophisticated mechanisms, automation and electronics and the achievements of biochemistry and microbiology. Yet, one should quite clearly realize that these complexes do not entirely solve the problem of providing the country with livestock and other produce.

[The speaker outlined measures to bring other branches of livestock husbandry up to the level achieved in poultry.]

The Central Committee calls for a thrifty attitude to supplementary economies in the private plots of collective farmers and other citizens. Without playing any substantial part in the state marketable produce, these economies are still a great help in providing the population with vegetables, fruit and animal products.

The draft Directives contemplate major steps in the technical re-equipment of agriculture. Modern agricultural production, remaining an important part of the national economy, is becoming ever more sophisticated, with increasing utilization of chemistry and mechanization, automation, electronics and agricultural aviation. At the same time we have to deal here with living organisms, developing according to intricate biological laws. And we have also to contend with the great influence of weather conditions on the results of human activities.

It is necessary to dwell briefly on some difficulties and urgent problems in the technical re-equipment of agriculture. Some 15-20 years ago the basic ploughing tractor with us was DT-54 which in its days had nothing to match it. Today our agriculture does not have a mass-scale powerful ploughing tractor conforming to all the modern requirements. The slow progress in improving the design of machines for the harvesting of grain, sugar beet, hay and for procuring silo, leads to crop losses.

117

Transport is an acute factor hampering the development of collective farms and state farms. Agriculture as a rule has to deal with a great variety of large freights. Therefore along with enlarging the output of good trailers for tractors, the automobile industry must develop a system of specialized heavy duty automobiles, with high cross-country capacity, based on alternating trailer platforms for various purposes.

Special attention should be paid to the supply of buses for agriculture. The process of merging small settlements into large modern townships is taking place in the countryside, and the transportation of people to the fields and livestock-breeding sections and the delivery of children to schools is usually handled by trucks; this leads to catarrhal diseases, and sometimes to road accidents. It is obviously necessary to increase the supply of buses to collective farms and state farms.

Scientific and technical progress, better utilization of machinery, solution of urgent problems sometimes arising unexpectedly, new forms of management: all these require that collective farms and state farms be provided with reliable means of radiotelephone communications, both mobile and stationary.

The problem of manufacture of the necessary machinery merits the closest possible attention. As many as 455 types of machines have been developed for the mechanization of livestock breeding sections and complexes alone. But as yet, industry puts out only 217 of these, and not always of perfect quality.

Building construction in agriculture is developing extensively. Special organizations contract for the erection of poultry factories, complexes, large animal farms, workshops, and dwelling houses. Buildings and structures are being constructed more soundly than before. At the same time, we agriculturists are alarmed by rising costs of construction, mainly due to the increase of overhead, prices of materials, and so on.

Specialization of collective farms and state farms and mass output of homogeneous produce on an industrial foundation provide favorable conditions for processing and storage of produce at the point of production. This will help to avoid losses, to preserve and provide the consumer with the entire crop grown, and will enable the smoother use of labor and transport facilities. Development of enterprises for the processing of agricultural produce on a group of specialized large collective and state farms leads to the establishment of agro-industrial complexes that, as Leonid Brezhnev reports, have a great future and, aside from being the new organizational form, are also an important socioecoomic phenomenon. In such associations the level of production will grow. Labor will become more skilled and attractive for educated youth. The production and cultural conditions and way of life in the countryside will be brought closer to those of the urban population, and thereby one of the basic policy goals of our Party will be achieved.

The agriculturists will not spare efforts to implement the Party's great program of construction of communism in our country!

PYOTR S. NEPOROZHNY

USSR Minister of Power and Electrification

THE CPSU CENTRAL Committee and the Soviet Government, in the period under review, have devoted very great attention to the solution of the complicated problems of priority development of our power industry. Thanks to their aid and the creative work of the power industry employees, we have fulfilled a vast program of further electrification of the country. At present our country has electric power stations with the total capacity of over 166 million kw. The annual commissioning of new power capacities in recent years reached a volume of 10-12 million kw, seven times as much as contemplated by the GOELRO* plan.

In 1970, the level of electricity output was 740 billion kwh. And currently, the Soviet Union generates more electricity than Britain, France, the FRG and Sweden put together.

In the eighth five-year period, the Soviet power industry achieved a qualitatively new and higher level of technical development. Thermal electric power stations were provided with generators, with superhigh steam parameters, having a capacity of 200,000 and 300,000 kw each.

The country also has 30 thermal electric power stations with a design capacity of over 1,000,000 kw, and among these there are the world's biggest: Konakovskaya, Zmiyevskaya, Pridneprovskaya and Burshtynskaya, each with a capacity of 2,400,000 kw. There has also been a further development of the heat supply for towns and industrial centers.

The past half-decade saw the commissioning of the world's biggest hydroelectric power stations—in Bratsk and Krasnoyarsk. Construction is under way of the even more powerful Sayano-Shushen-

---

*GOELRO—The State Electrification Plan, brain child of Lenin, worked out under guidance of Gleb Krzhizhanovsky, and adopted in 1920. The world's first plan of economic development.

skoye hydroelectric power station and major hydrostations in Siberia and Soviet Central Asia (Ust-Ilimskaya, Nurekskaya, Toktogulskaya, etc.). As for the sophistication and scope of the problems being tackled by us in hydropower station building and hydropower engineering, our country definitely is first in the world.

A beginning has been made in the establishment of a large-scale atomic power industry; superhigh tension lines with the world's greatest voltage have been built. In the period of extensive electrification it is already impossible to secure a reliable and effective power supply for the national economy from isolated power stations. In this connection great work has been done to develop and link power grids and to provide the country's territory with centralized power supply.

We have completed the establishment of the Single Power Grid for the European USSR with the total capacity of over 100 million kw. This grid, the biggest in the world, is controlled from a single operations center.

The past half-decade saw the construction of rural high voltage lines with a total length of 1,200,000 km. And currently, centralized electric supply from state grids ensures 93 per cent of electricity consumption on collective and state farms.

Electrification of public services and homes has been more intensively developed. There has been a particularly high growth in power consumption for utility purposes in the countryside.

The vast Soviet know-how in electrification and development of the power industry, in addition to being successfully used to develop our economy, has a direct influence on the advancement of the processes of integration of the economy in the socialist countries. It is common knowledge that the Mir power grid is now functioning successfully. It includes the grids of Bulgaria, Hungary, the GDR, Poland, Rumania, Czechoslovakia and the Soviet Union. Cooperation in the area of the power industry between our country and many Afro-Asian states is also developing successfully.

The long-range plan for the development of the power industry shows that in the next 10 to 12 years it will be necessary to commission additional capacities of about 200 million kw, including 67 million kw in the ninth five-year period. In the thermal power industry, we contemplate a further boosting of the capacities of power units, from 300,000 to 1,200,000 kw. Comrades, a generator of 1,200,-000 kw is the world's first single-shaft power unit with such a capacity —almost equal to the entire power output envisaged under the GOELRO plan! Special attention will be devoted to the introduction of automated systems for the control of power stations and grids. In the development of atomic power stations chief attention should be devoted to boosting the capacity of reactors to one million kw and more. Special attention will be paid to stepping-up research, designing and the construction of fast neutron reactors.

As to the hydroelectric power station construction, in the future we shall stick to our earlier policy of erecting large and highly profitable hydroelectric power stations, especially in Siberia and Central Asia, with a view to utilizing their cheap electricity to develop various local power consuming processes, and also to develop further construction of hydrostorage and other hydropower stations in the European USSR.

The great requirements in water, not only for the electric power industry but also for other needs of populated areas, especially the so-called Southern slope of the European USSR (the basins of the Dnieper, Dniestr, Volga, Kubanfi Terek and other rivers), as well as Central Asia (the basins of the Amu-Darya and Syr-Darya rivers), call for regulation of the river flow by erecting dams and water reservoirs attached to them. Some land in flooded in the process. Therefore the appropriate organizations must tackle creatively the problems of rational, multi-purpose utilization of water reservoirs, for more intensive fish farming, cultivation of special high-yielding varieties of rice in shallow places, and other purposes.

We power workers are taking measures to conserve land. We are building low-voltage power transmission lines along railways; we are working on the problem of transmitting large streams of electricity in special piping, using so to speak the phenomenon of superconductivity; we are laying cables. We too love our native land, comrade agriculturists!

ANDREY GRECHKO

Minister of Defense of the USSR

THE Armed Forces of our country covered themselves with unfading glory in the years of the great Patriotic War. Not only our contemporaries, but future generations will forever revere the memory of the heroic Soviet soldiers who saved the world from fascist enslavement and ensured the peoples of many countries in Europe and Asia freedom, independence and social progress.

The outstanding achievements of our socialist country and these military victories had an enormous impact on the destinies of the world and contributed to the growth of the liberation movement of the peoples and the development of the world revolutionary process. The Soviet Army convincingly demonstrated its historic mission as a defender of everything forward and progressive against the forces of reaction and aggression. In our days this noble mission of the Soviet Armed Forces as a powerful factor for preserving peace and stability on the earth is especially necessary.

Comrades, the tragedy of the Second World War is still alive in the memory of the peoples, the deep scars on the earth have not yet been reclaimed, human wounds have not healed. Grief at the loss of countless lives has not yet died, but the forces of reaction are already hatching plans for a new crusade against the Soviet Union and other socialist countries, again seeking to unleash an even more destructive war. The increasing aggressiveness of imperialism, spearheaded against the Soviet Union, is responsible for the tension of the international situation today. The US monopoly magnates seek to mobilize the entire arsenal of political, economic and military means of the capitalist world for the struggle against the socialist countries.

The US imperialists' preparations for aggression have never ceased and are continuing unabated. They have surrounded the socialist states with aggressive military-political blocs and entangled the world in the barbed wire of their military bases. They have been steadily building up and perfecting their means of war and increasing allocations for military purposes year by year.

The United States, a nuclear power, has chosen blackmail as the main instrument of its foreign policy. It has taken upon itself the role of world gendarme and created a multimillion-strong army, more than ten times larger than its prewar armed forces. A special threat to peace is the US-led aggressive military bloc of NATO which each year is arming itself more and more and has an army of six million.

The military and political leaders of imperialism are working out all kinds of strategies and doctrines for a future war. As a testing ground for their strategy they have chosen Vietnam where the US imperialists have for several years been waging a predatory and criminal war. But Vietnam has become the graveyard for imperialism's military doctrines. The heroic Vietnamese people and their armed forces, relying on assistance from the Soviet Union and other socialist states, have inflicted on the aggressors a number of heavy defeats and left them no hope of success in their military adventure.

Under cover of the old talk about a "communist threat," US ruling circles in every way possible have been fomenting militaristic frenzy and searching for a way out of the crisis of imperialism's political and military doctrines in increased preparations for war against the Soviet Union and the forces of peace and progress. Voices can still be heard in the United States that call for negotiating with the Soviet Union "from positions of strength." The invalidity of this "positions of strength" approach has been proved both by past experience and by the present course of events. The Soviet Union, together with the other socialist states, is capable of responding to force with a superior force. The lovers of such talk will do well to remember this.

The United States seeks, by political and economic pressure, military threats and provocations, to impose on other states a policy befitting its monopolies, and to establish the kind of "peace" that would ensure them the freedom of getting rich by exploiting and despoiling other countries. It is such a "peace" that the imperialists carry to the peoples of Indochina, the Arab Middle East and other states embarking on the path of independent development and strengthening their sovereignty.

War propaganda ranks prominently in the arsenal of the imperialists' means of aggressive policy. The ideologists of militarism are doing their best to prove that the cause of wars should be looked for not in the system of imperialism, but in the nature of man, in his inborn warlike psychology which, allegedly, makes war eternal and inevitable and denies completely its class nature.

Grossly distorting the Marxist-Leninist teaching about the class nature of war, the champions of aggression slanderously claim that socialism gives rise to war and that, therefore, nuclear warfare has to be regarded as a potentially essential means for wiping out socialism.

But the entire bloody history of imperialism shows quite convincingly that imperialism and its creation—state-monopoly capital—have been and remain the chief source of war. It is the aggressive objectives of imperialism that give rise to the reactionary policy which leads to numerous wars and conflicts aimed against the liberation movement of nations.

The Soviet Union has struggled consistently for real peace, for the freedom and equality of all nations, and for their inalienable right to decide their own future without interference from outside. However, in the conditions of acute international tension and unceasing arms race in imperialist states, our country has to take the necessary precautions and support its peaceful policy by strengthening the defense potential and extending the combat facilities and readiness of the Armed Forces.

We have no need for other people's territories. The Soviet people are strengthening their army not for offensive purposes, but solely for the defense of the Soviet state and other countries of the socialist community. The might and solidity of our Armed Forces lie in their unbreakable unity with the people. The army is connected with the people by thousands of threads. The successes of the Soviet people in labor, in the setting up of the material and technical basis of communism, in the fulfillment of the five-year plans, and in the development of science and culture increase the might and solidity of the Soviet Army. Close ties have been established by the personnel of military units with local government and party bodies and collectives of working people, who display constant concern for the servicemen, for their education, and cultural facilities. This concern has a great influence on the successful solution of many tasks in the army and navy, and we are deeply gratified for it.

An example of our loyalty to international duty is the disinterested aid being given to the heroic Vietnamese people, to the peoples of the Arab countries, and to the armies of the newly-developing countries in Asia and Africa, which are defending their freedom and independence against the encroachments of imperialist states. We can say in all boldness that the Soviet Army is an army of proletarian internationalism, rendering aid to all who are fighting against imperialism, for freedom and socialism.

YEVGENY TYAZHELNIKOV

First Secretary, Leninist
Young Communist League

K OMSOMOL Secretary Tyazhelnikov reported that over half of all Soviet youth—27,000,000—are now Komsomol (Young Communist League) members; since the 23rd Congress 1,350,000 have also joined the Party. He thanked the Party for its attention to the problem and interests of youth: "Our motherland," he said, "gives its best to its children and youth."

Recalling youth's pioneering role in all the big construction projects over the years, he declared that the Komsomol's primary task would be the construction of the key projects of the new Five-Year Plan:

> One of the largest power bases in the country is being built in West Siberia. Komsomol members are working together in the front ranks with Party members. The land of impenetrable taiga and marshes, rich in oil and gas, is becoming the land of new Komsomol exploits. We pledge to take a still more

active part in the development of the rich deposits of the Kursk Magnetic Anomaly and Karshi steppe, in the construction of the Kama motor works, the Ust Ilim hydropower station, in the technical re-equipment of farming, land improvement, the creation of Far East and Ural science centers and other priority projects.

Tyazhelnikov vowed also that all Komsomol organizations and student building teams would back up the Party's campaign to build more housing, for cultural and service institutions, amenities for town and countryside, and improvement in the conservation of nature.

The reporter spoke enthusiastically of the Komsomol's interest in training the new labor reserves required for this time of surging scientific and cultural revolution: "It is our job to help every teenager realize, while still at school, the role and grandeur of the workingman. We therefore support the proposal for a sizable increase in the number of vocational schools, to turn out skilled workers with a complete secondary education."

He noted also that a rising level of general knowledge is now required among *all* the youth. Already most of the Komsomol members have either a secondary or a higher education, but too many still have only eight years of schooling. The Komsomol should therefore strongly support the Party program for universal ten-year education.

Tyazhelnikov paid special tribute to older experienced workers who give their time and skill to training the young. Moreover every Soviet enterprise needs special educational measures for the creative development of the new *type* of worker required by the scientific and technical revolution. During this time Soviet society needs new methods and solutions, in the upbringing of youth as well as in economic management. More attention to the urgent problems of the communist education of youth is required, and scientific institutions engaged in such research have to be more closely related to schools and industrial and agricultural enterprises. Engaged in enriching the content of its Marxist-Leninist political education system, the Komsomol therefore proposes a special council for the coordination of scientific studies and youth problems.

Tyazhelnikov took note, finally, of the bitter ideological struggle for the minds and hearts of youth today, with anti-Communism as a main weapon. But Soviet youth, armed and steeled with the Party's ideology, would never yield to such propaganda. To the foreign delegates he promised:

The Leninist Komsomol will vigorously promote the fraternal friendship of the youth of the socialist countries, and the unity of the international communist and democratic youth movement. We shall extend still further

125

the movement for solidarity with heroic Vietnam, with peoples and youth everywhere fighting for national liberation and social progress, in a worldwide Youth Against Imperialism campaign.

S. P. RASHIDOV

First Secretary, Uzbekistan Communist Party

FIRST Secretary Rashidov of the Uzbek Party stressed the growth of the Uzbek Party's ties with the masses, and the enormous support it enjoys among all the working people of the Republic:

> The Party expresses the vital interests and daring dreams of the people, their brightest hopes and aspirations. The Party and the people are a single whole. Their unity is indestructible. The Party is the soul of the people, its mind and heart and conscience!

Reporting that both agriculture and industry had developed at an accelerated rate, he noted that due to the extensive irrigation and land reclamation program spark-plugged by the Party, Uzbekistan farmers in 1970 had produced the largest cotton harvest in the history of the Soviet Union—26.2 centners per acre.

In the warm, lyrical language characteristic of the people of this Central Asian Republic, he exclaimed:

> Cotton, our "white gold," this is the basic wealth of Soviet Uzbekistan, the priceless gift of our sun-drenched land. It is our pride, the main source whence comes the flowering of our republic, the symbol and material expression of our fraternal unity with all the peoples of the USSR.

The working people of Uzbekistan were fired with a desire to supply the fraternal peoples of their country with ever larger quantities of this precious raw material, and were resolved to raise cotton production to five million tons a year by 1975. For this they needed greater mechanization and better rotation measures. Above all they must get rid of the scourge of wilt. But to insure this, more effective help was needed from the All-Union Academy of Sciences than provided in the past.

Uzbekistan's role as a major gas producing region was growing, and their new gold-mining industry had tripled production in the past five years. Rashidov called upon the State Planning Commission to speed up action on the Uzbek Party's proposals for increasing the Republic's gold extraction. In light and food industry, meat and dairy production there was low labor productivity, unsatisfactory quality of output and other serious lags that must be overcome.

126

Rashidov said the triumph of the Party's Leninist national policy could be seen in all spheres of life, in the steady build-up of both productive forces and a flourishing culture "national in form and socialist in content." Paying tribute to the Russian people as "the older brother and faithful friend of all the Soviet peoples," he noted that the Russian language, as the second native language of all the peoples of the USSR, is a "powerful accelerator of the process of the drawing together of nations." Of the help to Tashkent by all the Soviet peoples after its great disaster, he said:

> The restoration and construction of Tashkent after the 1966 earthquake was a brilliant manifestation of the triumph of the Leninist nationalities policy. Here we saw with our eyes the deep current through which the fraternal friendship of the Soviet peoples carries its mighty constructive force and we felt the indestructible strength of this friendship with all our hearts . . .
>
> Our people have a saying: "A bird's strength is in its wings; a man's strength is in friendship." As the sun's rays warm the earth, so friendship warms our hearts. It gives us a marvelous feeling of being a single family, it inspires us and multiplies our strength. The friendship of the Soviet peoples, reared by Lenin's Party—this is the inexhaustible source of our might and the pledge of our future victories.

OF FLOWERS AND PEACE

I RECALL a moving moment of a truly symbolic nature. In the morning of March 31, on the second day of the Congress, the great vestibule of the Palace of Congresses was suddenly filled with the fragrant scent of flowers: there were fresh bouquets of red carnations lying on the tables where the delegates were getting registered—the flowers were presented to the woman participants of the Congress. The flowers came straight from the flower plantations of the fertile South of France. They had just been sent by French coop workers who had decided to mark in that way the centenary of the Paris Commune and to wish Lenin's Party a successful continuation of the work of the 24th Congress, in the name of peace and socialism.

The delegates and guests at the Congress welcomed this announcement with stormy applause. Then Suslov read out a note which had been sent to the presidium: "We, woman delegates of the 24th Congress of the Communist Party of the Soviet Union would like to express our great thanks to the French coop workers for the flowers they have sent. All women wish with their hearts for peace and friendship to reign on the globe: Let there always be red carnations and crimson roses blossoming on the whole of the earth, and may the conflagration of war never blaze. Long live peace!"

The red carnations were like the drops of hot blood shed on the barricades of the Commune. And when the woman delegates fastened the flowers to the back rests of their seats, it looked as if lights had started shining in the hall.

Yury Zhukov, *Pravda* commentator

Delegates Discuss the
Brezhnev and Kosygin Reports

IN THE speeches already presented, as well as in these briefer excerpts that follow, including government ministers and milkmaids, Presidents of Republics and steel workers, First Secretaries of top Party Committees, teachers, scientists, writers, Russians, Ukrainians, Asians and many minority peoples, a fascinating panorama unfolds of the development and future prospects of socialist Soviet society in all its infinite variety.

To read the texts available in English, going back as well to the originals printed in *Pravda* and *Izvestia*, is really to take a course on Soviet life. The temptation is strong to keep on excerpting and quoting, to give something from everyone. But if this account is to remain within limits, time and space cannot be stretched any further!

Many things are necessarily omitted in the excerpts that follow as well as in the foregoing summaries. Every participant in the discussion began with fervent expressions of approval for the overall proposals in the report of General Secretary Leonid Brezhnev for the Central Committee. Also warmly approved were the draft Directives for the new five-year plan in Premier Alexey Kosygin's report. There was no question about the unanimity of the delegates on these matters which they themselves had helped decide. We have omitted for the most part these opening statements since there were bound to be great similarities, except for differences in emphasis depending on the speaker's area, in geography or life.

The foreign press played up the special praise bestowed by the delegates on Brezhnev, implying the beginning of a new "cult of personality." There were indeed many examples of this praise. But the speakers emphasized above all the work of the Central Committee of the Party and its Politbureau and the collective leadership given by Party organizations everywhere. They hailed in particular the restoration of Leninist principles of Party work that now prevail.

All the delegates ended by pledging their own area or group or profession to new and stronger efforts to carry out the program that the Party, with the participation of all of them and the non-Party population as well, had charted for the future. These perorations and pledges, all on a very high level, also had to be omitted.

On the main content of the speeches, several aspects are notable. As was natural, every speaker recounted the achievements of his or her particular region, factory, farm, school or profession. Space limitations have compelled us to omit local statistics. We should only like to point out that the figures show vividly the greater rate of investment and the greater rate of development in the formerly backward republics, demonstrating the deep concern of the Soviet Government and the Party to bring them up to the level of the more advanced ones. There was vigorous approval by all of the foreign policy of the Soviet Government and the Party.

Finally, special note must be made of the sharply critical sections contained in every speech.

These were not criticisms of basic policies, which all had shared in making, but of failures to carry them out, to respond quickly enough to needs. The criticisms showed above all a determination to improve in every direction, to make things better. There was self-criticism, in relation to the delegates themselves and their own local Party organizations. There was also specific and sharp criticism of government ministries, and in a number of cases individuals were named. New proposals were brought forward regarding the plan, some already embodied in the Directives agreed on at the conference, some still under consideration for the final plan to be discussed and made law at the summer session of the Supreme Soviet.

Our excerpts by no means give the whole picture. We have tried to select items most characteristic of the life of Soviet society.

Delegates from Central Asian and Other National Republics

Dinmuhamed Kunayev, Kazakhstan Party First Secretary, described the huge social and economic changes in the Kazakhstan SSR. This formerly incredibly backward republic covering 1,100,000 square miles, peopled largely by nomads before the Revolution, has made huge strides in developing ferrous and non-ferrous metallurgy, coal mining, a chemical industry, aluminum production, power engineering and machine building. Kunayev assured those who complained of the lack of big all-purpose tractors for agriculture that mighty new Kazakhstan tractors were already coming from the assembly line. Light industry, the food, meat and dairy industries, were growing steadily. Speaking of the 1966-70 five-year plan, he said:

> In these years the sum of 23.8 billion rubles, 33 per cent more than in the previous five-year plan, was invested in the republic's national economy;

445 new industrial enterprises and large shops were built; industrial production increased by 55 per cent. New industrial centers, whole new branches of production have sprung up in all parts of our republic, including formerly uninhabited places. Fifteen new cities have risen, each connected with the birth of an industrial giant. A major oil and gas area has been developed. Mangyshlak oil is already flowing to the central regions of our country through the Uzen Kuibyshev pipeline.

Nearly a quarter of the population has received new or improved housing in this period, national income increased by 61 per cent, everyday and communal services have expanded and consumer goods increased.

Like the other speakers, the Kazakh First Secretary discussed shortcomings. These had been taken up in detail at the Kazakhstan Party Congress, which had discussed the Republic's failure to utilize all its reserves and make greater scientific and technical progress, and criticized government organs as well. He said much more help was needed than formerly received from various government ministries for improved irrigation, more mineral fertilizers and more powerful machinery to carry out their ambitious plans for increased production of grain, rice and livestock. Kunayev blamed the USSR State Planning Committee and Ministry of Non-Ferrous Metallurgy for not bringing up the level of ore extraction to production requirements, and the Ministry of Light Industry for being slow in supplying proper housing, kindergartens and other social facilities for the workers of a large new textile combine. Finally, he faulted Timofeyev, head of the USSR Lumber and Woodworking Industry, for failure to supply enough lumber to construction workers. In conclusion, he declared:

> Representatives of more than 100 nationalities and peoples of the Soviet Union live in Kazakhstan, working selflessly in all sectors of the economic and cultural construction. Our creative labor has strengthened and deepened still further the Leninist friendship of the peoples.

Baiken Ashimov, Chairman of the Kazakhstan Council of Ministers, expanding on some additional achievements and problems, noted the special importance of further improving cultural and service establishments due to the vast distances in Kazakhstan. Some progress had been made in putting clubs, shops, libraries and repair shops "on wheels" to serve the population of the small and remote inhabited points. But a whole fleet of specialized motor vehicles was needed to insure steady mobile service to the rural population.

Muhamednazar Gapurov, Turkmenian Party First Secretary, also reported on industrial and agricultural advances. Like the Uzbek delegate, he spoke with particular pride of the achievement of record harvests of cotton, their "white gold," in the Lenin Centenary year.

130

The whole region had been transformed by the Karakum Canal, built together by the Turkmenian and other peoples. He stressed the friendly mutual help and interchange in both production and culture among all the national republics which "predetermines the rapprochement of all our peoples' interests and their merging into a single all-national interest." Thus:

Many works of art and literature produced by one nation are increasingly acquiring an international character. By assimilating them, every nation gains access to the culture common to all nations and participates in the formation of a single culture of Soviet society. On the other hand, every condition is created for the progress of each nation and for the development of its finest traditions in the spheres of production, culture and daily affairs. Thus the harmonious process of the rapprochement of nations, as an objective law of our society, is being continuously enriched with new content.

Assailing attempts of imperialist propaganda to foment nationalistic sentiments and sow distrust among the Soviet peoples by malicious fabrications about "Soviet colonialism" and the allegedly unequal position of Central Asian Republics in the Soviet Union, Gapurov declared that none of this could halt the objective historical process, "the free and ever more rapid advance of the Central Asian republics within our multinational state—the Union of Soviet Socialist Republics."

Turdakun Usubaliev, Kirghiz Communist Party First Secretary, hailing from a wild and mountainous Central Asian land where semi-feudal conditions prevailed before the Revolution, also reported progress in building up modern industry and agriculture, due to a big increase in the Soviet state's capital investments. In the past five years over half a million of Kirghizia's three million population had received new apartments. The republic, where only three persons in a hundred could read and write fifty years ago, now has a hundred per cent literacy, with 160 university students for every 10,000 inhabitants. All these advances were due to the Leninist national policy of the Party. Of the Kirghiz Party's ideological work Usubaliev said:

We strive to get every working man of the republic to fully understand that the interests of the Kirghiz people and the interests of the whole country are indissoluble, that like every other Union Republic Soviet Kirghizia can continue to grow and flourish only in the close community of socialist nations of the Soviet Union. . . . The Party organization devotes special attention to work among the intelligentsia and youth. In the further strengthening of the fraternal friendship of the peoples, of their cooperation and mutual assistance, lies the main guarantee of new successes in building communism.

Refuting the "slanderous concoctions" of those who served the interests of imperialism about "Russification" of the Central Asian

Republics, Usubaliev declared: "The bourgeois falsifiers can no more succeed in hiding the truth of history than you can hide the light of the sun with your palm."

Geidar Aliyev, First Secretary of the Azerbaidzhan Communist Party, after enumerating the successes of Azerbaidzhan in the five-year period, continued:

> But Communists, the Party teaches us, must always see not only the positive side of the results of work but also the existing deficiences and blunders. This is especially important for us, since for a long time the rates of our republic's development lagged behind the average rates for the Union: there were serious shortcomings in industry and agriculture, for which the CPSU Central Committee repeatedly subjected the Azerbaidzhan Party organization to justified criticism.

These shortcomings had been exhaustively analyzed at plenary sessions of the Azerbaidzhan Party. In July 1970 the CPSU Central Committee and the USSR Council of Ministers had decided on a number of measures to aid Azerbaidzhan's economic development. As a result an upturn had already taken place. The new five-year plan provides for putting more than 100 new enterprises into operation in Azerbaidzhan, more than twice as many as in the past five years, with improvements in the oil, machine building, chemical, food and other branches of industry. Capital investments in agriculture, would be almost doubled, along with increased measures for irrigation and land reclamation, housing and cultural expansion. "But we realize," said Aliyev, "that we still have to do a great deal."

Speaking of the stress in the party program on the two interacting processes in national relations, the flowering of each of the nations along with their drawing together, Aliyev said:

> However, there is in our view a certain one-sidedness in the scientific elaboration of the problem of national relations under socialism. Many works, often on a high level, have been written about the flowering of the individual union republics, nations and nationalities; this is, of course, important and necessary. But at the same time scientific works do not sufficiently elucidate the problems of the drawing together of nations, and the formation of a new, historically constituted community of people—the Soviet people, including all the nationalities of the USSR.
>
> Well-reasoned works on the subject, based on the generalization of extensive factual material, would facilitate further intensification of the ideological work of party organizations and the internationalist upbringing of the working people, and would be a sharp weapon in the struggle with our adversaries.

Referring to the 50th anniversary of the victory of Soviet power in Azerbaidzhan, celebrated last year, Aliyev declared:

> Five decades is only a short period in the centuries-old history of the Azer-

baidzhanian people. But in the half century a real miracle has occurred in our land. Only yesterday, historically speaking, Azerbaidzhan was a backward outlying district of Tsarist Russia, but today it is a highly developed industrial-agrarian republic. In the recent past, the rich national culture of our people was fettered by the exploiter classes. Today this culture, filled with socialist content but national in form, has burst into luxurious bloom, sparkling with the many facets of its achievements.

Fikryat Tabeyev, First Secretary of the Tatar Region CPSU Committee, described the great headway made by the Tatar Autonomous Republic, a major oil extracting and processing area, an important industrial center which also has a well-developed agriculture. At the same time, he said:

> Critically assessing our work in local areas, it must be noted that not all possibilities have been used, that there were shortcomings in making full use of our reserves. There are still many unsolved problems in the life of our republic. We need more houses, schools and cultural and service establishments in the oilfields as well as in Kazan, capital of the republic.

Anton Kochinyan, First Secretary of the Communist Party of Armenia, said that the Armenian people, too, had something to report to the Congress:

> In the past five years the average annual increase in industrial output in our Republic was roughly 12 per cent. In the last year of the 8th five-year plan period our collective and state farms obtained record yields of grapes, fruit, potatoes and other crops. In five years approximately one family in three received a new apartment or better housing. The scale of construction of schools, kindergartens, hospitals, health resorts, workers' overnight sanatoria, cultural, service and other establishments is growing.

Among the Women Delegates

Klavdia Smirnova, milkmaid at the "Dawn of Peace" Collective Farm, Deputy to the Oryel Regional Soviet, expressed her gratitude to the comrades who had elected her a Congress delegate and to the Communist Party for its concern for agriculture and for the well-being of collective farmers. She told the story of her own farm, one of the first small and weak *kolkhozi* formed at the beginning of the collectivization period:

> No sooner had we grown strong enough to begin to enjoy the advantages of this new way of life, than the war came and churned up our fields, in 1941. Our native land did not need that kind of plowing.
> All our men and many women left for the front. I too fought against the fascist invaders. I was a machine gunner. When I came home I didn't recognize our green and flowering village of Urynok. Three times it had changed hands in fierce battles that left nothing but ashes and ruins.
> We former front liners could not rest after the war. We went into battle

again, this time against the ruins, and we rebuilt everything from scratch.

She described the new construction rising everywhere in Urynok:

In the past five years we have built nine sheds for cattle, four modern pig-barns—we can no longer call them sties—a repair shop, a storehouse for mineral fertilizers, eight granaries, a Palace of Culture, three brigade clubs, a public steam bath, a canteen and a bakery. This year we expect to complete construction of a secondary school. In this period our farmers and specialists have built 690 new homes! Now we have everything. Comfort and happiness in our homes, machines in the fields and in the livestock breeding stations. Our work has become much easier.

She reported that their collective farm board and Party organization—over 100 Communists and over 100 Communist Youth—were doing a lot for young people, who nowadays were not leaving the village as they used to. But things didn't always go smoothly:

Sometimes we have difficulties and misunderstandings. We are largely to blame ourselves. We don't always organize the work of our people the way we should, not all of us have the right attitude to our work, some are careless about collective farm property.

While Klavdia herself had gotten 4,500 kilograms of milk from each of her cows last year and pledged to raise this by another 500 in 1971, the work was not yet fully mechanized and there were too many breakdowns. She called upon the scientists, designers and agricultural executives to speed up provision of still better machinery. The question of combined fodder was not yet solved. While collective farmers were receiving better pay, there were not yet enough goods and social services available in the countryside. On the question of foreign policy, Smirnova said:

Comrades, our Party shows concern not only for human needs and living conditions. It also tries to provide us with peaceful conditions for life and work. Our collective farm is called the Dawn of Peace. That is a good name. It makes us think always of the sun rising with the dawn and bringing mankind warmth, light and life.

One feels bitter indeed thinking of the blood of innocent children, women, and old folk being shed every day. That is what US imperialism is doing in its dirty war in Vietnam and Laos, blatantly interfering in the affairs of other nations, threatening a world atomic war.

We completely support the foreign policies of the Party and the Soviet Government spearheaded against the evil designs of the world's reactionaries, and we will spare no effort to strengthen our country's power!

Yekaterina Garbuzova for many years has headed the Russian language chair of the Pedagogical Institute in Novozybkov, Bryansk Region. Recalling her childhood in the tiny village of Rudnya on the border of Russia and Byelorussia, a "world of sweet sounds and colors" that is difficult to find on any map, she continued nostalgically:

Everybody, I know, has some place especially close to his heart, a place where he belongs. For me this is the Bryansk area, one of great beauty which inspired Tyutchev, Tolstoy and Paustovsky. . . . I remember the prediction made just before the Revolution by Maximovsky, a member of the Bryansk Regional Council: "Schooling in the region presents a sorry picture. With the percentage of education carried out up to now, tens of thousands of years will pass and the people will still be as ignorant and illiterate as they are today."

Now the Bryansk Region has 1,650 general schools and 123 evening schools for working and village youth. Every third person in the region is studying or training.

Professor Garbuzova reported that the number of students at her institute has increased year by year. In 1966 they numbered 1,439. This year, including correspondence students, the number is 3,852, most of them girls. She concluded her speech:

Now our gardens are in full bloom. Soon will come this year's graduation. In this first year of the new five-year plan we are giving the country over 600 teachers. In this age of scientific and technical revolution the role of secondary and higher training cannot be overestimated. The inspiring aims presented by the Party give rise to a new flood of creative powers!

Nina Grachikova, sewing machine operator of the Oka shoe firm in Moscow, spoke of her pride as a worker in having a share of designing shoes as well as in making them quickly and well. This year 101 of their designs passed the test of the artistic council of the Light Industry Assortment Institute and 59 models were marked "excellent." Her factory produced 330,000 pairs above the plan, with 83.2 per cent of the production accepted as "first quality." She continued:

The workers of our factory are fully behind the plans of our Party for the coming five years, because they have but one aim—improving our living conditions. But we are well aware that there is only one way of achieving this and that is through increased productivity on the part of everyone of us. . . . In the third and fourth quarters of last year our firm took second place among the workers of the Russian Federation. We made an extra profit of 10,500 rubles, which was used for bonuses for the workers and in part for the construction of a Young Pioneer Camp.

Quoting further figures about their production, Grachikova added:

You needn't be surprised at my quoting figures. When you've been working in a factory for nearly fourteen years, have been elected to the shop trade union committee and are a member of the shop Party Committee, then you naturally learn to see a little farther than just your work place.

Natalia Shuropova, team agronomist at the Krasnoye Znamya Collective Farm, in the northernmost corner of the Rostov Region, described the 14,000 hectares (1 hectare=2.47 acres) of their *kolkhoz,* sown to wheat, rye, barley, sunflowers and corn, the increasing variety of farm machinery acquired each year and the high level of education being acquired by the farm workers. Many of them are given important technical jobs on the farm after finishing education by correspondence in agricultural schools and institutes. Shuropova reported that the farm girls as well as boys were satisfied with their work:

Many have become milkmaids, planners and economists. I, as a person closely tied to the soil since childhood, am very pleased that the young people choose to live and work on the collective farm. But then, why should they leave? Collective farm settlements are getting better with every year. Many families have acquired new houses—large well-built and beautiful homes. Practically every family has a motorcycle, some have cars. At the central settlement, Shumilinskaya, we have all the community services, a shop selling every imaginable kind of goods, a hospital and maternity home, an infirmary, a kindergarten, a boarding school and a canteen. And now we're building a new club. At our hamlet in Chetvertinsky we also built a club recently, where we have dances, movies and plays, and many amateur groups which give performances.

Amelia Gorskaya, a teacher from Syktyvkar, in the Komi Autonomous Socialist Soviet Republic (in the northern section of the RSFSR, reaching into the Arctic) spoke of her republic as an example of the triumph of the Leninist policy of equality and friendship of peoples. Soon to celebrate its 50th anniversary as an Autonomous Republic, the area had been transformed "from a downtrodden and backward outlying territory of Tsarist Russia into an industrially developed Soviet Autonomous Republic." Formerly without even a written language, the territory was now 100 per cent literate, with an extensive network of research institutions, its own higher educational establishments, a local branch of the USSR Academy of Sciences, and a national literature. She declared:

I am proud to be a teacher because teachers have a great role in the life of our country. The teacher has a hand in shaping the destiny of everyone growing up under socialism. I am especially happy that the work of the teacher is so highly valued by my Party and my people. . . . The new manifestations of attention of the Party and the government for the teachers and the school are a source of creative inspiration for us.

The Komi Republic needs still more schools, said Gorskaya, especially in the countryside. She said the fine government decision that schools and preschool institutions should be built simultaneously with each new enterprise must be carried out better in the future than in the past. She declared:

The plans outlined in the CPSU Central Committee's report are so realistic that now we can boldly dream about new schools with all the required specialized study rooms, light and spacious conference halls, cozy dining rooms, premises for after-school groups, for extra-curricular activities.

Our country has within it still another land—the land of childhood. And we who have grown up in the years of building socialism know how well the children of homeland are living. Everything that is being built by us, everything our people and our Party are thinking about is meant for children. Concern about children means concern about the tomorrow of our society. That is why the Party and the government view the cause of bringing up and educating children as a sacred cause for the entire nation.

Delegate Gorskaya spoke approvingly of the plans for improved teacher training in the draft Directives. She said that there was some fine scientific-pedagogical and methodological literature, but it was to be seen mainly at exhibitions and there was need for its wide distribution. She advocated both refresher courses and institutes for the advanced training of teachers to insure their living up to their high calling and responsibility for the future.

Another teacher who spoke dwelt on the need for greater understanding by men of the position of women in Soviet society. She was highly critical of the fact that men seldom taught at the grammar and high school levels, apparently feeling that such teaching was "women's work."

Alexandra Monakhova, woman director of a state pedigree farm in the Moscow region, told of the wonderful changes she had seen in her 30 years as a farm worker. She spoke expertly of the economic achievements on her farm, with special emphasis on the role played by the Party's political and organizational work with people. Dealing particularly with the work of women, she reported:

Our Party organization and the management have no fear of entrusting responsible key posts to women. We have women working as section heads and specialists and team leaders. Our women are highly skilled and efficient and enjoy great authority. Women make up more than 40 per cent of our party organization of 226 people and many of them are deputies to the Soviets.

Monakhova dwelt especially on the importance of warm human relations as one of the most important factors in making an organization run smoothly and achieving good production results. Their experience had convinced them of the value of "a kind word, greater confidence" in stimulating the best work. On the improvement of living conditions, she said:

During the past five years housing facilities at our farm have increased by 50 per cent. We have built a public dining room, a combined crèche and nursery, and a shopping center, a Palace of Culture and a Young Pioneer Camp are under construction. Now almost every family on our farm has TV and radio sets and a private library and subscribes to at least two newspapers. Our farm is a good example of how the gap between city and countryside is being eliminated.

Delegates from the Baltic States

A. J. *Snieckus, Lithuanian Communist Party First Secretary,* said that last year's celebration of Lithuania's 30th year as a Soviet Republic had provided the opportunity to review what the socialist order had given the Lithuanian people:

> When the bourgeoisie were in power, Lithuania was economically backward, with no serious prospect of development. Industry and agriculture were stagnant. Unemployment was rampant. Tens of thousands of workers were forced to emigrate across the sea in search of a piece of bread. But no golden mountains awaited them there, only the same exploitation, the same capitalist yoke.
>
> Now all that has irrevocably passed into history. Present-day Lithuania is a flourishing Soviet Socialist Republic, an equal among equals in the great family of peoples of the USSR. The most complex social problems have been solved —industrialization, the reconstruction of agriculture on a socialist foundation, the cultural revolution. All this has created a solid foundation for the tempestuous growth of our national economy and the transformation of the spiritual life of the people.

Turning to the question of ideological work [especially important in the Baltic states, which have been among the main targets of anti-Soviet propaganda, with Washington still recognizing and coddling representatives of the old bourgeois regimes], Snieckus said:

> In the Western world they talk a lot about the rights of man, cavalierly brushing aside any concern for his needs. But show me any capitalist country which would have such a clear and realistic program for raising the living standards of the working people. And the main thing is that this program is being unswervingly carried out. . . .
>
> The Party teaches us as the inviolable principle of organization and ideological work Lenin's behest—never to lose contact with the masses, to be a part of the life of the workers, to know the needs of the people, to win confidence by a comradely attitude to people and concern for their interests. Accountability of the leadership to the collective, through reporting and taking counsel with them regularly, is the most important element in socialist democracy.

Snieckus called for constant vigilance in the light of the diverse arsenal of weapons being used against the Soviet Union by bourgeois propagandists, "all kinds of revisionist and super-leftist elements, émigré nationalist and Zionist groups." He charged them with employing "the open services of criminals, sometimes acclaiming them as national heroes," as was done recently by "a reactionary nationalistic segment of the Lithuanian émigré community." He went on:

138

The principal content of hostile propaganda at present is an attempt to discredit the Soviet system and its ideological and political foundations, and to preach an abstract humanism, a so-called "pure" democracy and universal morality. Efforts are being made to spread the poison of bourgeois nationalism, to deaden people's class consciousness, and violent attacks are being made on our Party's nationalities policy, based on the friendship of peoples.

The Leninist national policy of the CPSU has always supported the development of the material and spiritual forces of all the Soviet nations, their flourishing and drawing together, their international unity. The Party demands that its members fight against any manifestation of nationalism and chauvinism, for the strengthening of the friendship of the peoples of the Soviet Union and their fraternal ties with the peoples of the socialist countries and the workers of the whole world.

A. E. Voss, First Secretary of the Latvian Communist Party, expressed special gratitude for the fact that the people of Latvia and the whole Soviet Union had been able to live and work in conditions of peace for the more than quarter century period since World War II, due to the wise foreign policy of the Soviet Government, guided by the Central Committee of the CPSU. This sentiment was voiced by all the delegates.

I. G. Kabin, First Secretary of the Estonian Communist Party, stressed that in the period since the 23rd Congress party leadership at all levels had made extraordinary efforts to adhere to the Leninist style of work. This meant that the main content of its activities has been work with people. He said:

> The policy of the Party can only be carried out through the people. This Leninist principle has profound meaning for our days, embodying the very essence of socialist democracy. . . .
>
> In the period under review, the CPSU Central Committee has persistently pursued a line aimed at overcoming the method of administrative fiat and of usurping the activity of the Soviet government and economic agencies, a method incompatible with party leadership. It has done everything possible to develop the initiative of Communists.

Kabin reported that Lenin's principle of the correct combination of old and young cadres was being implemented in the Estonian Party, where over half the personnel in the party apparatus are under 40, and special concern is given to the promotion of women. In working with people, he said, one of the primary tasks was not only to explain the policies of the Party and state but to "provide information on all the most important questions of international and domestic policy." With the many means of information at its disposal, he felt that the Party needed to make still greater efforts to render its agitation and propaganda work more intelligible.

The Estonian Party had introduced the regular practice of reports by party, Soviet and economic executives to the working people, with full opportunity for discussions, which often turned out to be quite lively. Delegate Kabin stressed the need to encourage suggestions by the workers followed by efforts to carry them out, to react swiftly to criticism and eliminate mistakes and shortcomings. It is necessary, he said, to listen to the people's opinions, to know what they are thinking, their needs and their problems.

From All Areas of the Country and of Soviet Life

V. I. Dolgikh, First Secretary of the Krasnoyarsk Territory Party Committee, dwelt on the special conditions of Siberia. The immense scale and forbidding quality of nature, with its mighty rivers and forests to be tamed and hewn for the service of man, the permafrost zones to be made livable—all this presents thrilling challenges to man's strength and ingenuity and arouses tremendous pioneering labor enthusiasm. At the same time, the harshness of the conditions make living difficult.

Krasnoyarsk, reported Dolgikh, is one huge construction site. While rates of industrial growth are higher than in some other areas, there has been a lag in agriculture. Higher wages must be paid to attract people to the North, and concessions on paid travel, vacations, and so on. Dolgikh suggested that there also be a pay increment for length of service in order to retain cadres. Speaking of the great need for more labor in Siberia, he said:

> Our tremendous construction growth means tremendous housing too, but we don't always keep up with the needs. We can retain workers from other parts of the country better if we have more facilities for them. And we don't yet make enough use of our women. We could have many more women workers by expanding the construction of kindergartens, nurseries and everyday service institutions.
>
> Our territory is a land of young people. Our Komsomol detachment numbers over 300,000. We must create better conditions for young people's study, education and sports activity to reduce labor turnover among our youth and create better conditions for their upbringing.

The immense amount of lumbering in this part of Siberia meant an increasing number of small settlements remote from the main cutting sites where it is impossible to create the necessary conditions for recreation and leisure time and education for the children. Lumber workers sometimes have to travel almost 100 miles a day over primitive roads to get to work. To correct this, Dolgikh proposed:

> We should establish base towns with all amenities for employees of lumber camps. It is possible to arrange lumbering according to a special schedule and still maintain the total number of hours per week. This would make possible

140

not only better living conditions but also improved labor productivity for lumber workers.

Gavril Chiriayev, First Secretary of the Yakut Regional Committee of the Party (Northern Siberia), welcomed the Central Committee's policy towards accelerated development of Siberia and the Far East. He declared that in Yakutia, with its fabulous natural resources, a large-scale mining industry has been developed. In the eighth five-year period fixed production assets grew by 170 per cent. However:

We still have big untapped reserves and unsolved problems. Industry has made its way far in the North. Now, a new, qualitatively higher stage in the development of the North begins. Key problems include the immediate and extensive equipment of enterprises with the latest and most highly efficient machinery, adapted for use in the North. This would make it possible to manage with a minimum labor force, the maintenance of which costs more in the North than in the temperate zone. Secondly, it is necessary to develop all types of transport and extend our aviation network. Finally, there is the problem of manpower, one of improving the housing and everyday conditions of life of the people working in the North.

Nikolay Baibakov, Deputy Chairman of of the USSR Council of Ministers and Chairman of the USSR Planning Committee (Gosplan), stressed the tremendous creative and collective work of the CPSU Central Committee which had made possible the draft Directives. He said over two years had been spent in the draft's preparation, in which all important central and local government organizations, enterprises and masses of the people had participated. Speaking of the importance of long-range planning, he said:

The lack of long-term plan projections not infrequently hinders the adoption of adequately grounded decisions as regards distribution of investments, deployment of big new enterprises, arrangements for geological prospecting, development of mineral deposits and scientific research and design work. That is why a long-term Soviet economic development plan, for a period of ten to fifteen years, is a significant precondition for the five-year plans, and an important factor for raising the standard of economic planning in general.

Yegor Proskurin, steelworker from Zaporozhye in the Ukraine, expressed gratitude for the confidence in the working class displayed in the report of the Central Committee. He said:

Comrades! I am 32 years old, and for eleven of those years I have worked at our factory. It was there I found my calling, my aim in life. I went through the school of the Komsomol, and was accepted into the Party, and elected shift chairman.

When I went to work I had only six years of schooling. But the advice and friendly support of my comrades enabled me to finish secondary school while on the job, and in 1968 I received my diploma as a metallurgical technician.

He spoke also of the wide and varied interests of Soviet workers:

> There is not a single important question in our internal or international life
> which has not been hotly discussed in our collective. The growing feeling of
> being master of your own enterprise, of your country, the good morale of the
> workers, the direct part we play in working out and putting into effect the
> policies of the Party and the government—these are the real facts of our
> daily life.

On the critical side, he said that their work in the past had sometimes been hampered by lack of long-range plans, and he welcomed
the decision to enter upon them for the future. His sharpest words
were for those workers who lacked discipline, changed jobs frequently
and did not have a responsible attitude toward their work. The steelworker urged greater strictness in this respect.

E. I. Lebedev, a grinder from the Kirov works (formerly Putilov)
in Leningrad, also expressed gratitude for the high evaluation of the
role of the workers in Brezhnev's report. He spoke of the tremendous
reconstruction and expansion of the Kirov works in the past five years,
the new shops with their modern equipment "where you go to work
as if you are going on a holiday." Kirov workers, he said, took great
pride in the machinery they were turning out and considered it a
major task to provide proper equipment for agriculture. He spoke of
the tremendous boost the economic reform had given to technical
progress, and to increasing participation of workers in the planning
process. The economies effected at the Kirov Works had provided
greater funds for social-cultural undertakings and housing construction:

> Suffice it to say, for example, that our plant, using a part of these funds, is
> now restoring a former grand duke's palace in a Leningrad suburb, which will
> become a workers' Palace of Recreation. We've gone down to Sochi, too, and
> are building a health resort there with our own funds.

Lebedev urged replacing obsolete machinery with new everywhere
possible, and stressed the need for better training for the younger
generation. He said sometimes there was too great a turnover of young
workers who didn't like their jobs because they were not well enough
trained to do them properly. He welcomed the provision in the Brezhnev and Kosygin reports for better technological training.

He spoke of the increasing participation of workers in political and
public life:

> Thousands of Leningrad workers today give talks on current events and
> politics. Workers make up 50 per cent of the deputies to our local Soviets.
> They also have a creative influence in production matters. Veteran workers
> take patronage over the young and are responsible to the collective for the

education and the training of our labor replacement. This is a good system.

Speaking of honorary titles for workers in science, culture and the professions, Lebedev asked if the time had come to establish such titles for workers too: " 'Honored Worker of the Republic.' How good that would sound!"

Vladimir Shcherbitsky, Chairman of the Council of Ministers of the Ukraine, spoke of the broad perspectives the new plan opens up for the Ukrainian SSR, and stressed the need for conservation measures:

> Our Republic will continue to develop as a major fuel-and-power, metal, chemical and engineering center of the Soviet Union. The light, food and local industries will be developed considerably, and this will make possible notable increases in the output and quality of consumer products. Gross farm output is planned to increase by 20 per cent. . . .
>
> Our Republic, as the rest of the country, will conduct large-scale housing, cultural and municipal construction. Important measures have been mapped out for the further development of health service, education, public service establishments and the municipal economy. Considerable efforts will be exerted to prevent water and air pollution and ensure the more rational use of water resources.

Mikhail Prokofiev, USSR Minister of Education, spoke of the importance of completing the transition to universal secondary education in the next five years. He reported:

> During the eighth five-year period over 16 million young people received complete secondary education. . . . The implementation of the Party's task as regards completing the introduction of universal secondary education will require great efforts. The number of the graduates of secondary educational establishments must grow from 3.2 million in 1970 to 4.5-4.7 million in 1975. Special attention must be paid to the further improvement of work of village schools.

Konstantin Gerasimov, Deputy Chairman of the Council of Ministers of the Russian Federation, Chairman of the Russian Federation's State Planning Committee, declared that the Soviet economy has now achieved a stage when it is fully possible to accept as one main task the fuller satisfaction of the material and cultural requirements of the Soviet people. On the question of conservation, he said:

> In our opinion, the time has come for our economic plans to include, beginning with the current five-year period, a special section on nature conservation. This section should cover complexes of measures setting time limits for taking action to improve land use radically and to improve the state of water resources and the surrounding atmosphere with the aim of raising the efficiency of their utilization and, what is most important, promoting the protection of the people's health.

Guests from Abroad
Greet the Congress

The speeches and greetings by the heads of the more than 100 delegations from Communist and Workers' Parties attending the Congress would make up a book by themselves. Taken all together they give a graphic panorama of the revolutionary movement in its many stages of development in the world today. Space limitations permit only a sampling. We have omitted the formal greetings and the words of appreciation unanimously expressed for the internal achievements of the Soviet Union, common to all the speeches. There was unanimous approval of the Soviet peace program and warm appreciation for its aid to national liberation movements and to newly independent countries, with special emphasis on Soviet aid to the peoples of Indochina and the Soviet role in seeking a peaceful solution in the Middle East. There was complete support for Soviet efforts to stabilize the situation in Central Europe and bring about a European Security Conference. A majority of the guests spoke harshly of China's splitting policy, expressed in new political attacks on the USSR on the eve of the Congress. All the delegates without exception condemned the aggressive policies of US imperialism in Indochina and elsewhere.

While reflecting their own special needs and problems, there was remarkable unanimity among both Communist and non-Communist parties in support of Soviet policies. A minority of the delegates made references to differences with the CPSU and the Soviet Government on specific issues. But each of these made a point of stressing that no differences could mar their basic friendship with the USSR nor the all-surpassing need of unity in the common struggle against imperialism.

We begin this section with the full text of the address by Gus Hall, head of the US delegation, which included Henry Winston, James Jackson and Matthew Hallinan. Excerpts from speeches of other guests from abroad follow.

GUS HALL

General Secretary, CPUSA

IN KEEPING with the teachings of Lenin, the Soviet Union continues to be the most consistent and stable working-class base of power in the world arena of the class struggle, and the struggle against imperialism.

In keeping with the teachings of Lenin, the Communist Party of

144

the Soviet Union continues to be the most consistent force for proletarian internationalism—for unity in the world communist movement, for unity of the anti-imperialist forces.

You are consistent because your ideological, political and theoretical moorings are firmly and unwaveringly secured on the working-class side of the class struggle—guided by the revolutionary science of Marxism-Leninism.

In the minds of millions in the capitalist world, there is growing a new criterion by which they measure and compare the two world systems.

The comparisons are not now limited to industrial charts or prices of goods. What is placed on the scales now is the overall quality of life. Standards of physical comfort remain very important in determining the quality of life, but the yardstick is much broader now. It includes the total spectrum of human values, the order of priorities dictated by the inherent laws of each system. It includes the moral, cultural and philosophical concepts nurtured by each system. Many of the new components that add up to a quality of life cannot be measured by charts.

How can you weigh the growing sense of insecurity, alienation and frustration, of not being involved, not being a factor, under capitalism, with that of being totally involved and relevant, of being able to determine the course of life, that flows from the inner nature of socialism?

How can one compare by charts the quality of life, of distortions, humiliations, the brutal suffering and pain that is the product of racism, fostered by capitalism, with the flowering of the quality of life under socialism, a life without racism, based on equality and dignity of each individual?

How can one weigh the racism that results in the attempt to frame up, and send to the gas chamber, a brave, young black woman Communist, Angela Davis?

There is no way of measuring the mental anguish resulting from mass addiction to drugs, or the corruption that permeates all phases of life, from top to bottom. The quality of life under capitalism is also measured by 800 murders a year in a city of one and a half million people.

The brutalization, the cold-blooded murder of women and children in the Mylais of Vietnam, Laos and Cambodia is a measure of the quality of life produced by capitalism. What is the quality of life in a system that issues orders—"kill everything that moves, burn everything that grows"? As capitalism decays and is less and less able and willing to respond to human needs, the quality of life disintegrates, and as

145

socialism increases its ability to respond to these needs, the quality of life unfolds into full bloom. The inability of the masses to find basic solutions under capitalism to the recurring economic crisis and recession, to the inherent drive towards fascism and repression, to the new problems of environmental contamination, to the growth of slum housing, to economic insecurity resulting from automation, to corruption—each contributes to the serious deterioration in the quality of life.

What vivid comparisons—in the United States an acute crisis of education, in the Soviet Union its continuous rise; in the United States and Great Britain anti-labor laws, and in the Soviet Union new laws of protection for labor.

This 24th Congress, Comrade Brezhnev's report, the new five-year plan, in sharp contrast, stand as a beacon light on the pathway to an ever-rising quality of life under socialism.

In the United States the declining quality of life is closely related to the aggressive war policies of US imperialism. It is related to the crisis of that policy. The ignominious defeat for the forces of US imperialism in Laos adds an important spike in US imperialism's coffin.

It is a victory history will record along with Stalingrad and Dienbienphu. There is maneuvering but there is no change in US world policy, and there is no basic change in its policy of aggression in Indochina. While Nixon tries to coo like a Quaker peace dove, he also announces a policy of unlimited adventuristic bombings. While Nixon talks about this being the "last war," his spokesmen are refusing any meaningful negotiations in Paris to end the war. It is the basic policy of the Nixon Administration to have no meaningful negotiations anywhere. A policy of aggression and a policy of negotiations are self-contradictory. For political reasons, Nixon wants to create the image of being reasonable and willing to negotiate. But the policy is not to settle any serious problems by negotiation.

The Nixon doctrine is a doctrine of aggression through indiscriminate, brutal and adventuristic use of air power.

But in spite of the demagogy, the Nixon plan is being exposed. That is the significance of the latest public opinion poll in which 73 per cent of the people of the United States are for withdrawal of US forces from Indochina by the end of the year.

What is new in this sentiment is that this overwhelming majority of our people are for withdrawal this year under all conditions.

What is becoming clear to ever greater numbers of Americans is that a politically-negotiated settlement at Paris is not in the plans of US imperialism. What is being exposed is that US imperialism has never accepted the concept of an independent neutral South

146

Vietnam, Laos or Cambodia! What is being exposed is that the withdrawal of all US armed forces from Southeast Asia has never been, and is not now, a part of US imperialism's plans! What is being exposed is that the basic aim of the Nixon plan of "Vietnamization" is for US political, economic and military domination in Southeast Asia.

The policy is headed for a new crisis. On the one hand, US imperialism cannot continue the withdrawal of troops much longer and also continue the policy of aggression. At home Nixon cannot stop the troop withdrawals and expect to be re-elected.

The essence of the Nixon plan is to attempt to ride out this dilemma. The plan is to continue the aggression in Southeast Asia and also to win his re-election. He is going to try to pull off this fraud by continuing troop withdrawals to satisfy enough of the electorate at home. On the other hand, he wants to withdraw only to the point where it will not endanger the aggression—where it will not endanger the puppet governments. But these are plans that do not take into account the reality either in Southeast Asia or in the United States.

Nixon's plans will be smashed by the heroic armed people of Vietnam, Laos and Cambodia. They will be smashed by the *new* wave of mass struggles now under way in the United States.

The Mideast crisis is also at a critical turning point. It is a crisis of US Mideast policy, but in a special sense it is Israel's crisis. Even the Zionist-CIA-created hysteria and provocations in the United States about "Soviet Jews" are not going to save Israel from this dilemma.

What is becoming clear to new millions is that the fundamental policy of Israel and the United States has been and is imperialist aggression. There is demagogy, there is maneuvering, US spokesmen talk from both sides of their mouths, but so far there is no change in policy.

The US dilemma is that US imperialist oil interests in the Mideast are in contradiction with Nixon's political interests in the coming elections. And some of the oil interests are beginning to hedge on their bets on Israel. And in a sense Israel is at the mercy of this contradiction.

The Communists of the United States, in the name of the progressive working people of our country especially, hail all the revolutionary advances of the national liberation movements in those lands under the yoke of US imperialism and their minions. We glory in socialist Cuba's every advance and are inspired and strengthened in our struggle by the great anti-imperialist victory of the Commu-

147

nists, the Socialists, the working people of Chile, who have brought to power a government of Popular Unity. We greet the social advances of the people of Peru and Bolivia as a blow against the common enemies of our peoples, the monopolists and Pentagon imperialists.

We express our wholehearted solidarity with the struggles of the African peoples to liberate the last of their peoples from imperialist domination!

Each advance made by the Soviet Union has a direct revolutionizing effect on the world revolutionary process. The effect is progressively greater because each advance corresponds to a deepening of the crisis of capitalism. Therefore, it should surprise no one that each advance brings forth a more shrill cry of vituperation from the center of world imperialism.

What continues to be a source of amazement to us is the left echo that accompanies and competes with the propaganda barrages of imperialism.

And whether the left echo is the open vilification and abuse from Peking, rivaling the anti-Soviet slander of the most fascist sectors of imperialism, such as we hear daily from the Pentagon-CIA and the most reactionary of the capitalist papers, or whether it is the left echo coming through the back door, speaking in general classless terms about the "domination of the big powers," or "of military blocs," or in classless terms about "superpowers," no matter what name you call it, it is still a form of begging for crumbs from the table of US imperialism. The left echo is a form of beautifying, of covering up for US imperialism, a form of accommodation, of finding common ground with US imperialism. Anti-Communism, including its anti-Soviet variety, is a major weapon of imperialism. How you react to this weapon in concrete terms is a cardinal class question. The report of Comrade Brezhnev clearly restates the position of the Communist Party of the Soviet Union on these matters.

The values, the order of priorities, the quality of life under socialism is fed and nurtured by the most humane and beautiful of all human concepts. The perspective of "from each according to his ability, to each according to his needs" is the loftiest expression of social consciousness.

The 24th Congress of the Communist Party of the Soviet Union is the highest, the clearest expression, of this concept.

You, Soviet Communists, are the advance guard in giving real life a quality, a beauty that till now appeared only in poetry and song.

Glory to the Revolutionary Party of Lenin!

Glory and all power to the revolutionary working-class movements and peoples of the world!

HENRY WINSTON

National Chairman, Communist Party, U.S.A.

THE 24th Congress of the Communist Party of the Soviet Union is an epoch-making event. The implementation of its decisions will have a profound significance for building the material and technical base of communism, and at the same time, will help to strengthen the socialist nations, the international working-class and communist movement and the movement for national liberation.

The report of L. I. Brezhnev points the way to the peace movement in the world and to the anti-imperialist struggle, which, if followed, can create that powerful force which can defeat all of the machinations of world imperialism in general and US imperialism in particular. US imperialism is the "top dog" in the imperialist world. It is the organizer of the criminal aggression against the people of Vietnam, Cambodia and Laos. It is at the same time the main support of the Israeli aggressors in the Middle East. Its policies are based on racism, anti-communism in general and anti-Sovietism in particular, and threaten humanity with the danger of a new world war.

The Soviet Union is the bastion of peace and its most powerful defender. It represents that force which opposes imperialist aggression everywhere and brings decisive support to all oppressed peoples. The lofty dreams of the peoples are to be found in the peace policies of the Soviet Union. And because of this there is a strengthening of the ties between the Soviet Union and the peace-loving people of the world. The unity of these forces can compel US imperialism to move in the direction of peaceful coexistence, which is the policy for which the Soviet Union fights. It is this united force that will check imperialism, compel it to retreat and ultimately lead to its final defeat.

The main goal of the Communist Party of the United States today begins with the struggle for peace. The most urgent problem is the organization of all peace forces—black, white, yellow, brown and red —for ending the war in Indochina and for the immediate and complete withdrawal of US troops. In the Middle East, its policy is full support for the just struggle of the Arab people and complete ex-

149

posure of policies which support the Israeli aggressors. Our position in this respect is similar to that taken by the 24th Congress of the CPSU. We also struggle to end the embargo on trade with Cuba and oppose any attempt on the part of reaction to invade this Island of Freedom. In the spirit of proletarian internationalism, we fully support the people of Chile in their nationalization program.

The Communist Party of the United States undertakes to expose fully the demagogy of the Nixon Administration and its anti-Soviet policy. Nixon's foreign policy is directly related to his domestic policy. The huge military budget and the billions of dollars used by the CIA are factors which continue to aggravate all the social and economic problems of the people at home. Thus, for example, there are crises on every front. There is a growth in unemployment, which hits the Black workers in the first place. There are increases in monopoly prices for all consumer goods. There is an increase in taxation and in rents. There is a crisis in public education and in the field of public health.

This picture of the social and economic malaise affecting the most powerful capitalist country in the world is in glaring contrast to that in the Soviet Union, a socialist country which has made the satisfaction of the growing material and spiritual needs of its citizens the law of political and economic development.

The US Communists see that the struggle against US imperialism is directly related to the struggle for the economic and social interests of the people of the United States. There is a growing movement in the country which is uniting on the basis of a multi-issue program. The US monopolies make use of their two main weapons—racism and anti-communism—in an effort to discredit the movement of opposition at home. The sharpest attack is directed against the Black liberation movement. The symbol of this racism and anti-Communism is the political frame-up of Angela Davis. This attack is part of a general offensive of pro-fascist reaction which is also directed against other fighters for civil rights and social justice—Ruchell Magee, Bobby Seale and Ericka Huggins, the Soledad brothers, Arnold Johnson and Chicano, Puerto Rican and Indian victims of racism. Angela Davis was framed for her political beliefs, for her active participation in the fight against racism, repression and the US aggressive war in Vietnam. The Communist Party, therefore, relates the struggle for freedom for Angela Davis with the fight for freedom for all political prisoners, against suppression of democratic liberties in America.

The influence of the Communist Party is growing in the United States among workers, black and white. Its press is also growing

150

and there are wider opportunities for struggle. This enables the Communists to give greater help in the building of the movement for peace and democracy and the advocacy of socialism in the country.

ANGELA DAVIS AND THE 24th CONGRESS

HENRY WINSTON reported on his return home that the whole Soviet Union was rooting for the freedom of Angela Davis. It was impossible to keep an Angela Davis button. The US delegation had brought a substantial number with them, but had to send home for thousands more. Soon the buttons appeared all over the Congress floor. The Americans were told they could go into any village, and everyone over five years old would know who Angela Davis was!

Winston said he received many letters and telegrams from people in the Soviet Union, congratulating him on his sixtieth birthday which was celebrated while he was there, and asking him to convey to Angela Davis their concern for her health and their support in the struggle to save her from death in California's gas chamber. Winston continued:

I met Professor S. S. Shauyman and his wife from the Academy of Sciences. His father was one of the 26 Commissars executed by the British in Baku during the armed foreign intervention that followed the Revolution. They told me their 11-year old daughter Katherine and her schoolmates had not only sent letters and telegrams and signed petitions to President Nixon, but they had also started a special project calling on every student to work to get only fives (the highest mark) in honor of Angela Davis.

Asa, a medical worker I was talking with, asked about her prison conditions and when I told him of her solitary confinement without light or air, he took the ring off his finger for me to give her, saying it bore the national seal of Ossetia, where he lived, a small autonomous region in the Georgian Soviet Republic.

Winston said he had known before going to the Soviet Union of the massive fight its people were waging for the freedom of Angela Davis and other victims of imperialist reaction, but he was not prepared for such a staggering campaign as he found. *Pravda*, central organ of the CPSU, with a circulation of 14 million, campaigns editorially for Angela Davis and carries reportage from all over the world about her case. *Izvestia* and *Komsomolskaya Pravda*, also with circulations in the millions, do the same, as do other newspapers and periodicals of all kinds, both central organs and local publications. In addition, Soviet television and radio have Angela Davis programs, connecting her fight for freedom in the United States with that of other victims of imperialist reaction in the dungeons of South Africa, Mozambique, Angola, Guinea-Bissau, Spain, Greece and elsewhere. The US Communist Party Chairman added:

> The 14 million members of the Communist Party of the Soviet Union are actively leading this fight. Joining with them are the Komsomol with its 24 million members and the 93-million member Soviet trade union organizations. It can be said that there is not a single factory in the USSR which is not involved. Every collective and state farm, every Soviet citizen in every walk of life knows the name of Angela Davis and supports the cause of her freedom.

In addition, practically every public organization in the Soviet Union has passed resolutions and taken other actions in support of Angela Davis.

LE DUAN

First Secretary,
Vietnamese Working People's Party (DRV)

THE VIETNAMESE people sincerely desire peace. The United States must end its aggression against Vietnam and other states of Indochina, and immediately, completely and unconditionally withdraw its troops and those of its satellites from South Vietnam and other countries of Indochina so that their peoples may solve their internal problems without foreign interference.

Until the American imperialists abandon their aggressive acts, the Vietnamese people will never give up their determined fight for final victory, for the liberation of the South, the defense of the North and the subsequent peaceful unification of our motherland.

Neither the policy of "Vietnamization" of the war, nor the "Nixon Doctrine," nor any other tricks of the aggressors will save the United States from the complete failure of its designs or bring the people of Vietnam and the fraternal peoples of Laos and Cambodia to their knees.

Our victories in the struggle against the American aggressors and for the salvation of the motherland are inseparably linked with powerful support and tremendous aid from the Soviet Union, China and the other socialist countries, from the international communist and workers' movement, the national liberation movement, and the progressive and peace-loving people of the world, including the American people.

Dear Comrades! Both in the past war of resistance against the French colonialists and in the present struggle against the US aggressors, the Vietnamese people have enjoyed the constant support and enormous and valuable assistance of the CPSU, the Soviet Government and the whole Soviet people. From the very moment the US imperialists unleashed their aggression in South Vietnam and their destructive war against the DRV, the Soviet Union has been firmly on the side of the Vietnamese people. This support is a powerful stimulus that inspires the fighters of our entire country to new and greater victories, and strengthens still more the friendship of the Vietnamese people for the fraternal Soviet people.

LANSANA DIANE

National Political Bureau,
Democratic Party of Guinea, West Africa

IT IS an honor to bring the 24th Congress the friendly and militant greetings of the Democratic Party and the entire Guinean people. We are especially happy to express to Comrade Brezhnev and the CPSU Central Committee feelings of unbreakable friendship on behalf of Comrade Ahmed Sekou Touré, General Secretary of the Democratic Party of Guinea and leader of the Guinean revolution.

Our participation in the work of your Congress is a historical necessity brought about by our common goals and struggles.

The decisions of your Congresses are of the greatest interest to the Guinean people, because the Soviet people are the pioneers of socialist construction and their experience is of great importance to the Democratic Party of Guinea, which wants the people of Guinea to be in the front ranks of builders of socialism in Africa. Together with the CPSU the Democratic Party of Guinea is taking part in the great struggle against imperialism, colonialism, neo-colonialism and all forms of human exploitation in order to establish a new society based on the principles of lasting peace, justice and social progress.

Your struggle is our struggle. Your victories are our victories. Hence your Congress is as much ours as yours.

Your Congress is likewise the Congress of all nations which still live under colonial exploitation and those putting up a grim struggle against the criminal intrigues of imperialism.

We therefore take this opportunity to pay due tribute to the CPSU for its tremendous contribution to the cause of liberation of the oppressed peoples of Africa, Asia and Latin America.

On November 22, 1970, Portuguese imperialism mounted a treacherous attack on the Guinean people with the help of inhuman, outcast mercenaries.

Despite the strength and suddenness of this foul aggression, the Guinean people, inspired and led by the Supreme Commander of the People's Revolutionary Armed Forces, Comrade Touré, were immediately mobilized for a heroic resistance against the hired murderers and won a great victory.

We take this opportunity, before this representative forum of socialist forces, once again to express the sincere gratitude of Guinea to all who helped us in this struggle. We especially appreciate the Soviet Government's effective material and moral assistance. It will help to safeguard our security. Our confidence in the future was especially strengthened by Comrade Brezhnev's far-reaching report with its constructive and dynamic proposals for securing the unity of the socialist camp and establishing world peace.

GUSTAV HUSAK

First Secretary, Communist
Party of Czechoslovakia

UNDER the leadership of their Leninist Party the Soviet people have made a fresh step along their heroic road, overcoming the difficulties in the way. Thanks to their selfless creative work they have achieved outstanding successes in production, science, technology, education, and in raising their living standards and cultural level. As a result the Soviet Union is today the main bulwark of peace and progress all over the world.

All of us realize that your successes have tremendous significance not only for the Soviet Union but also for us, for Czechoslovakia, for the other fraternal socialist countries and for the progressive and peace-loving forces of the whole world.

We shall this year observe the 50th Anniversary of the founding of the Communist Party of Czechsolovakia. And once again we realize what the glorious Party of Lenin meant for the Communist Party of Czechoslovakia, what it has done for our Party from the moment it appeared and how deep are the roots of the friendly relations between our peoples.

The Communist Party of Czechoslovakia was formed and shaped during its first years with the direct assistance of Vladimir Ilyich

Lenin. And later as well the Communist Party of the Soviet Union helped our Party mold itself into a force that was able to lead our people to victory over the bourgeoisie.

The Soviet Union and its Party became the strong support and hope of the Czechoslovak people in the period of the Munich deal and in the period of the enslavement of our country by Hitler fascism. Our people will never forget that it was the heroic Soviet army that liberated Czechoslovakia and thus saved our peoples from extermination by the fascists.

In the struggle for our freedom, Czechoslovakia army units commanded by Army General Ludvik Svoboda, now President of the Czechoslovak Socialist Republic and member of our delegation, fought shoulder to shoulder with the Soviet army. Our strong friendship, cemented with the blood we shed together, was forged in this struggle.

The entire course of history convinces us that close and comradely relations with the Soviet Communists were always a prerequisite for success in the struggle of the Czechoslovak Communists against capitalism, in building socialism. Any weakening of these relations brought harm to our Party and our peoples. We again convinced ourselves of the immutability of this truth in the crisis of 1968-1969 when the anti-socialist forces in our society, together with the right-wing opportunist and revisionist forces in the Communist Party of Czechoslovakia, and with the all-round support of international reaction, tried to overthrow the socialist system in Czechoslovakia. The logical consequences, had that attempt succeeded, would have been to endanger the position of socialism in Europe and to open the possibility of a revision of the results of the Second World War. These intentions were frustrated only thanks to the timely internationalist assistance of the Soviet Union and other socialist countries.

From the tribune of this congress we want to express our sincere gratitude to the Communist Party of the Soviet Union, the Soviet Government and the Soviet people for treating with understanding the anxiety of the Czechoslovak Communists for the cause of socialism and responding to their appeal for assistance. This internationalist assistance saved our country from civil war and counterrevolution, and helped to defend the gains of socialism.

We Czechoslovak Communists can confirm from our own example the truth and wisdom of Lenin's ideas about the role and responsibility of the Communist Party in building a new socialist society. Our experience shows how great the danger to socialism is when, under slogans of so-called "improvement" and "reformation" of socialism, the party leadership loses unity and the ability to act, when socialism loses its revolutionary content, when the Party renounces its leading role, when under the influence of petty-bourgeois opportunism the Party is in a state of ideological ferment, is weakened organizationally and is incapable of taking united action, when principles of democratic centralism are rejected, when class principles of the socialist state are buried in oblivion and proletarian internationalism is replaced by nationalist and chauvinist hysteria.

Such deviation from the basic Leninist principles, from the general natural laws of building socialism, was the chief cause for the development of the crisis and the gradually increasing offensive of the counterrevolutionary forces in Czechoslovakia in 1968. In scale and depth this was an offensive which endangered not only the revolutionary gains of the working class but the very existence of the socialist system.

The history of the revolutionary movement and the past period in the history of our Party have also convinced us that the Communist vanguard of the working class must never lose sight of the fact that, after the Communists take power into their hands, the defeated forces hostile to socialism do not cease their activities. In order to carry out their plans these forces seek allies, they support the subversive activities of imperialism which is ready, when socialism has been weakened from within, to take any risk and embark on any venture.

The forces of reaction and imperialism have learned by our example, the example of Czechoslovakia, that the well-known Bratislava (1968) statement of six fraternal parties on the need for the international defense of the socialist gains was more than just a declaration. They learned that any attempt at counterrevolutionary penetration of the socialist system inevitably meets with a vigorous rebuff from the united internationalist forces.

The plans of imperialism and reaction in Czechoslovakia in 1968-1969 failed utterly. There can be no doubt that the breaking away of Czechoslovakia from the alliance of socialist states which these forces were working for would have been a victory for imperialism and a loss and defeat for the forces of the world revolutionary and anti-imperialist movement. But to the contrary, the saving and consolidation of socialism in Czechoslovakia has strengthened the position and the confidence of the revolutionary and anti-imperialist forces in their struggle against imperialism.

Our experience irrefutably shows that a socialist state preserves its sovereignty only when the power of the working class led by the Communist Party is stable, strong and invincible. And if as a result

156

of the offensive by counterrevolution that power is seriously endangered, this creates a threat also for the very sovereignty of the socialist state, which can find itself dependent on imperialism. An abstract notion of sovereignty of a socialist state does not exist. The real expression of this sovereignty is the power of the working class, the realization of the leading role of the Communist Party. As the result of the victory won in this struggle by the healthy forces of our Party and society, with the fraternal support of our socialist friends, our socialist republic's sovereignty was strengthened and consolidated.

We want to assure you, dear comrades, that we have learned a clear lesson from this experience: we shall never again allow anyone to weaken and demoralize the Communist Party of Czechoslovakia, to drive a wedge between our Parties and thus to undermine friendship between our peoples. We shall forever be faithful to Klement Gottwald's slogan: "With the Soviet Union forever!"

Dear comrades, our entire Party is now actively preparing for its 14th Congress, which will end a hard but also instructive period in the life of our Party and our entire society. We have to recover from the tremendous damage inflicted by counterrevolution on the Party and the socialist state in every sphere of activity.

Only two years ago we were having serious economic difficulties. A wave of inflation was rising in our country, the market and planned management of the economy were in danger of collapse and the chaos resulting from the right-wing opportunist activity made itself felt in the sphere of production. The situation today has radically changed. Planned management of the national economy has been reestablished, dangerous elements of inflation have been overcome, prices and the market have been stabilized, planned targets in the sphere of production and national income are being overfulfilled and our economy is becoming ever more dynamic.

Conditions for the peaceful life and work of our people have been fully restored in Czechoslovakia. The Czechoslovak working people actively support the political line of the central committee of our Party, intended further to develop socialism, with which they associate their social and political confidence. An expression of that confidence is the high quality of the work and the great initiative that is going into the preparation for the 50th anniversary of the Party and the 14th Congress of the Communist Party of Czechoslovakia.

The general course of preparation for our congress, the activity of the Communists and of all working people, give us ground to conclude that our mass Party, numbering more than 1,200,000 members, has again become united ideologically and organizationally, that it firmly adheres to the positions of Marxism-Leninism and is the leading force of our society, as well as a reliable unit in the international communist movement.

In the present world divided into two opposing systems, the Soviet Union's peaceful foreign policy fully corresponds also to the vital interests of the Czechoslovak Party. We consistently support the Vietnamese people and other peoples of Indochina in their heroic struggle against US imperialism's brazen aggression. We support the Arab peoples in their just struggle to end Israeli aggression and to bring about a peaceful settlement of the situation in the Middle East. We believe that our common active efforts in international relations to carry out the ideas of peaceful coexistence will be successful in the measure that we struggle actively to strengthen the unity of the socialist community, and our alliance within the framework of the Warsaw Treaty, and develop the process of economic integration of the Council for Mutual Economic Assistance countries.

We shall continue striving to defeat the right-wing opportunist and revisionist trends in the communist movement. At the same time, we denounce the malicious slander campaign and the splitting actions of the leaders of the Communist Party of China against Czechoslovakia and other socialist countries, the Soviet Union first of all, because this undermines the unity of the socialist states, the international communist movement and all revolutionary and anti-imperialist forces. Such a policy does great damage not only to the common interests of all socialist countries but also to the vital interests of the Chinese people themselves, since it objectively serves the aggressive plans of world imperialism.

Comrades, the clear analysis of the situation and the prospects outlined in the report of the Central Committee of the Communist Party of the Soviet Union made by comrade Leonid Ilyich Brezhnev, as well as the vivid, businesslike and frank discussion by congress participants are for us, too, a school of tremendous importance; they give us more strength and confidence in our work.

WHILE LISTENING to the speeches of our foreign friends and brothers, we felt with renewed strength that we were an inalienable, integral part of the great international movement called upon to transform the world. And we realized with particular force the worldwide significance of what our Party and our people are doing. . . . Dear foreign brothers and friends! Permit me on behalf of the Congress, on behalf of all our Party and the entire Soviet people, to thank you for the great contribution you have made.
LEONID BREZHNEV, closing speech, April 9

"Your today is our tomorrow . . ."

Revolutionary Forces
From Many Lands

Delegates from Asian Countries

Nguyen Van Hieu, Member of the Presidium, National Liberation Front of South Vietnam, told the Congress of the South Vietnamese people's love for the fraternal Soviet people and the heroic Land of Soviets, and their delight at its achievements.

The NLF delegate told the Congress that the South Vietnamese people had always enjoyed the sympathy and support of friends all over the world as well as the immense help of the Soviet Union, China and the other fraternal countries. Speaking of the ever-increasing mass movement throughout the USSR to increase support for the Vietnamese and other peoples of Indochina, Hieu declared:

> Allow us to take this opportunity, on behalf of the people and the National Liberation Front of South Vietnam, to express deep gratitude to the Communist Party, the Government and the people of the Soviet Union for their sympathy and support, for their massive and valuable assistance. The ties of brotherhood and friendship are binding the Vietnamese and Soviet peoples ever closer together, and we shall spare no effort in strengthening these ties.

Hieu also expressed gratitude to the other socialist countries, the Communist and Workers Parties and the progressive forces of the United States for their support of the National Liberation Front.

Keison Phomvihan, Vice Chairman, Laotian Patriotic Front, in bringing greetings to the Congress, pointed out that it was the October Socialist Revolution and the Soviet people's victories over the fascist aggressors in World War II which created favorable conditions for the revolutionary movement in Laos and other countries. He hailed the Soviet Union's constant support of national liberation movements, the working class and all exploited peoples in their fight against imperialism and reaction:

> While fighting against the American imperialists for a peaceful, independent, neutral, democratic and prosperous Laos, our people enjoy the generous help and support of the CPSU, the Soviet Government and the entire Soviet peo-

159

ple. And today, on behalf of the Laotian people, we express our sincere and deep gratitude for this priceless help and support.

Vice Chairman Phomvihan made a scathing attack on Nixon's efforts to destroy Asians by the hands of Asians, and on the attack on Laos by the Saigon puppets, with US air support. This attack had met with a crushing defeat by the Laotian armed forces and people, with the cooperation of the liberation forces of South Vietnam and Cambodia, who would never cease resistance until the Americans were driven out. He continued: "All our recent victories are inseparable from the tremendous assistance of the Soviet Union and other socialist countries. We once again want to express our deep gratitude."

Yumzhagiin Tsedenbal, First Secretary, Mongolian People's Revolutionary Party, Chairman, Mongolian People's Republic Council of Ministers, paid tribute to the CPSU as a powerful source of strength and knowledge in the building of a new socialist way of life. He declared that Mongolian Communists would continue learning from its rich world-historic experience, and would be forever grateful to the CPSU and the Soviet Government for their constant fraternal assistance. Scoring the schismatic activities of the Chinese leaders and the new anti-Soviet attacks launched by them on the eve of the 24th Congress, the Mongolian leader declared that nothing could shake Mongolian-Soviet friendship:

> Alliances of friendship, brotherhood and unity with the peoples of the Soviet Union and the other socialist countries are the foundation of foundations, the alpha and omega, as it were, of the foreign policy of the Mongolian People's Revolutionary Party and the Government of the Mongolian People's Republic.

Kim Ir, Political Committee Member of the Korean Labor Party, First Deputy Chairman of the Council of Ministers, Korean People's Democratic Republic, brought greetings from Kim Il Sung, leader of the Korean Party's Central Committee, and expressed gratitude for Soviet support for Korea's struggle for independence and reunification. He declared:

> We are confident that the traditional relations of friendship and cooperation between the parties and peoples of our two countries will steadily gain strength and develop on the basis of the principles of Marxism-Leninism and proletarian internationalism, and we wish the Congress every success in completing its work.

Chandra Rajeswara Rao, General Secretary of the Indian Communist Party, paid tribute to the Party of Lenin for its pioneering role in establishing the world's first socialist state, saving the world from fascism, extending the frontiers of socialism to one third of humanity,

160

and opening the way to the collapse of the colonial system over the major part of the globe.

Stressing the decisive role of the USSR in the anti-imperialist struggle, the Indian Communist leader mentioned especially its tremendous aid in the present two main centers of conflict:

> The glorious struggle of the peoples of Vietnam, Laos and Cambodia against American aggression and the struggle of the peoples of the Arab world against Israeli aggression backed by American imperialism.

Delegate Rao also spoke gratefully of the friendship and cooperation between the Soviet Union and India and the mighty Soviet aid in building a powerful national base for Indian industry and in preserving the independence of India.

The Head of the East Pakistan CP Delegation recalled gratefully the role of the Soviet Government and Premier Kosygin in the signing of the Tashkent Declaration in 1965, ending the war between India and Pakistan. He expressed gratitude as well for the enormous assistance given by the Soviet Union to the people of East Pakistan during the cyclone and flood disasters of last year, in the administering of which 17 Soviet people lost their lives. The delegate from East Pakistan also expressed appreciation of the deep concern manifested by the Soviet Government and people in connection with the military administration's current use of armed force against the people of East Pakistan, and President Podgorny's recent call for an end of the bloodshed and a political solution.

Tomio Nishizawa, head of the delegation from the Communist Party of Japan, reported on the fight carried on by his Party, which has increased its membership nearly nine times in the past ten years, against the revival of Japanese militarism under the aegis of the USA.

Nishizawa said internal Party difficulties had been straightened out and the Party strengthened by expelling those who were carrying out splitting machinations on the basis of both right and "left" opportunism.

Referring to difficulties in the international communist movement, he felt these could be ironed out by comradely exchanges of opinion between Marxist-Leninist parties and mutual relations of independence and equality.

On recent talks between the Communist Parties of Japan and the Soviet Union, he said:

> Both sides have acknowledged the agreement reached during their talks in Tokyo and Moscow in 1968 and agreed on concrete measures to remove obstacles preventing normalization of relations between the parties. Both sides expressed their readiness to improve mutual relations on this basis and pro-

161

mote cooperation. We believe the implementation of this agreement will develop the friendship between the Japanese and Soviet people and help to restore cohesion in the international movement.

Delegates from Africa and the Middle East

Claude Ernest Ndala, First Secretary, Congolese Workers' Party of the People's Republic of the Congo (Brazzaville) said his Party shared the views of the CPSU and the Soviet Government on international issues. The visit to their country of the CPSU delegation in 1971 had strengthened the ties between the two parties and the two countries. He emphasized the importance of the idea expressed in the Brezhnev report that the socialist countries, the international working class movement and the national liberation movement "should be united into a single powerful mainstream in order to speed up the defeat of world imperialism." Ndala declared:

> The Congolese Workers' Party contends that anti-Communism in the national liberation movement is a crime. Our Party and our people do not accept the philosophical concepts and fabrications intended to isolate the Africans from the rest of the world. We are men of creative endeavor—we have no right under the pretext of Black exclusiveness to live aside from the rest of the world and to counter the universal truth of Marxist-Leninist teaching.

John Marks, Chairman of the Communist Party of South Africa, hailed the growing strength of the Soviet Union not only for its benefits to the peoples of the multinational USSR, but "because it is directed towards strengthening and extending the world socialist community." The Black African leader declared:

> It is no exaggeration to say that the stronger the Soviet Union becomes under the Leninist leadership of the CPSU, the more powerful are the moral, political and material resources available to the working-class, revolutionary democratic and national-liberation forces in their struggles against capitalism, imperialism, neo-colonialism and racism and for national liberation, peace and socialism.

Of immense importance to the struggle against the terrorist white supremacy autocracy of the Pretoria regime, declared Marks, is the material support from the Soviet Union and other socialist countries, along with the fraternal support of the independent African states, the Asian countries and the working-class and democratic movements in the imperialist countries.

Daudi Mbakabago, Central Committee and National Executive member of the African National Union of Tanganyika, told how highly the people of Tanganyika value the support of the Soviet Union in

162

their struggle against colonialism and all forms of exploitation. He said the Soviet experience in carrying out their great five-year plans had great lessons for the people of Tanganyika who were entering on the road to socialism.

Mohammed Yusuf Elemi, member of the Supreme Revolutionary Council of Somalia, praised especially the concrete proposals for world peace in the Brezhnev report, with their sharp warnings to the imperialists and instigators of war. He said the Somali people, headed by the Supreme Revolutionary Council, had chosen the non-capitalist road of development, and considered socialism the only possible road of liberation from imperialist exploitation, hunger, illness and illiteracy, "those age-old enemies of the Somali people and all mankind." He told the 24th CPSU Congress, "The Revolutionary Council and the working masses of Somali march in close formation with you in the ranks of the anti-imperialist struggle."

Amilcar Cabral, General Secretary of the African Party for the Independence of Guinea and the Cape Verde Islands, paid tribute to the CPSU and to the great liberating genius of Lenin as an inexhaustible source of inspiration to all fighters against imperialism. He said he spoke not only for his Party but for the African people of Guinea-Bissau and the Cape Verde Islands, the oldest Portuguese colonies in Africa, who in eight years of struggle against the Portuguese fascist colonialists had liberated two thirds of their territory. He declared:

> Our confidence in victory is all the greater since your Party's Central Committee, through its General Secretary, has once again reaffirmed the CPSU's determination to go on giving moral, political and material assistance to the liberation movements. For us this means that the Soviet Union will, as in the past, stand steadfastly by our people, exposing the heinous war of the Portuguese colonialists and their accomplices and helping our Party to bring its struggle to victory.
>
> We are not in any way belittling the importance of African solidarity and the solidarity of the other anti-colonial forces when we frankly say that it is from the Soviet Union that we receive the bulk of the aid for our struggle.

Agostino Neto, Chairman of the Popular Movement for the Liberation of Angola, reported on the Angolan people's liberation struggle against the Portuguese colonialists and expressed gratitude for the Soviet Union's constant support.

Mashel Samora, head of the liberation front of Mozambique, FRELIMO, also told of the bitter struggle of his people against the Portuguese colonialists, armed with modern weapons received from NATO. He thanked the Soviet people for their aid, and said the 24th Congress would decisively aid the consolidation of all anti-imperialist forces, hastening the end of imperialism and colonialism.

Abdel Mohsen Abu al-Neur, General Secretary of the Arab Socialist Union of the UAR, brought greetings and gratitude from the ASU and its leader, President Anwar Sadat. Lauding the Soviet Union as the leader of the world forces of freedom, socialism and peace in the struggle against the forces of colonialism and imperialism led by the USA, he said that his people would forever remember the all-round aid and support of the Soviet Union for the freedom-loving forces of the Arab world:

> Arab-Soviet friendship has traversed a long path of fruitful cooperation and is profound and strong today. We associate this friendship, above all, with our immortal leader Gamal Abdel Nasser, whose dedicated and purposeful efforts, together with the efforts of the outstanding Soviet leaders, have created the magnificent edifice of this friendship and opened up the prospects of successful and constructive cooperation between our countries.

Expressing gratitude for the Soviet role in transforming the life of the people of the UAR through the Aswan High Dam, the steelworks in Helwan, the electrification of the Egyptian countryside and other projects, he pointed especially to "Soviet support in the struggle against imperialism and Zionism."

Khaled Bagdash, General Secretary of the Syrian Communist Party, thanked the Soviet Union for its services to mankind, especially in its program for world peace and its aid to the Arab cause. Noting certain recent changes in Syria, the Communist Party leader declared:

> The leadership of the ruling BAATH party has been replaced. Our party decided to support the course of the new leadership as laid down in an official policy statement: the policy of continuing the anti-imperialist struggle and the progressive socioeconomic reforms, of building a national front composed of all progressive forces, of strengthening cooperation with the UAR and other progressive Arab states, of struggle for Arab unity, the policy of reinforcing friendship with the Soviet Union and other socialist countries.
>
> To help implement this program our party agreed that two Communists should enter the government.

Mohammed Djaber Badjboudj, of Syria's Arab Socialist Renaissance Party, also attended the conference. He expressed gratitude for Soviet support and assistance in the fight against imperialism, colonialism and Zionism. He also stressed Soviet aid in creating the material and economic basis of a new society advancing along the road of socialist transformations; for helping to establish their own oil extraction industry and to end a major aspect of imperialist domination; for aiding the construction of the great dam on the Euphrates which will mean irrigation of over 1,500,000 acres of land; for providing military assistance in the struggle against occupation and aggression.

Meir Vilner, General Secretary of the Communist Party of Israel,

164

brought greetings from the progressive Jews and Arabs of a country "whose rulers and Zionist leaders are carrying out an unbridled anti-Soviet campaign," thereby "insulting the memory of the six million Jews destroyed by the Nazis, and joining forces with the most aggressive and reactionary forces of the imperialist states." But they and their American patrons could never erase from the memory of the peoples the unforgettable fact that the Soviet Union had made the decisive contribution to the salvation of mankind, including millions of Jews, from the Nazi barbarians. He expressed his appreciation of the Soviet policy directed at ensuring peace in Middle East. The Israeli Communist leader continued:

> The constructive, realistic position of the UAR, entirely lacking in extremism, its acceptance of Dr. Jarring's proposals and its readiness to conclude a peace agreement with Israel on condition that Israeli troops are withdrawn from occupied Arab territory on the basis of the complete implementation of the Security Council's resolution of November, 1967, have aroused a positive response in Israel.

He declared that the main obstacle to peace in the Middle East is the policy of American imperialism.

Delegates from Latin America and Canada

Osvaldo Dorticos Torrado, Politbureau and Secretariat member of the Communist Party, and President of the Republic of Cuba, hailed the CPSU and the Soviet people for the victory of the October Revolution, for saving the working people of the world from fascist aggression in World War II, and for the high level of economic and cultural development in which "revolutionaries all over the world rejoice." Stressing especially Cuba's debt to the Soviet Union, Dorticos declared:

> It is appropriate to point out at this Congress not only the historic results of your great achievements but also to emphasize the significance of the very existence of the Soviet Union and its economic might for the working people's revolutionary struggle and the national liberation movement. This is eloquently shown in the effective support the Soviet Union has given to Vietnam, the Arab peoples and Cuba at the decisive moments of their histories.
> The consolidation of the Cuban revolution and Cuba's socialist gains, attained despite the imperialists' aggression and blockade, became possible only in the historical era opened by the October Revolution. We owe a great deal to the economic, technical and military assistance received from the Soviet Union. This assistance enabled Cuba to wage a steadfast struggle against imperialism's powerful center, only 90 miles away from us.

The Cuban President concluded that "there is no more fitting place to stress the role which this cooperation has played in the Cuban revolution and its consolidation and to express our confidence in the unbreakable friendship between the Soviet Union and Cuba and between the Communist Party of the Soviet Union and the Communist Party of Cuba."

Luis Corvalan, General Secretary of the Communist Party of Chile, expressed the determination of his Party to go hand in hand with the CPSU and other fraternal parties in the common world struggle against imperialism, for peace and socialism. He spoke of the progress of the Allende Popular Unity Government toward nationalizing the copper mines and other big mining and industrial enterprises and the biggest private banks, and in land reform. No efforts of US imperialist or native reactionaries could stop this advance.

Noting that the Chilean Government was formed by a bloc of parties, Corvalan expressed great satisfaction that there was also present at the 24th Congress a delegation of the Socialist Party of Chile. Corvalan stated firmly:

> In our country we view all questions, including socialist construction, from the standpoint of cooperation, with no time limits, between the Communists and Socialists and among all the parties making up the Popular Unity Bloc. There is no other road for us. We are satisfied with the road we have taken, for our choice was dictated by the social and political realities of our country.

Hernan Del Canto, delegate from the Socialist Party of Chile, told the Congress it was a great honor for the Chilean Socialists to attend such a Congress for the first time in history. This Congress was of worldwide significance due to the impact of the Soviet Union on the world revolutionary struggle. Many years of friendship had enabled Chilean Socialists to get acquainted with the tremendous achievements of the Soviet Union, and their theoretical views, based on Marxist-Leninist teaching, coincided.

The Chilean Socialist declared that elementary revolutionary honesty required acknowledgment that "on certain aspects the assessments of Chilean Socialists differ from yours," but, he stressed:

> Historically and politically we have cast our lot with the working class, revolution and socialism. Following this path we are fighting for the well-being, happiness and progress of the Chilean people.

Del Canto emphasized the importance of strengthening still further the unity of Communists and Socialists in carrying through the construction of socialism in Chile. He expressed confidence in the leadership of Allende and in the victory of the Revolution:

> We are aware that the reactionary forces will seek to provoke clashes and violence. Our answer is: we do not want violence, nor do we seek it. We have

no intention of playing into the hands of our enemies. But if they resort to violence they will meet with a firm, resolute and organized resistance on the part of the people and the working class.

Felix Ojeda, General Secretary of the Puerto-Rican Communist Party, said it was the greatest honor of his life to attend the 24th Congress. He described the humiliating colonial conditions imposed by the United States on the people of Puerto Rico. Yet under conditions of the harshest US repression the Puerto Rican people are stepping up their struggle for independence.

Ojeda paid tribute to the CPSU policy which opens up all the cultural riches of the country to the working class and gives full scope to their creative powers, making science and technique serve the wellbeing of the people. Furthermore, he said:

> The most remarkable of all things I have seen at this historic Congress is the carrying out in practice of the Marxist-Leninist teachings on criticism and self-criticism and the actual realization of the principle of democratic centralism.

Arnold Martinez Verdugo, General Secretary of the Mexican Communist Party, declared that the achievements of the Soviet Union helped in the struggle against imperialism throughout the world, and thus played a revolutionary role on a world scale. He reported that the Mexican Communists, along with other revolutionary forces, were carrying on an intense struggle against the ruling Mexican bourgeoisie, which was serving imperialist interests and carrying on crude anti-Soviet provocations to divert attention from its own internal problems. He declared that the Mexican people know that the only enemy of their freedom is US imperialism, and are aware the Soviet Union is their real friend and ally. He expressed gratitude to the Soviet Union and the entire Communist movement for their support for the students and other political prisoners in Mexican jails.

Jorge Colle, First Secretary of the Communist Party of Bolivia, declared that support from the socialist camp, especially the Soviet Union, is helping to consolidate the powerful upsurge of the revolutionary and anti-imperialist movement now sweeping the entire Latin American continent. US imperialism is trying to nullify the positive changes achieved as a result of the frustrating of the military-fascist coup in Bolivia last October. But the important part played by the working people in the developing struggle "unfolds new prospects for a revolutionary deepening of the political process now taking place. . . . The People's Assembly, created by the Bolivian Workers' Center and democratic revolutionary political parties, is capable of directing the current process along a popular, anti-imperialist path."

167

Jorge del Prado, General Secretary of the Peruvian Communist Party, informed the delegates that transformations that began in Peru October 3, 1968 due to the powerful liberation struggles of their people, which substantially altered the outlook of a considerable part of the military, are continuing despite US repression, threats and interference. Establishment of diplomatic and trade relations with the socialist countries has formed a real barrier to imperialist aggression and promotes Peru's independent development. He expressed profound gratitude to the Soviet Union for its tremendous contributions to the people in the stricken areas of Peru and restoration of the towns destroyed by the earthquake in May 1970:

> It is with deep respect and sorrow that we pay tribute to the Soviet pilots and doctors who tragically met their death while carrying out their humanitarian mission. We are also grateful for the emergency aid we received from socialist Cuba, the fraternal people of Chile and many other countries.

Luis Carlos Prestes, General Secretary of the Communist Party of Brazil, spoke of the growing resistance in Brazil to the fascist military dictatorship established following the 1964 military coup and supported by US imperialism, which tries to make Brazil the gendarme of Latin America. He deplored the splitting activities of the Chinese Party leadership, which complicate the struggle, and expressed warm gratitude to the CPSU for its effective support.

William Kashtan, General Secretary of the Communist Party of Canada, reported on the inflationary recession arising from growing US domination of Canadian economy leading to a growing offensive against labor by their own monopolies, resulting in severe repression and unemployment. The main victims are the youth and the French-Canadian people whose national rights are ignored, while their economic and social inequality has been further aggravated. This was at the root of the political crisis in Quebec which still continues. All these developments have at the same time led to a marked increase in the militancy of the working class and "a marked growth of opposition to US domination and US policies amongst a majority of the Canadian people."

From the Socialist Countries of Eastern Europe

Edward Gierek, First Secretary, Polish United Workers' Party, paid tribute to the key role of the CPSU in strengthening unity among the socialist states, and among the Communist and Workers' Parties. One's attitude toward the CPSU and the Soviet Union, he said, is "the best criterion of one's real attitude toward the unity of socialist and anti-imperialist forces." Those who did not understand this and take an anti-Soviet position, trying to split the international communist movement, harm the cause of socialism and their own vital interests. Of his own country, he said.

> As you know, Comrades, we have recently had difficulties, which we are overcoming thanks to the support of our working class, which is profoundly linked with socialism, the inner strength of our Party and to the help of all our friends. Our entire Party and our entire people are profoundly grateful to the Communist Party of the Soviet Union and its leadership for their understanding of our problems and for their friendly help in solving them. . . .
> Our entire experience teaches us graphically that the basic condition for the successful development of socialist society is the firm and consistent implementation of the leading role of the Party and strengthening its bonds with the working class, with all the working people. In day-to-day practical activity we are carrying out Lenin's teachings that the state of the dictatorship of the proletariat . . . draws its strength from the consciousness of the masses, from the broad democratic participation of the working people in the administration of the state.

The Polish First Secretary expressed gratitude to the Soviet Union for policies which had preserved peace on the European continent for 25 years, for bearing the primary burden in the worldwide struggle against imperialism and for consistent support of all peoples fighting for their freedom. He pledged support to the movement for European security and declared that the Polish people would forever march by the side of the Soviet Union in the struggle for socialism, peace and liberation.

Janos Kadar, First Secretary, Hungarian Worker's Party, speaking of the steady growth of the ideas of socialism and communism throughout the world, noted also the lack of complete unity in the communist movement:

> Nationalist, revisionist and other anti-Marxist views have emerged in our ranks and cause damage. Particular harm has been done by the disruptive activity of the Chinese leaders, which our Party, as is well known, sharply condemns. . . . We most emphatically oppose all anti-Communist and anti-Soviet trends and all varieties of right and "left" opportunism, from any direction.

The Hungarian First Secretary stressed the efforts of the Hungarian Socialist Workers' Party and the Hungarian state for unity and cooperation with all socialist countries, with all Communist and Workers' Parties and all progressive forces.

Todor Zhivkov, First Secretary of the Bulgarian Communist Party and Chairman of the Council of Ministers of the Bulgarian People's Republic, told the Congress: "Your today is our tomorrow." His country, he said, was proud that the views of Bulgarian Communists on all the main problems of the time fully coincided with the position of the CPSU and the great majority of fraternal parties. The Bulgarian First Secretary declared:

> Our Party will unswervingly continue its struggle for the purity of Marxism-Leninism, against anti-communism, against bourgeois nationalism, against rightwing and "left" revisionism and against any manifestations of anti-Sovietism. . . . We Bulgarian Communists resolutely reject the attacks and slander which the present Chinese leadership is making against the CPSU and the Soviet Union, against the world socialist system and against the entire international communist movement.

Walter Ulbricht, [*] *First Secretary, Socialist Unity Party of Germany and President of the State Council of the German Democratic Republic,* expressed full support of the CPSU Central Committee report, on behalf of the working people of the German Democratic Republic. Noting his delegation's complete agreement with the statements in the Brezhnev report, he said:

> With respect to peace and security in Europe, he [Brezhnev] emphasized the fact of international recognition of the GDR by many states and the immutability of the existing borders in Europe. He unequivocally indicated that the ratification and, consequently, the entry into force of the Moscow and Warsaw treaties with the FRG must be considered a top-priority task in the interests of European security.

Nicolae Ceausescu, First Secretary of the Romanian Communist Party and Chairman of the State Council of the Socialist Republic of Romania, noted with satisfaction that "firm political, economic, scientific, technical and cultural relations have been established and are developing between the Romanian Communist Party and the CPSU and between our peoples and countries." He said the new Treaty of Friendship, Cooperation and Mutual Assistance signed between Romania and the USSR last year opened up new prospects for all-around cooperation between the two countries. Ceausescu called for:

> . . . relations of a new type among socialist countries, relations that are diametrically opposite to the relations existing in the capitalist world, and . . . the socialist countries' voluntary cooperation in the spirit of the principles of Marxism-Leninism and socialist internationalism, respect for independence and national sovereignty, equal rights and non-interference in internal affairs and comradely mutual assistance and mutual advantage.

Mijalko Todorovic, from the League of Communists of Yugoslavia, brought greetings from Josif Broz Tito, head of the Party and State of

---

[*]On June 15, at the Congress of the Socialist Unity Party, Walter Ulbricht, due to advanced age and ill health, was succeeded as First Secretary by Erich Honecker. Ulbricht remains head of state.

Yugoslavia, declaring: "We rejoice in every one of your achievements in the economic, scientific, cultural and other fields." The head of the Yugoslav delegation said:

We are gratified to see the favorable development of relations between Yugoslavia and the Soviet Union on the principles of equality, mutual respect and non-interference. We are confident that favorable conditions and common enduring interests exist for further cooperation between our countries and our peoples.

He also stressed the importance of cooperation between the Yugoslav League of Communists and the CPSU and the useful exchange of opinions and experience arising therefrom.

Delegates from Capitalist Countries of Europe

Georges Marchais, Deputy General Secretary of the French Communist Party, brought warm greetings from the ailing General Secretary, Waldeck Rochet. He praised the creative initiative displayed in Brezhnev's report, and the fact that efforts to make the CPSU renounce the policy adopted by the 20th Congress had been rejected. He praised CPSU support for the independence of oppressed peoples, its defense of the peoples of Indochina and the Arab peoples against imperialist aggression, and its work for peaceful coexistence. He scored manifestations of anti-Sovietism from any source as a crime against the interests of the working class.

He reported on successes of the French Communist Party in the direction of achieving greater unity among the trade unions and left-wing political organizations, and in exerting influence among the youth. [The French Communist Party has about 400,000 members, and a potential 5,000,000 votes in a national election.]

On the question of unity of the socialist countries and their Communist Parties, he declared:

Dear Comrades! Relations between the French Communist Party and the CPSU have always been ones of fraternity, solidarity and cooperation. These relations have never been and never will be shaken by any trial.

Unity of all the socialist countries, of all Communist Parties, in the struggle against imperialism, for peace and independence of the peoples, is an urgent necessity in face of the aggressive policy of US imperialism.

We set much store on the principle of the independence and sovereignty of every Communist Party, and the observation of this principle in relations among the fraternal parties. We consider that achieving proletarian internationalism and unity of action of all the Communist Parties on the basis of Marxism-Leninism is a sacred duty and an essential condition for success in our struggle.

In conclusion Marchais said that French Communists:

. . . call for the unity of the world communist movement, convinced that differences on some questions . . . must never result in a weakening of the basic links uniting our parties, that they must not become an obstacle to the joint struggle of all our forces against imperialism.

Enrico Berlinguer, Deputy Secretary General of the Italian Communist Party, brought greetings from Secretary General Luigi Longo. He stressed the significance of Soviet plans for economic advancement, and for increased aid to all peoples fighting for freedom and independence, above all the Vietnamese and Arab peoples. Stressing the vitality of the solidarity of his Party with the CPSU, the Soviet Union and all socialist countries, he declared that this did not mean that the views of the Italian Party always coincided with those of each socialist country and each Communist and Workers' Party:

Our internationalism is based on recognition of the complete independence of each country and of each party. This does not exclude differences, which have occurred and may do so again. This however does not impair our solidarity and does not prevent us from participating in the struggle to achieve the great objectives that unite us.

Berlinguer said his Party resolutely rejected any calls to renounce its international commitments or "to deviate from them within the great worldwide communist and revolutionary movement"; it had always fought any manifestations of anti-Sovietism and would continue to do so. He sharply attacked US imperialism's aggressive policies, especially its war of extermination against the peoples of Indochina and its dangerous policies in the Mediterranean; solidarity with the people of Indochina was linked closely with the Italian people's struggle against the US presence in their own country. He urged the necessity for a European Security Conference.

The Italian Communist leader spoke of the growing influence of the 1,500,000-strong Italian Communist Party, which polls nine million votes. He reported growing unity in Italy among all Left-wing forces, both secular and Catholic, and growing unity of action on the part of trade unions. All this has inevitably sparked off a ferocious onslaught by reactionary forces, against which "the people and all anti-fascist forces are being mobilized on a growing scale."

Dolores Ibarruri, legendary revolutionary leader, Chairman of the Communist Party of Spain, banned in its homeland, gave good news to the Congress of the growth of the anti-Franco movement, now encompassing ever wider sections of society in addition to the workers —influential sections of the bourgeoisie, the Catholic Church, intellectuals, engineers, technicians, students and peasants. "Even in Franco's army a thaw has set in, heralding the spring of hope for our country."

There are vast potentialities for a Freedom Pact, championed by the Communist Party of Spain as a basis for mobilizing the whole country to overthrow the Franco dictatorship. The main adverse factor is "the American bases located in strategic points on Spanish territory and spearheaded against the Soviet Union and our people . . . and used for internal political pressure."

Ibarruri expressed deep appreciation on behalf of her Party for the campaign of solidarity with the young Basque freedom fighters in which the Soviet Union and other socialist countries took part, and which developed on an unprecedented scale in France, Italy, Belgium and other countries. Mentioning differences in the international movement she declared: "No discord can justify anti-Sovietism, which we denounce most resolutely."

John Gollan, General Secretary of the Communist Party of Great Britain, declared that differences, on which the British Party had stated its position at the World Meeting of Parties in 1969, have not stopped and will not stop the solidarity and joint action of British Communists with the CPSU and other socialist countries in the common struggle against imperialism and for socialism.

Kostas Koliannis, First Secretary of the Communist Party of Greece, said that despite the fascist terror of the ruling military junta, openly supported by US imperialism, the junta had been unable to break out of its isolation, the Greek people remained unsubdued and their anti-imperialist and anti-American mood was growing. He said the Greek Communist Party was in the front ranks of the struggle for the overthrow of the dictatorship, and in this struggle was receiving warm internationalist support, "above all from the Soviet Union and other socialist countries."

Lavaro Cunhal, General Secretary of the Portuguese Communist Party, reported that the fascist dictatorship of Caetano was continuing the colonialist policy of Salazar. Supported by the NATO countries, and closely allied with the racist government of South Africa and Rhodesia, it is stepping up military operations against the peoples of Angola, Guinea-Bissau and Mozambique. While forced to work underground, the Portuguese Party is doing everything possible to defend the peoples of these countries and to mobilize the working class and democratic forces to wipe out the fascist dictatorship.

The preceding selections, while necessarily incomplete, should convey a sense of the broad experience, confidence, and deep solidarity of the foreign delegations, making the 24th Congress of the CPSU a truly international forum for peace and revolutionary change.

I. V. KAPITONOV

Who Are the Delegates?

THE genuinely representative nature of the CPSU Congress, as shown by its diverse composition and the broadly varied backgrounds of its delegates, was the subject of a report by the Chairman of the CPSU Congress' Credentials Commission, I. V. Kapitonov. The Congress, analyzed sociologically, can be seen to be not only a cross-section and microcosm of the Party itself, but a miniature version of Soviet society—economically, occupationally, geographically, educationally, generationally, by sexes and in other ways. One wonders about how many congresses and parliaments a similar statement could seriously be made!

After referring at some length to the extensive and broadly-based preparations for the Congress, and its significance as an index of the Party's leading role, Mr. Kapitonov detailed some of the mechanics of the Congress' election procedures before going on to discuss the constituency itself. All 4,963 of the delegates were elected by secret ballot at their respective regional and territorial Party conferences, or in some cases at Party congresses of the Union Republics. These elections in the candidates' home areas were carried out "in full accord with the Party Rules and norms of representation." An indication that what is commonly called "seniority" did not determine who was elected can be seen in the fact that about three quarters of the delegates—3,691 to be exact—were elected to a national Congress of the CPSU for the first time.

All areas of the multinational Soviet state, as well as 61 nationalities, were represented at the Congress in proportion to the respective size of their party organizations, each delegate representing 2,900 members of his Party. Kapitonov reported that:

> The Congress represents all the regional, territorial and Republic party organizations. The biggest delegations come from the party organizations of Moscow, 314 members; Leningrad Region, 175; Moscow Region, 158; Rostov Region, 92; Krasnodar Territory, 89; Gorky Region, 79; Sverdlovsk Region, 75; Kuibyshev Region, 69; and Saratov Region, 65. The 1.5 million-strong detach-

---

I. V. KAPITONOV was the Chairman of the Credentials Commission of the 24th CPSU Congress. This summary was prepared by David B. Buehrens.

ment of the Communists of Siberia and the Soviet Far East, which are rapidly developing parts of the country, is represented by over 500 delegates.

The party organizations of the constituent Republics are represented proportionally, as are such newly formed central Asian regions as Taldy-Kurgan and Turgai in Kazakhstan; Namangan in Uzbekistan; Mari, Tashauz and Chardshou in Turkmenia and others.

Mr. Kapitonov prefaced his examination of the *social* make-up of the Congress with a reference to Leonid Brezhnev's report, which stressed that the Party must constantly show its concern "to have its composition help solve in the best way the problems confronting it. And this is duly reflected in the composition of the Congress delegates—workers and government ministers, collective farmers and scientists, military men and cultural workers, and old and young party members."

The Soviet working class was represented at the Congress more widely than ever before, as befits its leading role in the construction of communism. Among the 1,195 delegates were metallurgists and miners, machinists and textile workers, weavers, oilmen, railway workers and skilled builders of automated instruments and sophisticated electronic computers, "all models of a truly communist attitude toward their work,"* according to Kapitonov.

Another 870 delegates were from the countryside: rank-and-file collective farmers, state farm workers, and section, team and livestock-breeding leaders comprised two-thirds of this number. Said Kapitonov: "These are people who spare no effort to implement the Party's program for a further development of agriculture, persistently striving for high yields of crops and an increased output of animal husbandry produce in order to strengthen the economy of the collective and state farms."

Thus we see that industrial workers like Yegor Ivanovich Drozdetsky, noted miner from Kuzbas and Maria Ivannikova, Moscow weaver, or agricultural workers like Victor Stasevich, a Byelorussian agricultural machine operator and Vaike Nutt, Estonian milk-maid—people employed directly in the production of material values—comprised over 40 per cent of the delegates to the recent CPSU Congress.

Another sizable and important group of delegates included the leaders of various Soviet industrial and agricultural enterprises. "Participating in the Congress," Mr. Kapitonov reported, "were 370 heads of industrial enterprises and construction projects, production associa-

---

*About 98 per cent of *all* the delegates had been awarded Soviet medals and citations of various sorts for patriotic, occupational, public and other achievements.

tions and firms; 82 state farm directors; and 148 collective farm chairmen. And this shows that our executives enjoy well-deserved prestige in the country."

Professional full-time party workers—"functionaries"—were also present and active at the CPSU Congress. The great majority of this group, which made up almost a quarter of the delegates, were recently workers, collective farmers and professionals. They included hundreds of secretaries of regional, territorial, republic area, city and district party committees.

Youth, government and trade union interests were represented by the "556 Soviet government, 126 trade union and YCL officers participating in the Congress. We have among the delegates 1,284 deputies to the USSR Supreme Soviet and the Supreme Soviets of the constituent and autonomous republics."

Kapitonov reported that scientists, academicians, educators and creative people in the arts made up over seven hundred of the delegates present:

> We have among the delegates 86 Academicians and Corresponding Members of the USSR Academy of Sciences, of the branch Academies and those of the Union Republics; 363 Doctors and Candidates of Science, and 138 professional research workers. The Congress is also attended by 120 cultural workers, educators, writers, composers, artists and actors. We have among the delegates such prominent men of science and culture as Academician Mstislav Keldysh, three times recipient of the Hero of Socialist Labor award; the famous writer Mikhail Sholokhov; sculptor Nikolay Tomsky, and others.

In this period of women's liberation movements, many American readers will be interested to learn that every fourth delegate to the Congress was a woman, a much higher percentage than at the 8th Party Congress in 1919. The important and ever-increasing public role of women in the USSR is indicated also by the fact that, as reported in the Soviet *Economic Gazette* of November 1969, every third engineer in the USSR is a woman, while in the U.S. only one out of fifty is female; women comprise over 70 per cent of the doctors, a rate ten times higher than in the US. They also account for half the employees in factories and offices throughout the USSR. A national policy of generous four-month pregnancy and maternity leaves with full pay, and a wide network of children's out-patient clinics, nurseries, and kindergartens in addition to maternity grants and other services: all these are the material conditions for the growing role of Soviet women, as shown by their extensive participation in the Congress as elected delegates.

Incidentally, to implement further the participation of women in non-domestic work, the 24th Congress adopted the following national goals: "An increase in cash allowances for children where the (monthly) income per family member does not exceed 50 rubles; an increase in the number of paid days allowed for care of a sick child; and 100 per cent paid pregnancy and maternity leaves for all working women, regardless of length of employment." Previously this payment was scaled according to length of employment. Thus there may be even more women delegates to the next Congress.

Concerning the "generation gap," which, like other bourgeois problems, is supposed to be universal and common to all countries, the Congress presented a picture of the continuity of age groups, not of their clash. Actually, only 26 per cent of the delegates were over fifty. The remainder were distributed by age as follows: under 30, 5.1 per cent; 31 to 35, 12.8 per cent; 36 to 40, 13.9 per cent; and 41 to 50, 41.6 per cent. There are only 5.9 per cent over the age of 60. Clearly the Congress was not "dominated" by old people, a frequent aspect of the "generation gap" charge. The statistics on the length of party membership similarly support the thesis of the continuity of generations in the USSR.

All of these considerations, taken into account along with the unprecedented progress of the country as a whole, according to Kapitonov, will "help to increase still more the prestige of our Leninist Party which is confidently guiding the Soviet people along the road to communism."

GENNADY F. SIZOV

CPSU Budget and Finances

THE importance of the spirit of serious businesslike responsibility, earnest self-examination and self-criticism, in order better to carry out party goals, was the subject of a report by Gennady Sizov, Chairman of the CPSU Central Auditing Commission. In Mr. Sizov's report we are given a frank assessment of party shortcomings as well as achievements, and a reminder of the need for continued devotion to high standards of party operations in meeting the new challenges of the present and future.

"An important stage in the work of translating communist ideals

GENNADY SIZOV is Chairman of the Central Auditing Commission of the CPSU Central Committee. This summary was prepared by David B. Buehrens.

into life" is how Sizov characterizes the period between the 23rd (1966) and 24th Congresses of the CPSU. "Conditions have been created in our country after the 23rd Congress for the work of party functionaries and economic executives that insure a respectful and attentive attitude towards them, and greatly encourage businesslike initiative and political activity in every functionary."

In that connection Mr. Sizov takes note also of the improvement during that period "in the style of party leadership and the further development of inner-party democracy which have invigorated the work of the various auditing commissions—both the Central Commission and the local party commissions." All of this, he continues, has helped put "our socialist country on a fresh, mighty upgrade," and the Party's ties with the labor and political activities of the masses have been correspondingly strengthened.

Mr. Sizov points to a general improvement in the management and efficiency of Central Committee operations during the recent five-year period, noting that his commission is concerned chiefly with the Party's financial operations. Revenues for the Party's budget have had sizable annual increases, he reports, the period since the last Congress showing a growth of almost 40 per cent. Membership dues make up about two-thirds of these revenues, and the correct and prompt payment and accounting of dues is therefore an important financial matter as well as one of "the foremost duties of a Communist"—a matter of observing party discipline and duties as recorded in the Party Rules.

Commenting that party and candidate members on the whole strictly observed the fixed order of payment of party membership dues, Sizov gives some specific examples of party organizations and members falling short in this matter. He also chides particular party organizations for laxity in accepting dishonest statements of income from dues-paying members, failing to maintain proper accounting and banking procedures, and carelessness in the matter of losing membership cards.

Calling attention to the substantial portion of the Party's revenue which derives from its publishing activities, Sizov details the very large increases in circulation of such party publications as *Pravda*, 6.4 to 9 million; *Selskaya Zhizn* (Agricultural Life), 5.3 to 6.6 million; *Kommunist*, 704,000 to 820,000; and *Partinaya Zhizn* (Party Life).

In 1970, 274 party newspapers were published, with a circulation of 67 million, and 226 magazines with a circulation of 69.4 million copies. This, he says, "testifies in the first place to the increasing political activity and spiritual and cultural requirements of our people." Further, "all the publishing houses and printing shops have now been changed over to the new methods of planning and incentives," substantially increasing their efficiency, but there is still a need for much expansion and new construction of publishing facilities in the new five-year period in order that "the legitimate desire of the Soviet citizen to have newspapers and magazines should be fully met."

Coming to the question of the handling of letters, applications and complaints to the Party's Central Committee and its various editorial offices, Sizov talks about the change "in the nature of letters received in recent years—besides complaints of a personal character, questions of social importance are raised more and more frequently, showing the increased political maturity and sense of responsibility of the Soviet people for the success of the common cause, their deep interest in the speedy development of our economy and culture, and in the pursuance of our Party's domestic and foreign policy."

By giving due attention to these questions, Sizov concludes, as well as by expanding its exchange of experience in these areas with the commissions of a number of fraternal Marxist-Leninist Parties, the Party will be able to satisfy the legitimate needs of the people, as well as its own responsibilities, even more fully.

DAVID LAIBMAN

The Draft Directives:
Pre-Congress Discussion

THE DRAFT Directives of the Ninth Five-Year Plan, 1971-75, were published months before the 24th Congress for purposes of nationwide discussion. It is vital to realize that the form of the Directives at the Congress, as embodied in the report of Kosygin, and the nature of the discussion at the Congress itself, was shaped by the discussion that occurred throughout the pre-Congress period. This discussion took place in local Soviets, in work places, in numerous specialized organizations dealing with particular problems, and in the press. *Pravda* and *Izvestia,* the two leading Soviet dailies, carried continuous streams of contributions, which, according to Alexey Kosygin, testify to the Soviet people's "active participation in tackling the basic problems of the development of Soviet society." All of the contributors to the discussion fully support the positions set forth in the Directives, and take pride in the accomplishments of Soviet society; it is in that context that the criticisms of shortcomings and problems yet to be solved take on their meaning, as an inseparable part of the process of implementing the Directives and moving toward the goals set forth in them. To show the reader something of the seriousness and importance of the discussion, we have concentrated on the participants' criticisms of the existing situation and their proposals for change, which shows socialism as process, as constant improvement.

An official of a government planning committee describes the increasing complexity of planning: In a year more than *four billion* documents are circulated among the various levels of management. The problem is that many of these documents are drawn up in different ways, and terminology is not standardized; this is preventing the wide-scale introduction of automated management systems throughout the country. "A major problem we face is the creation of a single system of documentation for the entire country." Work on the theory and practice of classification systems, and the training of cadres for this, is becoming urgent.

An economist discusses the problems of manpower in Siberian agriculture. The ten-year decline of 17 per cent in the rural population of Siberia has not been counterbalanced by rising mechanization and productivity in agriculture, and plowland per worker remains way above the country's average. Something must be done to stabilize the number of workers on the farms. With higher pay, only 15 per cent of those who leave the countryside do so for "financial reasons," but "dissatisfaction with cultural, everyday and trade services, the quality of housing, labor organization and the work routine are more and more frequently cited as reasons for migrating." Bad roads cause people in small villages to feel cut off from civilization; thus, especially in Siberia, road construction is a major means of solving *both* economic and social problems.

An agricultural specialist points to a knotty problem. Due to the past concern in the country over the shortage of bread, wheat was encouraged at the expense of food-grain crops for livestock feeding. Now wheat production continues to expand, while the requirement for feed crops is increasing. This means that rising proportions of the wheat harvest are devoted to this use, and this is highly unprofitable, since the yields per unit outlay are much greater in rye, barley, etc. The new situation requires a drastic shift in the structure of sown areas. Another contributor to the discussion on problems of agriculture focuses on the state farms, where he sees a contradiction between the present pay and bonus system and optimal planning:

180

Farms are rewarded more for *over*fulfillment of their plans than for fulfillment; this leads them to avoid taking on sufficiently steep plans. "To increase the weight of the plan, in our view, it is necessary to increasingly encourage fulfillment, not overfulfillment. Then the plan targets will to a larger extent take into account the achieved level of production and the latest gains in science and technology." Other discussants go into problems in the way the incentive funds are formed, issues too complex to follow in detail here. Some core problems: Contradictions in the pay and bonus system due to the complexity of the methods for forming incentive funds, a hindrance to full worker understanding and participation; lack of economic accountability of higher agricultural agencies; the need for more streamlined, harmonious organization.

Similar problems are discussed with reference to industry. Even where an enterprise has an incentive to set itself the highest possible plan (where enterprise funds depend more upon fulfillment than upon overfulfillment), it can be demoralized in the longer run by revisions of the technical indices on which its profitability is calculated.

From Taganrog: "I would like to express a few thoughts that trouble us production workers and that have not yet been fully reflected during the introduction of the economic reform." One of those thoughts: mechanical application of the reform may hurt enterprises which are introducing new technology or new products, since productivity will be low during the period when the new methods are first being assimilated. This is unfair, since the pioneering enterprise is making a great contribution in breaking new ground.

From an engineer: a proposal on how to pay engineers: "At present, an engineer is paid according to the position he holds. It would be more expedient to establish his pay rate according to his qualifications and performance. . . . The criteria for this should not be age and seniority but solely the person's abilities and knowledge. . . . Therefore, I suggest that the Directives of the Party Congress state the necessity of the further activization of the creative efforts of engineering and technical personnel and of improving the organization of labor and the system of their material and moral incentives."

The Deputy Minister of Local Industry of Lithuania writes on behalf of local industry: Many consumer goods are below the best standards because local industrial firms are not given the same equipment provided to other enterprises. He also proposes more specialization, less duplication.

One letter delves into the experience in Leningrad with the formation of research-and-production associations (see the article by G.

Romanov, p. 185). These combines have great potential, especially in the area of scientific research. At the same time, there are obstacles in the path of the associations, impeding their creation. "As a rule, the executives of enterprises and organizations making up the associations do not want to lose their independence and are reluctant to part with a position in which they are constantly in view." This "psychological" barrier must be overcome. In addition, "the existing pay system and standard table of organization do not facilitate the creation of such associations." There are all sorts of contrivances designed to maintain salaries and keep all the previous cadres within the new organization, including the creation of imposing titles, such as "First Deputy General Director for Production and Director of the Okhta Chemical Combine." "Such 'complexities' in the titles of positions are poor allies in the development of science and production."

Other problems for scientific workers: The current payment scheme makes it overly profitable for institutes to concentrate on short-term projects, to the neglect of long-term ones. The higher a scientific worker's qualifications, the more his time gets taken up with administrative duties. Criteria for evaluating the efficiency of scientific workers are too vague, and this occasionally leads to unjustified inflation of staffs. And so on.

Some of the contributions consider demographic problems, problems in the siting of productive forces. The rapid industrialization of the USSR led to the overly rapid growth of large cities, argues one participant. These large cities have problems expanding the productive facilities they contain, and providing housing and cultural services for the population; much would be gained by focusing on the development of smaller and medium-sized residential areas. But the dogma of size continues in force:

> We cannot agree with those economists who at times counterpose large cities to small ones and elevate the advantages of large cities to the status of an absolute. Practice has confirmed the correctness of the great attention that our planning agencies have devoted to the fate of small cities in recent years. . . . Current ideas notwithstanding, the enterprises of the up-to-date and most progressive branches of the manufacturing industry that have been set up in small and medium-sized cities are in no way inferior to plants of the same type in the large centers.

The rector of Odessa University raises some critical questions about the role of the universities in Soviet society. While flourishing and making great contributions, the universities have occasionally been somewhat divorced from practical problems, and the case of

182

engineering is cited. Higher technical schools (not considered to be on the university level in the USSR) turn out good engineering specialists, who can work within their narrow area of competence within guidelines already laid down. What is needed, however, is increased training of *research engineers*, with broad knowledge and the ability to do creative research. The universities must shoulder the task of training cadres for the higher, technical and secondary schools. New departments should be created at the junctures of the various sciences, "taking into account the strongest aspects of each university"; thus, at Odessa, a department of theoretical and applied cybernetics is planned.

An academician issues a call for improving the teaching of scientific communism, and elevating the subject to the status of a discipline with higher degrees, a publication, an institute, etc.

In this connection, it would probably be advisable to insert in the draft Directives of the 24th CPSU Congress, after the statement on economics, a clause reading approximately as follows: "In the field of scientific communism, to devote chief attention to: the comprehensive generalization of social and political processes in the implementation of the new five-year plan; the fuller and more comprehensive disclosure and practical utilization of the laws governing the construction of communism; the elaboration of the problems of social administration; and the integrated mastery of the laws governing the preparation for, the emergence of and the development of the world socialist system."

Discussion contributions poured in continuously on aspects of socialist organization and management; even a partial summary would exceed our space limitations. One suggestion is to eliminate the practice of calculating profit on the basis of the value of output, which includes materials purchased by the enterprise. As a result, enterprises become interested in embodying the most expensive possible materials in their product, since this increases the ruble value of their output, hence their profits and bonuses! Orders come to be divided into "profitable" and "unprofitable," the latter containing a low proportion of components or ingredients purchased from outside. "In our view, certain indices of the enterprise's work should be based not on its total outlays, not on the 'gross' but on the 'net,' which objectively reflects the degree of the achievements of the enterprise."

Other problems: Bureaucratic inertia and plan-sidestepping in the medical equipment industry. Accounting procedures which place firms manufacturing components and parts, as distinct from finished goods, at a disadvantage. Problems of improving the efficiency of the job placement process, particularly for youth. A gap between the production of mineral fertilizers and the production of fertilizer spreaders; developing the agro-industrial complex. A low "shift coefficient," i.e., too much idle time and down time at industrial installations. The organizational changes demanded in the wake of technical change in the computer industry. The penalization of lines of production in which progress does not immediately lead to an increase in output. The discussion contains examples of problems of socialist construction, which highlight the working of Soviet democracy. One example, from the Sheksna District Party Committee, is worth quoting at some length:

> The specialization and cooperation of production is a very important question. But here we run into obstacles, particularly on the psychological level. The collective farms, for instance, are not always willing to agree to set up mixed-feed production on a shared basis or to cooperate in the marketing of output. This "conservatism" is partly explained by the fact that the farms have already accumulated bitter experience in this area. It sometimes happens, and there is no need to deny this, that the intercollective farm organizations are run not by the collective farmers but by a third party. After all, the Rural Road-Building Trust was essentially set up with the money of the district's collective farms. But then the province gave it the assignment of building a road to the Kipelov Brickyard, which is under construction. After receiving this assignment, the Rural Road-Building Trust excluded the roads to the collective farms from its plan.
>
> It goes without saying that everyone needs the road to the new brickyard. Perhaps we really should have thrown the forces of our construction workers there. But this should not have been done by sending down an order. The collective farmers, who are the masters, should first have been convinced that this decision is in the interest of the district and in their own interests.

Many Americans will be glad to know that problems of conservation and pollution figured in the discussion of the draft Directives. *Pravda* published a survey of letters, having received too many for individual publication. One writer proposes the establishment of a single agency for the protection of nature. Others urge that enterprises be converted to a closed cycle of technological supply (recycling), "without the discharging of sewage into rivers or lakes." Still others are concerned with the protection of the forests; when the lumbermen cut down the trees that make the best lumber, natural selection is upset and the quality of the whole forest stand deteriorates. Laws are proposed requiring lumbering companies to plant trees to replace the ones cut down. Agronomists call for the planting of forest strips in agricultural areas to aid in the prevention of soil erosion. On a broader scale, the rector of Rostov University is concerned with man's "Interacting with Nature"; he describes a new lecture course, "The Study of the Biosphere," which he hopes will "instill in future specialists a broad understanding of the basic planetary processes and to give them the key to the correct utilization and, when necessary, to the protection of natural resources." Man now influences all natural processes on the planet, and must learn to take full responsibility for them.

The above examples should make it clear that, far from being simply a rubber-stamp formal operation, participation in the discussion of the draft Directives is a serious process, involving large numbers of Soviet people directly in "tackling the basic problems of the development of Soviet society."

GRIGORY ROMANOV

How the Communist Party Works

This article describes the working of inner-Party democracy in the CPSU, and what democratic centralism means in practice. The day-to-day functioning of party bodies is much misunderstood in the West, yet the topic forms an essential background for understanding the discussion and implementation of the decisions of the Party Congress. The article first appeared in Soviet News (London), April 1971, through whose courtesy we reprint it. The author is First Secretary of the Leningrad Regional Committee of the CPSU.

THE PRIMARY organization of the Communist Party of the Soviet Union, according to the Soviet Party Rules, is the basis of the Party. These primary organizations are formed at the places of work of the party members—in factories, on state farms and collective farms, in units of the Soviet Armed Forces, educational establishments, etc.—wherever there are at least three members.

The highest body of the primary party organization is the party meeting of its members, which is convened as a rule at least once a month. For the conduct of current business a bureau or committee is elected. Wherever the membership is less than 15, however, only a secretary and assistant secretary are elected.

As a rule, in organizations with a membership of less than 150— and 90 percent of the organizations come within this category—the secretary carries out his functions on a voluntary basis, in his spare time, as a party duty.

Concern for enhancing the vanguard role of Communists in the sphere of labor has an important place in the work of the primary party organization. It appears here as the organizer of the workers' socialist emulation movement for fulfilling the state plans and the obligations undertaken by the collective, and helps to develop in every way the people's initiative directed towards discovering and making better use of reserves in production and raising the level of efficiency of production.

With these aims in view, the primary organization directly connected with production has considerable rights in controlling the work of the administration.

Naturally, each primary party organization is guided in all its activities by the CPSU Program and the Party Rules, as well as being bound by the decisions of the higher party organs.

In short, the primary party organization is the cell of the Party in which all the tasks of communist construction are decided in practice, for it functions directly among people.

On October 1, 1970, the Leningrad party organization, including the region, had 445,000 members, including 12,000 candidate members—Communists serving a probationary period before being admitted to full membership of the Party. The social composition of our organization is as follows: workers and collective farmers account for 52.4 per cent and the others are white-collar workers. Of the latter, 75 per cent are engineering and technical personnel, agronomists and specialists of the most diverse branches of the economy, science and culture. So far as the ages of our members are concerned, more than half (52 per cent) are between 26 and 50.

All members belong to primary party organizations of which we have more than 6,000. There are 35 district and town party committees in Leningrad and the Leningrad region, formed on the territorial principle and providing daily guidance for these primary organizations.

The activities of the regional party organization are guided by the regional party committee, elected at the regional party conference which, under the newly-amended Party Rules, is held twice every five years. We hold plenary meetings of the regional committee, on an average, once in four months. In order to provide guidance for the party organization's current activities, the regional committee elects an executive body, the bureau of the committee, including the committee secretaries, and also appoints the heads of the departments of the committee. These departments of the regional committee are formed to deal with specific aspects of the work of each regional party organization.

We have, for example, a department for propaganda and departments concerned with guiding the work of industry, agriculture, construction, transport and communications and cultural, scientific and educational institutions.

In addition, attached to the regional committee there is a party commission which is responsible for considering appeals by party members and for dealing with a number of other questions.

Democratic Centralism

THE RANGE of problems dealt with by the regional party committee and its apparatus is very wide. One of the main tasks in all our activities is the selection, appointment and education of personnel as well as implementation of party directives.

The organizational structure of our Party is based on democratic centralism. This, according to the Party Rules, means: the election of all leading bodies, from the lowest to the highest; regular reports by party bodies to their party organizations, on the one hand, and to higher bodies, on the other; party discipline and subordination of the minority to the majority; the decisions of the higher bodies are binding on lower bodies.

The entire leadership of our organization—from the party group organizer to the regional party committee—is elected at party meetings or conferences.

Discipline and responsibility in the Party presume broad inner-party democracy and a membership that is well informed. Take the question, for example, of bodies being accountable to their organizations and members. In our party organization all the district and town committees of the Party reported to their organizations in 1969-70. Reports were given not only at district and town conferences—as required by the Rules—but also directly in primary organizations (at factories, on collective farms and state farms and in offices) between conferences. Members had the possibility of being informed about the activities of their party committees, of expressing their own ideas and proposals and of criticizing the party committees for shortcomings and omissions in their work.

All this ensures that rank-and-file members are drawn into the activities of the party committees, broadens their opportunities for administering public and state affairs, and for taking and carrying out decisions, and opens up wide vistas for every party member to display initiative.

Let me give one example. Not so long ago the regional party committee discussed the question of further enhancing the role of the workers of Leningrad and the Leningrad region in the production work and sociopolitical activities of various collective bodies and also the tasks of party organizations. A big group of policy activists, 150 in all, were drawn into making a study of the question and preparing recommendations that could serve as a basis for the regional committee's decisions. Half of these activists were workers.

All the members of the commission visited the organizations concerned, familiarized themselves with the work of the Party, trade union and Young Communist League organizations and economic executives, and made a study of statistical material. On the basis of an analysis of the information obtained, the trends and phenomena most characteristic of the Leningrad working class today were determined, and recommendations were drawn up for raising the level of its activities in the sphere of production and in the political field. Thus, all the preparations for the plenary meeting were conducted on a broad democratic basis.

Democracy was also strictly observed during the discussion at the plenary meeting. The 20 speakers included workers, peasants, scientists and factory heads. Shortcomings were criticized and suggestions put forward. The meeting set up a committee to draw up a draft of an appropriate resolution of the regional party committee. This draft was duly discussed and a decision taken. From that moment it became obligatory for all party organizations of the Leningrad region, i.e., one of the aspects of democratic centralism went into effect.

Every member who has made a proposal that has not received the support of the party organization has the right and opportunity to press his point of view. This right is inscribed in the Party Rules, where the section on the rights and duties of a member states that he has the right "to address any question, statement or proposal to any party body, up to and including the CPSU Central Committee, and to demand an answer on the substance of his address."

Many people abroad have a wrong idea about the leading role of the Communist Party. It is sometimes believed that the Party assumes the functions of state, economic and other bodies. This is not true.

The point is that the Communist Party is the party in power. Since that is so, its decisions are obligatory for all other organizations functioning in our country. It should be borne in mind, however, that the Party does not take decisions on questions that do not come within its sphere. What, for instance, is the role of the Party in drawing up the plans for the development of the national economy?

The Party does, indeed, adopt at its Congress the Directives for the country's economic development for the next five years. These Directives, which represent only the Party's political decision in the sphere of economics, do not, however, envisage concrete targets, but control targets for the development of this or that branch of the national economy in the five-year period.

I want to emphasize this: *control* targets. These assignments proceed from the realistic possibilities of our economy, take into account all the ever-growing demands of the population and, finally, reflect the level of social production reached and the ways and means for further developing it.

Proceeding from these Directives, state, economic and other bodies determine the measures required in order to reach the targets indicated by the Party and to carry out the management of the economy. All the material, financial and other resources are at their disposal, and they handle them as they see fit.

In these conditions, the local party organizations, such as the one in Leningrad, are entrusted with the task of exercising supervision over the implementation of the Party's Directives and the state plans. There is no question here of replacing any other bodies.

This can be shown by the work of our Leningrad party organization. We became convinced of the need for further concentration and specialization of our industry. We reached this conclusion following a tremendous amount of work by specialists and scientists who studied this problem at our request. On the basis of their recommendations, the regional party committee submitted a request to the state bodies, asking that production and scientific-production amalgamations should be brought about. We ourselves cannot decide such questions, for they are not within our competence.

The government and the appropriate ministries considered our proposals and decided to organize a number of big production associations in Leningrad and the Leningrad region. Today we already have over 50 of these associations, and they account for 30 per cent of our total industrial output.

The main task of every local party organization is to ensure the fulfillment of the Directives of the Party on major questions, to cope with questions of personnel and to be exacting in the demands it makes on personnel with regard to any task with which they are entrusted. This is the essence, the fundamental significance, of the leading role played by the Party and its local organizations.

THE PEOPLE are the decisive force in the building of communism. *The Party exists for the people, and it is in serving the people that it sees the purpose of its activity.* To further extend and deepen the ties between the Party and the people is an imperative condition of success in the struggle for communism. The Party considers it its duty always to consult the working people on the major questions of home and foreign policy . . . and to attract the more extensive participation of non-members in all its work. *From the Program of the CPSU*

Congress Documents

FREEDOM AND PEACE TO THE
PEOPLES OF INDOCHINA

ON behalf of the Soviet Communists, on behalf of the entire Soviet people, the 24th Congress of the CPSU extends passionate fraternal greetings to the heroic Vietnamese people and its militant vanguard, the Party of Working People of Vietnam; to the courageous patriots of Laos and Cambodia; to the fearless fighters against US imperialism, for freedom, independence, and the peaceful future of the countries of Indochina.

We wish the invincible defenders of the Democratic Republic of Vietnam further victories in repelling imperialist aggression and new achievements in the construction of socialism.

We declare our full solidarity with the forces of liberation in South Vietnam and wish them new successes in the struggle to rid their homeland of the interventionists and the corrupt Saigon regime, for asserting the right to decide their destiny themselves.

Our sympathy and our support go to the patriotic forces of Laos and Cambodia, which are waging a decisive struggle against the imperialist intervention of the United States, in defense of their righteous cause.

The Soviet people are full of pride for the victories of the heroic Vietnamese people, the glorious patriots of Laos and Cambodia, who are dealing crippling blows against the American interventionists and their hirelings.

The adventurist schemes of the American aggressors have turned into a continuous chain of ignominious failures. Neither bombs nor shells, nor the ruses of political intrigues will enable them to break the will of the people of a socialist country, the Democratic Republic of Vietnam, or of the patriots of South Vietnam, Laos and Cambodia, and this will be the case in the future, too.

The implementation of the so-called "Vietnamization"—the brutal policy of making "Asians kill Asians"—will not help the US imperialists attain their criminal ends. The staunchness and courage of the freedom-loving peoples of Indochina, along with the unfailing support of the Soviet people, the peoples of the other countries of socialism, the international communist movement and all progressive forces, serve as a guarantee of their victory in the struggle against the enemy.

The Soviet Union is deeply convinced that the proposals set forth by the Government of the Democratic Republic of Vietnam, the Provisional Revolutionary Government of the Republic of South Vietnam, the Patriotic Front of Laos and the National United Front of Cambodia, offer a constructive basis for the solution of the problems of Indochina.

Soviet Communists believe that in the prevailing situation there is an urgent need to strengthen solidarity with the embattled peoples of Indochina and to come out vigorously against the aggressive policy of the US ruling circles, everywhere and in every way.

The Soviet Union has given and is giving all-out support and aid to the Democratic Republic of Vietnam in the building of socialism, in strengthening its defense capacity, in repelling imperialist encroachments. It has been coming out consistently and resolutely on the side of the liberation movement in South Vietnam, Laos and Cambodia, which is making an outstanding contribution to the cause of the peace and national independence of the peoples. The 24th Congress of the CPSU solemnly declares that the Soviet Union will continue to follow this course.

The 24th Congress of the CPSU calls on all those who cherish freedom, peace and progress:

To raise still louder the voice of protest against the sanguinary aggression of American imperialism in Indochina!

To expose resolutely and boldly the crimes of the American military, to proclaim support of the heroic peoples of Vietnam, Laos and Cambodia!

May the worldwide movement for an end to the imperialist aggression in Indochina, for the withdrawal of all the troops of the United States and its allies, for the realization of the legitimate rights of the peoples of Vietnam, Laos and Cambodia to be masters in their own land, grow wider and stronger!

Out of Indochina with the American aggressors!

The just cause of the heroic peoples of Vietnam, Laos and Cambodia will triumph!

FOR A JUST AND LASTING PEACE IN THE MIDDLE EAST

WE, representatives of the 14-million-strong army of Soviet Communists, expressing the will of the peoples of the Soviet Union, sharply denounce Israel's imperialist aggression against the Arab states, conducted with support from American imperialism, and express our fraternal solidarity with the courageous struggle of the Arab peoples for the elimination of the consequences of Israeli aggression, for the triumph of the ideals of freedom, independence and social justice.

The struggle of the peace forces against Israeli aggression has now entered a stage marked by the utter exposure of the expansionist designs of the Israeli ruling clique and the Zionist circles. The international isolation of the Israeli aggressors and their patrons, the imperialist circles of the United States, hypocritically expressing a desire for peace while in fact encouraging the Israeli extremists, is increasing.

The constructive position of the Arab countries, first of all of the United Arab Republic, creates favorable conditions for the full implementation of the Security Council's resolution of November 22, 1967.

The stubborn refusal of the Israeli rulers to withdraw their troops from captured Arab lands is an open challenge to international public opinion and the decisions of the United Nations.

That is why it is the duty of all peaceloving forces to curb the Israeli aggressors by joint efforts and to make them respect generally recognized norms of international life and the lawful rights of the Arab states, and withdraw their troops from captured Arab territories.

The 24th Congress expresses the firm conviction that attempts by the imperialists and their hangers-on to impose their diktat on the peoples of the Arab countries, to undermine progressive regimes in the Middle East and to defeat the national-liberation movement in this part of the world, are doomed to failure. The legitimate rights and interests of all the Arab peoples, including the Arab people of Palestine, will triumph. The Israeli aggressors will have to get out of the Arab territories they seized in 1967. The unbending will of the Arab peoples in their struggle for independence, freedom, peace and social progress, their close alliance with the peoples of the Soviet Union and the other socialist countries and with all anti-imperialist and peaceloving forces, are an earnest of this.

The 24th CPSU Congress declares that the Soviet Union, unswervingly promoting the Leninist policy of peace and friendship among the peoples, will consistently uphold the just cause of the Arab peoples subjected to Israeli aggression, will support their efforts directed at restoring their violated rights, at ensuring a just political settlement in the Middle East and in defense of the lawful rights of the Arab people of Palestine.

We call on the fraternal Parties, on all peaceloving peoples and states to strengthen solidarity with the peoples of the Arab countries and to give them active support in their struggle.

For the unity of action of all forces coming out against imperialist aggression, for a just and lasting peace in the Middle East!

Long live the inviolable Soviet-Arab friendship and may it grow stronger!

COMMUNIQUE ON THE PLENARY MEETING OF THE CENTRAL COMMITTEE OF THE COMMUNIST PARTY OF THE SOVIET UNION

A PLENARY Meeting of the CPSU Central Committee elected by the 24th Congress of the Communist Party of the Soviet Union was held on April 9, 1971.

The Plenary Meeting unanimously elected Comrade L. I. Brezhnev to the post of General Secretary of the CPSU Central Committee.

The Plenary Meeting unanimously elected the Politbureau of the CPSU Central Committee: Members of the Politbureau, Comrades L. I. Brezhnev, G. I. Voronov, V. V. Grishin, A. P. Kirilenko, A. N. Kosygin, F. D. Kulakov, D. A. Kunaev, K. T. Mazurov, A. J. Pelse, N. V. Podgorny, D. S. Polyansky, M. A. Suslov, A. N. Shelepin, P. Y. Shelest and V. V. Shcherbitsky;

Alternate Members of the Politbureau, Comrades Y. V. Andropov, P. N. Demichev, P. M. Masherov, V. P. Mzhavanadze, S. R. Rashidov and D. F. Ustinov.

Comrades L. I. Brezhnev, P. N. Demichev, I. V. Kapitonov, K. F. Katushev, A. P. Kirilenko, F. D. Kulakov, B. N. Ponomarev, M. S. Solomentsev, M. A. Suslov and D. F. Ustinov have been elected Secretaries of the CPSU Central Committee.

The Plenary Meeting confirmed A. J. Pelse as Chairman of the Party Control Committee of the CPSU Central Committee.

The Central Auditing Commission of the Communist Party of the Soviet Union met on April 9, 1971. It elected Comrade G. F. Sizov to the post of Chairman.

Pravda, April 10